TEST OF ENGLISH FOR INTERNATIONAL COMMUNICATION

TOEIC®
公式ガイド&問題集

日本語版

Bo Arbogast
Jerome Bicknell
Trina Duke
Melissa Locke
Rhonda Shearin

 ETS Educational Testing Service

 IIBC

財団法人 国際ビジネスコミュニケーション協会
TOEIC運営委員会

Acknowledgments

The following individuals provided invaluable assistance in the development of this book: Susan Chyn, Rex Corlett, Krista Curran, Denise Gianetti, Sean Hainer, Monica Hemingway, Barbara Hogan, Catherine Newman Jerris, Lauren Levine, Linda Lizotte, Ron Love, Sheridan MacInnes, Noriko Schneiderman, Joanne Sher Grumet, Maxine Susman, and Gina Wright.

Visit www. TOEIC. com for more information about TOEIC and TOEIC-related products.

はじめに

「たくさんの日本人が世界中のあらゆる分野で活躍し、多くの友好関係を築くために、国際共通言語としての英語をコミュニケーションの手段として必要とする時代がやって来る。来るべき時代に対応するには、コミュニケーションに役立つ英語とは何なのか、何が学習の目標なのかを明確にした上で英語能力の向上を図らなければならない。そのために世界基準の英語能力テストを開発する必要がある。」そのように私たちが考えたのは、今から20年以上前のことです。当時、国際的なビジネス分野で活躍できる人材の育成は日本の産業界からの要請でもありました。こうしたニーズを受け、世界最大の公共教育研究機関である米国のETS (Educational Testing Service)に開発を依頼し、誕生したテストがTOEIC （トーイック、Test of English for International Communication)です。ETSがTOEICテストを制作し、全世界で実施されるTOEICプログラム・サービスの拡充と運営管理・統轄にあたっています。

TOEICテストが日本で初めて実施されたのは1979年です。現在では英語能力評価の「モノサシ」として、企業・団体・教育機関等の各方面で幅広くその有効性が認知されるまでになりました。近年は、日本のみならず、世界約50カ国で実施され、年間約140万人以上の方々が受験されており、真に英語能力評価の国際基準となりつつあります。

ここ数年来、社会では英語コミュニケーション能力の必要性が高まっており、TOEICテストが社会人、学生を問わず、多くの方々に認知され、受験していただいております。受験者数は近年大幅に伸び続け、それにともなって、TOEICテストの内容に関するお問い合わせをいただく機会が増えてきました。

TOEICテストは英語におけるコミュニケーション能力を測定するテストとして、評価基準を一定に保つために、テスト問題は非公開としております。しかしながら、TOEICテストが実施されてから20年が経過し、日本国内での受験者数がすでに年間80万人を超えた昨今、テスト形式を一人でも多くの方々にお知らせすることは、社会的な要請であると自認するに至りました。そこでこの度、受験者の皆様のご要望にお応えするために、ETSが過去に実施されたテスト問題の一部を公開し、日本でTOEICテストの運営・実施にあたる（財）国際ビジネスコミュニケーション協会TOEIC運営委員会が英語版公式ガイド・問題集を翻訳し、補足的な説明を加え、公式問題集を発行する運びとなりました。本書にはTOEICテストの制作者であるETSによる英語のコミュニケーション・スキルを向上させるためのアドバイスも掲載しましたので、読者の皆様がテスト形式を熟知することにとどまらず、各々が英語学習を継続し、ご自分の目標を達成するためにもご活用ください。

TOEICテストに関心を持たれる皆様が本書によりTOEICテストの内容を把握し、実際のテストにおいて正確な実力を反映されることを切に希望します。また、本書に掲載されたテスト問題（第6章：TOEIC練習テスト）は自己採点により、参考スコアへの換算が可能ですので、学習進捗レベルの自己評価にもご活用ください。

本書が英語能力評価と国際コミュニケーションの促進に役立つ手引書として、多くの方々のお役に立てることを願っております。

2000年2月
（財）国際ビジネスコミュニケーション協会
TOEIC運営委員会

目次

第5章

TOEICサンプル・テスト問題と解説

第6章

TOEIC練習テスト（200問）

付録A

付録B

INTRODUCTION

イントロダクション

Contents

イントロダクション

本書の特長

本書はTest of English for International Communication (TOEIC)受験のための公式学習ガイドブックです。本書には実際に出題された400問のTOEICテスト問題、TOEICテスト制作者が書き下ろした受験のコツ、アドバイスと総合的な英語能力を高めるための練習問題と方法が収められています。

本書の内容は以下の通りです。

- 正規のテストと同じ問題数（200問）から成る、実際に出題されたTOEICテスト問題を組み合わせて作った練習テスト（スコア換算表付き）

- TOEICテストの問題形式と内容の説明

- TOEICテスト制作者が書き下ろしたテスト受験の方法

- TOEICテストのパート別アドバイス

- 総合的な英語能力を高めるための方法と練習問題

本書の対象者

- 英語能力を高めたいと思っている方

- TOEICテストについてもっと詳しく知りたいという方

- TOEICテストの受験準備をしたいという方

- 従業員に対してTOEICテストを実施している企業担当者

- TOEICテスト準備講座を担当している教師

本書の構成

イントロダクション

イントロダクションでは以下のような問いにお答えします。

本書をどのように使用するか？
TOEICテストとは何か？
どのような人がTOEICテストを受験するのか？
TOEICテストの内容はどのようなものか？
TOEFLテストとTOEICテストの違いは何か？

■ 第1章：TOEICミニ・テスト

TOEICミニ・テストは実際のTOEICテストに出題された問題を使用した短縮版（70問）のテストです。Listeningの音声は付属のCDに収録されています。正解、解説、Listeningの音声スクリプトは付録Aに入っています。

■ 第2章：TOEICテストを受けるに当たってのアドバイス

第2章ではテストの要点を概観し、TOEICテストを受けるための方法を見ていきます。また、テスト受験当日の準備と総合的な英語能力を高める方法についても述べてあります。

■ 第3章：TOEIC Section I Listening

第3章ではSection I Listeningの準備として、アドバイス、受験の方法を見ていき、練習問題も行います。

■ 第4章：TOEIC Section II Reading

第4章ではSection II Readingの準備として、アドバイス、受験の方法を見ていき、練習問題も行います。

■ 第5章：TOEICサンプル・テスト問題と解説

第5章ではTOEICテストの短縮版を正解と不正解それぞれの解説を1問ずつ参照しながら行います。学習しやすいように、解説はテスト問題のとなりに載っています。

■ 第6章：TOEIC練習テスト問題（200問）

実際に出題されたTOEICテスト問題が正規のテストと同じ200問収録されています。付属のCDに録音されている音声は実際のTOEICテストと同じ音声を使用しています。このテストを受けた後、付録Bにあるスコア換算表から参考スコアを算出することができます。正解、解説、録音された音声のスクリプトも付録Bに入っています。

本書の使い方

英語学習者とTOEICテスト受験者へのご提案

本書はTOEICテストの概要を知る目的で、または英語能力を高め、TOEICテストの受験準備を目的とした体系的な学習を行うためのガイドブックとして使用することができます。

概要を知るために

TOEICテストの概要を知るのであれば、以下の各章を参照するのがとても便利です。

- イントロダクション：TOEICテストとその主な内容について一般的な情報を見ることができます。

- 第2章：TOEICテストの要点を簡潔にまとめており、テストを受験するための方法を見ることができます。

- 第3，4章：この2つの章の最後の部分ではテストの各パートに取り組む際のアドバイスを抜粋しています。

- TOEICテスト練習問題：第1，5，6章では実際に出題されたTOEICテスト問題を見ることができます。第1，6章の正解、解説、Listeningのスクリプトは本書の付録に収められています。

体系的な学習を行うために

本書を完全に使いこなすのであれば、

- イントロダクションを読んでから、第1章のミニ・テストを受けてください。ミニ・テストを受験することによって、どのパートが自分のもっとも苦手なパートであるかがわかります。付録Aの解説を読んで、解答の正誤理由を理解してください。

- ミニ・テストを終えたら、第3，4章にあるアドバイス、実力強化課題、自己学習課題に集中して取り組んでください。

- 第3，4章を一通り終えたならば、第5章にあるサンプル・テスト問題に1問ずつ解説を参照しながら取り組んでください。

- 第5章のサンプル・テスト問題を難しいと感じたならば、第3，4章を見直し、もう一度練習してみてください。

- 最後に第6章のTOEIC練習テスト（200問）を受けてください。このテストで得られるスコアは実際のTOEICを受験して得られる正規のスコアではありませんが、おおまかな自分の予想スコアを知ることができます。

> 注意：本書はTOEICテストを熟知するためのガイドであると同時に、英語スキルが向上するように導くものでもあります。しかしながら、言語の習得には多くの時間と練習が必要です。本書を使用しても、必ずしもテスト・スコアが上がるとはかぎりません。

英語教師へのご提案

本書は自己学習用として、または教室での授業で活用できます。本書に掲載されたテスト問題を練習することによって、正規のTOEICスコアを算出することはできません。ただし、これらのテストの結果から、学習者の得意な分野と不得手な分野が明らかになります。

第2章には学習者が総合的な英語能力を高められるように、教室内での課題と自己学習用の課題が収めてあります。実際に使われている英語の話し言葉と書き言葉をどこから探し出すか、また、その活用方法が述べられています。

第3，4章にはTOEICテストの全7パートに関する役立つ情報を収めています。各パートには以下の内容が入っています。

アドバイス

TOEICテストの問題についてのアドバイスと正解するための戦略を述べています。

実力強化

TOEICテストに必要なスキルを実践するための練習です。

自己学習

英語を使いこなすために必要なスキルをさらに磨き、発展させるためのアドバイスと課題を収めています。

第3，4章はTOEICテスト準備クラスに利用できます。公式TOEICテスト準備教材として、これらの章をクラスでお使いください。

CDを活用する
本書にはCDが付いています。CDのマークが付いている箇所ではCDで音声を聞いてください。

TOEICルーラー®の使い方
本書には学習をさらに効果的にするためにTOEICルーラーが付いています。TOEICルーラーを使えば、第5章にある練習問題に取り組むときに解説が見えないようにかくすことができます。そうすれば問題に集中でき、解説を1問ずつ参照していくことができます。

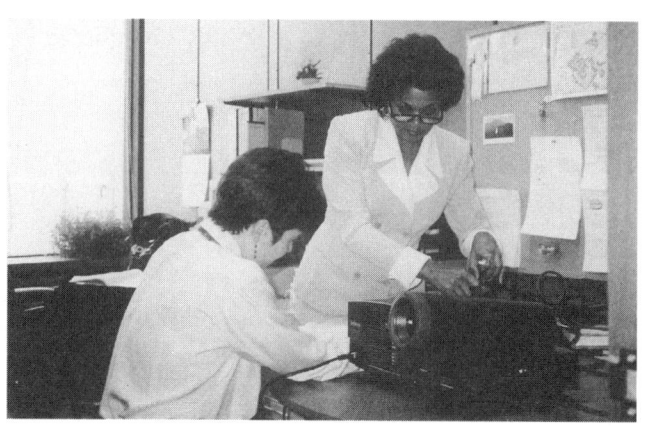

Example Question 1 (not recorded)

On the recording, you will hear:

(A) They're leaving the office.

Example Question 1　解説
(A)　人々は待っているように見えるが、ホテルの中にいる。
(B)　人々はまだ部屋の中にいる。

TOEICテストについて

TOEICテストとは何か？

TOEICはTest of English for International Communicationの頭文字を取って表記したものです。TOEICテストは英語を母語としない人たちのための英語能力テストです。TOEICスコアはグローバルな職場における個人が持っている英語コミュニケーション能力の程度を示します。専門知識や専門用語は必要ありません。日常生活のなかで使われる英語のみをテストの対象としています。

TOEICテストは職場で必要とされる英語能力を測定する世界でもっとも普及しているテストです。世界中で4,000以上の企業がTOEICテストを使用し、年間約290万人が受験しています。

TOEICテストの形式はどのようなものか？

TOEICテストの試験時間は2時間でマークシート方式による多肢選択テストです。テストは200問からなり、2つのセクションに分かれています。各セクションに要する時間は異なります。

■ **Section I ： Listening**

このセクションは全部で100問あり、問題の音声はカセットテープで流れます。4つのパートで構成されており、英語で録音されたいろいろなコメント、質問、短い会話、アナウンスを聞き、聞き取った内容に基づいて質問に答えます。Section I Listeningの試験時間は全体で45分です。

- ◆ Part I ：写真描写問題　20問（四肢択一）
- ◆ Part II ：応答問題　30問（三肢択一）
- ◆ Part III ：会話問題　30問（四肢択一）
- ◆ Part IV ：説明文問題　20問（四肢択一）

■ **Section II ： Reading**

このセクションは全部で100問あり、問題は問題用紙に印刷されています。いろいろな英文を読み、自分のペースで英文の内容に基づいて解答を進めていきます。Section II Readingの試験時間は全体で75分です。

- ◆ Part V ：文法・語彙問題　40問（四肢択一）
- ◆ Part VI ：誤文訂正問題　20問（四肢択一）
- ◆ Part VII ：読解問題　40問（四肢択一）

受験者は(A),(B),(C),(D)のなかから正解と思われるものを一つを選び、問題用紙とは別の解答用紙に鉛筆でマークします。試験時間は2時間ですが、受験者の個人データを解答用紙に記入したり、最終学歴と職業に関する短い質問に答える時間は試験時間に含まれません。

TOEICテストの内容はどのようなものか？

TOEICテストはビジネス界のニーズに応えるように制作されました。テスト問題は職場で英語が使われている世界中のさまざまな国々の話し言葉と書き言葉をもとに作られます。テスト問題は以下のようにいろいろな場面と状況から出題されます。

- ビジネス一般 – 契約、交渉、マーケティング、セールス、事業企画、会議

- 製造 – 工場管理、組立てライン、品質管理

- 財務および予算作成 – 銀行業務、投資、税金、経理、請求書作成

- 企業の開発事業 – 研究、商品開発

- オフィス – 取締役会議、委員会、手紙、メモ、電話、ファックスと電子メールのメッセージ、事務機器と備品、オフィス業務

- 人事 – 人材募集、採用、退職、給与、昇進、求職、人材募集広告

- 購買 – ショッピング、注文、出荷、請求書

- 技術分野 – エレクトロニクス、テクノロジー、コンピューター、実験室とその備品、仕様書

- 住宅／法人財産 – 建築、設計書、住居の購入および賃貸、電気、ガス

- 旅行 – 電車、飛行機、タクシー、バス、船、フェリー、切符、スケジュール、駅や空港でのアナウンス、レンタカー、ホテル、予約、遅延、キャンセル

- 外食 – ビジネス・ランチおよびインフォーマルな昼食、バンケット、レセプション、レストランの予約

- 娯楽 – 映画、演劇、音楽、美術、メディア

- 健康 – 医療保険、医師、歯科医の受診、医院、病院での受診

これらの場面で使用される英語からテスト問題が出されますが、受験者は特殊なビジネス用語や専門用語を知っている必要はありません。TOEICテストに出題される英語は、英語以外の言語を母語とする人たちがあらゆる環境で使用すると考えられる英語です。

どのような人がTOEICテストを受験するのか？

TOEICテストの受験者は以下のような方々です。

- 会社、ホテル、病院、レストラン、航空業界、国際会議、コンベンション、スポーツ・イベントなどの日常業務で英語を使う方

- 英語力が必要な国際的なビジネス、商業、産業の管理、営業、技術部門の従業員の方

- 職業上のトレーニングを英語で受ける方

- 履歴書に記載するため、国際的に認定された英語能力の測定値を必要とする方

どのような人が、どのようにTOEICテストを利用しているのか？

企業・団体 − TOEICテストは、将来の、あるいは現在の従業員の英語習熟度を評価する必要がある世界中の多くの団体の評価基準として認知されるようになりました。団体でのTOEICテストの適切な利用法には以下のようなものが挙げられます。

- **採用、昇進、配属** − 各種団体は、特定の任務を遂行するのに必要な英語レベルに基づいたスコア基準を設定するためにTOEICを利用することができます。これらの基準は人事決定の際の参考になります。

- **専門的なトレーニング** − TOEICスコアは、従業員が英語で行われるトレーニングに参加し、トレーニング内容を学び取るに十分な英語能力を持っているかどうかを判定するために利用することができます。

- **海外任務** − 従業員が英語圏の任務についたときに十分任務を遂行し、意志疎通がはかれるかどうかをTOEICスコアから判定することができます。

- **英語研修** − TOEICスコアはさらなる英語研修を必要とする従業員を特定し、習得目標を設定し、向上度をチェックするために利用できます。

集中英語プログラム − 英語研修プログラムの責任者の方々はTOEICテストが能力別クラス分けの有効な手段であり、研修後の効果測定に貴重なデータを提供するテストであると認めています。

学校 − 大学及び高等教育機関には、在学中に学生にTOEICテストの受験を義務づけているところが多くあります。

どのような人がTOEICテストを開発したのか？

教育にかかわる効果測定および精神測定学と教育学の研究を専門とする米国の団体、Educational Testing Service®（ETS®）が、日本の実業界の依頼を受けて1979年にTOEICテストを開発しました。年月を経て、TOEICテストは他の多くの国々で採用されるようになり、その後短期間のうちに、職業に従事する人々の英語能力を評価するグローバル・スタンダードとなりました。また、テストの制作もETSが行っています。

TOEICテストとTOEFLテストの違いは何か？

TOEICテストとTOEFLテストはそれぞれ異なった目的に応えるために開発されました。それゆえ、テスト形式、内容、英語の文脈、測定する英語能力の範囲も異なります。TOEFLテストは北米の大学に入学を希望する外国人の学生のためにETSが制作したテストです。北米の大学あるいは大学院の学位取得を希望する学生がTOEFLテストを受験します。従業員の英語能力を把握しようという団体、職場で使用する英語能力を証明しようという方はTOEICテストを受験する方が望ましいでしょう。

TOEICテストのスコアはどのようにして算出されるか？

受験者は解答用紙に鉛筆で解答をマークしていきます。スコアは正答数で決定されます。Listening, Reading各セクションの正答数が5点から495点の間の点数にそれぞれ換算されます。この2つのセクションのスコアを合わせたものが10点から990点の合計点となります。不正解に対しての罰則はありません。

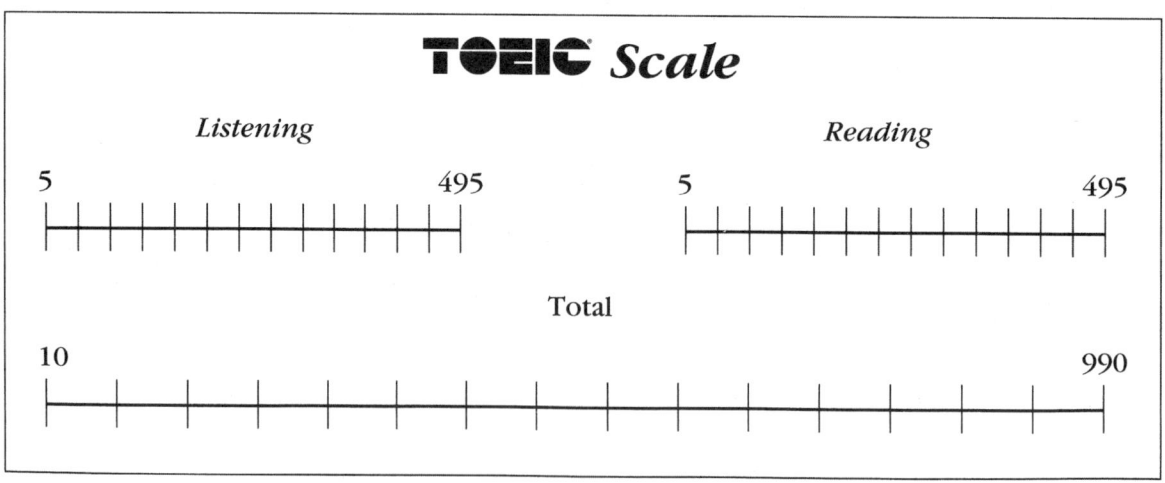

TOEIC スコアが意味するものは何か？

TOEIC スコアとコミュニケーション能力との関係を示す Proficiency Scale が目安として以下の通り設けられています（Proficiency Scale は Official Score Certificate とともに受験者へ送られる「スコアの読み方」に記載されています）。

Proficiency Scale
TOEIC レベルとコミュニケーション能力レベルとの相関表

レベル	TOEIC®スコア	評価（ガイドライン）
A		**Non-Native として十分なコミュニケーションができる。** 自己の経験の範囲内では、専門外の分野の話題に対しても十分な理解とふさわしい表現ができる。 Native Speaker の域には一歩隔たりがあるとはいえ、語彙・文法・構文のいずれをも正確に把握し、流暢に駆使する力を持っている。
	860	
B		**どんな状況でも適切なコミュニケーションができる素地を備えている。** 通常会話は完全に理解でき、応答もはやい。話題が特定分野にわたっても、対応できる力を持っている。業務上も大きな支障はない。 正確さと流暢さに個人差があり、文法・構文上の誤りが見受けられる場合もあるが、意思疎通を妨げるほどではない。
	730	
C		**日常生活のニーズを充足し、限定された範囲内では業務上のコミュニケーションができる。** 通常会話であれば、要点を理解し、応答にも支障はない。複雑な場面における的確な対応や意思疎通になると、巧拙の差が見られる。 基本的な文法・構文は身についており、表現力の不足はあっても、ともかく自己の意思を伝える語彙を備えている。
	470	
D		**通常会話で最低限のコミュニケーションができる。** ゆっくり話してもらうか、繰り返しや言い換えをしてもらえば、簡単な会話は理解できる。身近な話題であれば応答も可能である。 語彙・文法・構文ともに不十分なところは多いが、相手が Non-Native に特別な配慮をしてくれる場合には、意思疎通をはかることができる。
	220	
E		**コミュニケーションができるまでに至っていない** 単純な会話をゆっくり話してもらっても、部分的にしか理解できない。 断片的に単語を並べる程度で、実質的な意思疎通の役には立たない.

どうしたらTOEICテストの受験申し込みができるのか。また、受験についての情報を得られるのか？

主要書店、大学生協において、お申し込みの取り扱いをしております。お近くに書店がない場合には、はがきかFAXでTOEIC運営委員会東京業務センター申込書請求係へご請求ください。

〒100-0014
東京都千代田区永田町2-14-2　山王グランドビル
財団法人 国際ビジネスコミュニケーション協会
TOEIC運営委員会東京業務センター申込書請求係

TEL: 0120-40-1019
FAX: 03-3581-4783

TOEICテストは公式ホームページからのお申し込みもできます。詳細はホームページをご覧ください。

TOEIC®公式ホームページ　　http://www.toeic.or.jp

CHAPTER 1

第1章

TOEIC ミニ・テスト

■ TOEIC ミニ・テストのもっとも効果的な活用法
■ 解答用紙
■ TOEIC ミニ・テスト

1 第1章

TOEICミニ・テストのもっとも効果的な活用方法

実際のTOEICテストの問題数は200問ですが、この章のTOEICミニ・テストは、過去に出題された問題のなかから70問を出題しています。さらに、

- 問題形式とテストの構成についての簡単な説明があります
- ミニ・テストを行なうことによって、さらに学習が必要となる分野がわかります

以下にTOEICミニ・テストのもっとも効果的な活用法を挙げます。

■ サンプルの解答用紙を使いましょう

次のページには、実際のTOEICテストに使用される解答用紙に準じたサンプルの解答用紙があります。ミニ・テストを受ける際には、解答用紙に正確にマークする時間を取りましょう（247ページにもミニ・テストの解答用紙がありますので使用しましょう）。

■ ミニ・テストが終了したら付録Aへ進みましょう

付録Aには、ミニ・テストの正解と、正解・不正解それぞれの選択肢の解説があります。正解をチェックし、解説を注意深く読んで、解答の正誤理由を理解しましょう。また、付録AにはListeningの音声スクリプトも収められています。

■ できなかった分野をチェックしましょう

第3，4章にあるテストのパート別のガイドに進むことができます。

TOEIC ミニ・テスト

(21ページ)

ANSWER SHEET

REGISTRATION NO.
受験番号

フリガナ

N A M E
氏　名

LISTENING (Part Ⅰ～Ⅳ)

NO.	ANSWER A B C D
1	Ⓐ Ⓑ Ⓒ Ⓓ
2	Ⓐ Ⓑ Ⓒ Ⓓ
3	Ⓐ Ⓑ Ⓒ Ⓓ
4	Ⓐ Ⓑ Ⓒ Ⓓ
5	Ⓐ Ⓑ Ⓒ Ⓓ
6	Ⓐ Ⓑ Ⓒ Ⓓ
7	Ⓐ Ⓑ Ⓒ Ⓓ
8	Ⓐ Ⓑ Ⓒ Ⓓ
9	Ⓐ Ⓑ Ⓒ Ⓓ
10	Ⓐ Ⓑ Ⓒ Ⓓ

NO.	ANSWER A B C D
11	Ⓐ Ⓑ Ⓒ Ⓓ
12	Ⓐ Ⓑ Ⓒ Ⓓ
13	Ⓐ Ⓑ Ⓒ Ⓓ
14	Ⓐ Ⓑ Ⓒ Ⓓ
15	
16	
17	
18	
19	
20	

NO.	ANSWER A B C
21	Ⓐ Ⓑ Ⓒ
22	Ⓐ Ⓑ Ⓒ
23	Ⓐ Ⓑ Ⓒ
24	Ⓐ Ⓑ Ⓒ
25	Ⓐ Ⓑ Ⓒ
26	Ⓐ Ⓑ Ⓒ
27	Ⓐ Ⓑ Ⓒ
28	Ⓐ Ⓑ Ⓒ
29	Ⓐ Ⓑ Ⓒ
30	Ⓐ Ⓑ Ⓒ

NO.	ANSWER A B C
31	
32	
33	
34	
35	
36	
37	
38	
39	
40	

NO.	ANSWER A B C
41	
42	
43	
44	
45	
46	
47	
48	
49	
50	

NO.	ANSWER A B C D
51	Ⓐ Ⓑ Ⓒ Ⓓ
52	Ⓐ Ⓑ Ⓒ Ⓓ
53	Ⓐ Ⓑ Ⓒ Ⓓ
54	Ⓐ Ⓑ Ⓒ Ⓓ
55	Ⓐ Ⓑ Ⓒ Ⓓ
56	Ⓐ Ⓑ Ⓒ Ⓓ
57	Ⓐ Ⓑ Ⓒ Ⓓ
58	Ⓐ Ⓑ Ⓒ Ⓓ
59	Ⓐ Ⓑ Ⓒ Ⓓ
60	Ⓐ Ⓑ Ⓒ Ⓓ

NO.	ANSWER A B C D
61	
62	
63	
64	
65	
66	
67	
68	
69	
70	

NO.	ANSWER A B C D
71	
72	
73	
74	
75	
76	
77	
78	
79	
80	

NO.	ANSWER A B C D
81	Ⓐ Ⓑ Ⓒ Ⓓ
82	Ⓐ Ⓑ Ⓒ Ⓓ
83	Ⓐ Ⓑ Ⓒ Ⓓ
84	Ⓐ Ⓑ Ⓒ Ⓓ
85	Ⓐ Ⓑ Ⓒ Ⓓ
86	Ⓐ Ⓑ Ⓒ Ⓓ
87	Ⓐ Ⓑ Ⓒ Ⓓ
88	Ⓐ Ⓑ Ⓒ Ⓓ
89	Ⓐ Ⓑ Ⓒ Ⓓ
90	Ⓐ Ⓑ Ⓒ Ⓓ

NO.	ANSWER A B C D
91	
92	
93	
94	
95	
96	
97	
98	
99	
100	

READING (Part Ⅴ～Ⅷ)

NO.	ANSWER A B C D
101	Ⓐ Ⓑ Ⓒ Ⓓ
102	Ⓐ Ⓑ Ⓒ Ⓓ
103	Ⓐ Ⓑ Ⓒ Ⓓ
104	Ⓐ Ⓑ Ⓒ Ⓓ
105	Ⓐ Ⓑ Ⓒ Ⓓ
106	Ⓐ Ⓑ Ⓒ Ⓓ
107	Ⓐ Ⓑ Ⓒ Ⓓ
108	Ⓐ Ⓑ Ⓒ Ⓓ
109	Ⓐ Ⓑ Ⓒ Ⓓ
110	Ⓐ Ⓑ Ⓒ Ⓓ

NO.	ANSWER A B C D
111	Ⓐ Ⓑ Ⓒ Ⓓ
112	Ⓐ Ⓑ Ⓒ Ⓓ
113	Ⓐ Ⓑ Ⓒ Ⓓ
114	Ⓐ Ⓑ Ⓒ Ⓓ
115	
116	
117	
118	
119	
120	

NO.	ANSWER A B C D
121	
122	
123	
124	
125	
126	
127	
128	
129	
130	

NO.	ANSWER A B C D
131	
132	
133	
134	
135	
136	
137	
138	
139	
140	

NO.	ANSWER A B C D
141	Ⓐ Ⓑ Ⓒ Ⓓ
142	Ⓐ Ⓑ Ⓒ Ⓓ
143	Ⓐ Ⓑ Ⓒ Ⓓ
144	Ⓐ Ⓑ Ⓒ Ⓓ
145	Ⓐ Ⓑ Ⓒ Ⓓ
146	Ⓐ Ⓑ Ⓒ Ⓓ
147	Ⓐ Ⓑ Ⓒ Ⓓ
148	
149	
150	

NO.	ANSWER A B C D
151	Ⓐ Ⓑ Ⓒ Ⓓ
152	Ⓐ Ⓑ Ⓒ Ⓓ
153	Ⓐ Ⓑ Ⓒ Ⓓ
154	Ⓐ Ⓑ Ⓒ Ⓓ
155	Ⓐ Ⓑ Ⓒ Ⓓ
156	Ⓐ Ⓑ Ⓒ Ⓓ
157	Ⓐ Ⓑ Ⓒ Ⓓ
158	
159	
160	

NO.	ANSWER A B C D
161	Ⓐ Ⓑ Ⓒ Ⓓ
162	Ⓐ Ⓑ Ⓒ Ⓓ
163	Ⓐ Ⓑ Ⓒ Ⓓ
164	Ⓐ Ⓑ Ⓒ Ⓓ
165	Ⓐ Ⓑ Ⓒ Ⓓ
166	Ⓐ Ⓑ Ⓒ Ⓓ
167	Ⓐ Ⓑ Ⓒ Ⓓ
168	Ⓐ Ⓑ Ⓒ Ⓓ
169	Ⓐ Ⓑ Ⓒ Ⓓ
170	Ⓐ Ⓑ Ⓒ Ⓓ

NO.	ANSWER A B C D
171	Ⓐ Ⓑ Ⓒ Ⓓ
172	Ⓐ Ⓑ Ⓒ Ⓓ
173	Ⓐ Ⓑ Ⓒ Ⓓ
174	Ⓐ Ⓑ Ⓒ Ⓓ
175	Ⓐ Ⓑ Ⓒ Ⓓ
176	Ⓐ Ⓑ Ⓒ Ⓓ
177	Ⓐ Ⓑ Ⓒ Ⓓ
178	Ⓐ Ⓑ Ⓒ Ⓓ
179	Ⓐ Ⓑ Ⓒ Ⓓ
180	Ⓐ Ⓑ Ⓒ Ⓓ

NO.	ANSWER A B C D
181	Ⓐ Ⓑ Ⓒ Ⓓ
182	Ⓐ Ⓑ Ⓒ Ⓓ
183	Ⓐ Ⓑ Ⓒ Ⓓ
184	Ⓐ Ⓑ Ⓒ Ⓓ
185	
186	
187	
188	
189	
190	

NO.	ANSWER A B C D
191	
192	
193	
194	
195	
196	
197	
198	
199	
200	

LISTENING COMPREHENSION

In this section of the test, you will have the chance to show how well you understand spoken English. There are four parts to this section, with special directions for each part.

PART I

Directions: For each question, you will see a picture in your test book and you will hear four short statements. The statements will be spoken just one time. They will not be printed in your test book, so you must listen carefully to understand what the speaker says.

When you hear the four statements, look at the picture in your test book and choose the statement that best describes what you see in the picture. Then, on your answer sheet, find the number of the question and mark your answer. Look at the sample below.

Sample Answer

Ⓐ ● Ⓒ Ⓓ

Now listen to the four statements.

Statement (B), "They're having a meeting," best describes what you see in the picture. Therefore, you should choose answer (B).

1.

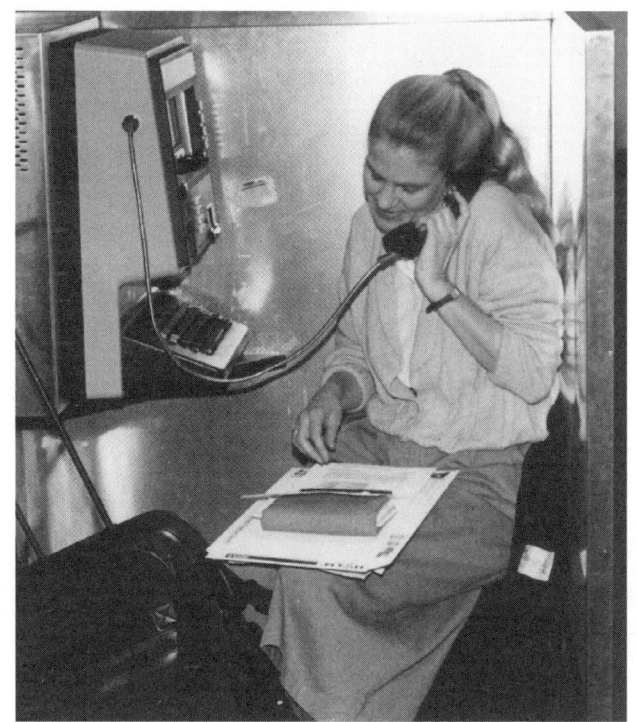

2.

GO ON TO THE NEXT PAGE

3.

4.

5.

6.

GO ON TO THE NEXT PAGE →

7.

PART II

Directions: In this part of the test, you will hear a question spoken in English, followed by three responses, also spoken in English. The question and the responses will be spoken just one time. They will not be printed in your test book, so you must listen carefully to understand what the speakers say. You are to choose the best response to each question.

Now listen to a sample question.

Sample Answer
● Ⓑ Ⓒ

You will hear:

You will also hear:

The best response to the question "How are you?" is choice (A), "I am fine, thank you." Therefore, you should choose answer (A).

21. Mark your answer on your answer sheet.

22. Mark your answer on your answer sheet.

23. Mark your answer on your answer sheet.

24. Mark your answer on your answer sheet.

25. Mark your answer on your answer sheet.

26. Mark your answer on your answer sheet.

27. Mark your answer on your answer sheet.

28. Mark your answer on your answer sheet.

29. Mark your answer on your answer sheet.

30. Mark your answer on your answer sheet.

GO ON TO THE NEXT PAGE

PART III

Directions: In this part of the test, you will hear ten short conversations between two people. The conversations will not be printed in your test book. You will hear the conversations only once, so you must listen carefully to understand what the speakers say.

In your test book, you will read a question about each conversation. The question will be followed by four answers. You are to choose the best answer to each question and mark it on your answer sheet.

51. How long will Mr. Olmos be away?

(A) Four days.
(B) One week.
(C) Two weeks.
(D) Over one month.

52. What does the woman want to do?

(A) Get directions to the office.
(B) Get a special line.
(C) Make an international call.
(D) Change the office phones.

53. How will the man probably travel?

(A) By train.
(B) By car.
(C) By plane.
(D) By bus.

54. What are they discussing?

(A) A vacation.
(B) An upcoming conference.
(C) A sports event.
(D) A party.

55. Who faxed the notes?

(A) Ms. Tanaka.
(B) The sales representative.
(C) The accounting supervisor.
(D) Mr. Mizuno.

56. When will the customer's order arrive?

(A) In two days.
(B) In four days.
(C) In eight days.
(D) In ten days.

57. Why is the woman relieved?

(A) She did not miss her flight.
(B) The ticket information is correct.
(C) The plane is an hour early.
(D) She has time to eat.

58. Where does the conversation probably take place?

(A) In a lecture hall.
(B) At a theater.
(C) At a stadium.
(D) In a waiting room.

59. What is the man looking for?

(A) A copy machine.
(B) A pharmacist.
(C) A package.
(D) A job.

60. Where is the woman going?

(A) To a medical office.
(B) To a taxi stand.
(C) Downtown.
(D) To the station.

PART IV

Directions: In this part of the test, you will hear several short talks. Each will be spoken just one time. They will not be printed in your test book, so you must listen carefully to understand and remember what is said.

In your test book, you will read two or more questions about each short talk. The questions will be followed by four answers. You are to choose the best answer to each question and mark it on your answer sheet.

81. Who is speaking?

(A) A police officer.
(B) A weather forecaster.
(C) A radio announcer.
(D) A bus driver.

82. According to the report, what is causing the traffic delays?

(A) Traffic accidents.
(B) Fog.
(C) Road construction. ✓
(D) Floods.

83. How are the apartments described?

(A) They are up-to-date in design.
(B) They have two bedrooms.
(C) They are in the middle of the city.
(D) They are very small.

84. What is included in the rent?

(A) Country-club fees.
(B) Gardening services.
(C) Health-club membership. ✓
(D) A video.

85. What is the speaker doing?

(A) Showing photos of the southwest region.
(B) Talking about her company on television. ✓
(C) Presenting an award to an employee. → ✓
(D) Introducing a new sales campaign.

86. Who will speak next?

(A) The company president.
(B) Joan Berry.
(C) Jill Smith. ✓
(D) Someone from the president's office.

87. Why is the construction being rescheduled?

(A) The government has requested a delay.
(B) The building codes are being changed. ✓
(C) The designers' workload is being decreased.
(D) The client has requested a new building site. ✓

88. When are the design plans due?

(A) Today.
(B) In two weeks. ※
(C) By March of next year.
(D) By November of this year. ✓

This is the end of the Listening Comprehension portion of the test. Turn to Part V in your test book.

GO ON TO THE NEXT PAGE

READING

In this section of the test, you will have a chance to show how well you understand written English. There are three parts to this section, with special directions for each part.

PART V

Directions: Questions 101-114 are incomplete sentences. Four words or phrases, marked (A), (B), (C), (D), are given beneath each sentence. You are to choose the **one** word or phrase that best completes the sentence. Then, on your answer sheet, find the number of the question and mark your answer.

You will read:

Because the equipment is very delicate, it must be handled with -------.

(A) caring
(B) careful
(C) care
(D) carefully

Sample Answer
Ⓐ Ⓑ ⬤ Ⓓ

The sentence should read, "Because the equipment is very delicate, it must be handled with care." Therefore, you should choose answer (C).

Now, begin work on the questions.

---

101. The publishers suggested that the envelopes be sent to ------- by courier so that the film can be developed as soon as possible.

(A) they
(B) their
(C) theirs
(D) them

102. Board members ------- carefully define their goals and objectives for the agency before the monthly meeting next week.

(A) had
(B) should
(C) used
(D) have

103. For business relations to continue between our two firms, a satisfactory agreement must be ------- reached and signed.

(A) yet
(B) both
(C) either
(D) as well as

104. The corporation, which underwent a major restructuring seven years ago, has been growing steadily ------- five years.

(A) for
(B) on
(C) from
(D) since

105. Making advance arrangements for audiovisual equipment is ------- recommended for all seminars.

(A) sternly
(B) strikingly
(C) stringently
(D) strongly

106. Two assistants will be required to ------- reporters' names when they arrive at the press conference.

(A) remark
(B) check
(C) notify
(D) ensure

107. The present government has an excellent ------- to increase exports.

(A) popularity
(B) regularity
(C) celebrity
(D) opportunity

108. While you are in the building, please wear your identification badge at all times so that you are ------- as a company employee.

(A) recognize
(B) recognizing
(C) recognizable
(D) recognizably

109. Our studies show that increases in worker productivity have not been adequately rewarded by significant increases in -------.

(A) compensation
(B) commodity
(C) compilation
(D) complacency

110. Conservatives predict that government finances will remain ------- during the period of the investigation.

(A) authoritative
(B) summarized
(C) examined
(D) stable

111. Mr. Kobayashi spoke quite ------- while he was making his sales presentation.

(A) exciting
(B) excitable
(C) excitedly
(D) excitement

112. It is essential that we operate ------- the parameters of time and a limited budget.

(A) among
(B) about
(C) within
(D) onto

113. The success ------- the new manufacturing process has doubled the number of requests for the product.

(A) to
(B) of
(C) for
(D) by

114. Interviewees should be given the company brochure to read ------- they are waiting for their interviews.

(A) during
(B) after
(C) with
(D) while

GO ON TO THE NEXT PAGE

PART VI

Directions: In **Questions 141-147,** each sentence has four words or phrases underlined. The four underlined parts of the sentence are marked (A), (B), (C), (D). You are to identify the **one** underlined word or phrase that should be corrected or rewritten. Then, on your answer sheet, find the number of the question and mark your answer.

Example:

Sample Answer
● B C D

All employee are required to wear their
   A   B

identification badges while at work.
    C   D

The underlined word "employee" is not correct in this sentence. This sentence should read, "All employees are required to wear their identification badges while at work." Therefore, you should choose answer (A).

Now begin work on the questions.

---

141. According to the press release, the
            A   B
company is planning on introduce several
                    C
new machines in the coming year.
          D

142. A total of ten thousands of dollars was spent
              A   B
on radio advertising, despite recent
              C
requests for budget-cutting measures.
       D

143. Employees will be reimbursed for business
            A
travel expenses incurred while on
              B
assignment away from the normal
         C
work located.
   D

144. The staff was told by their supervisor that
           A
the new safety inspection schedule would
       B   C
take effect on the end of the year.
       D

145. Your new credit card will bring you benefits
   A   B
that provides greater financial flexibility.
     C   D

146. Last week the President has announced
                A
more taxes on many crops grown for
     B   C
overseas markets.
     D

147. The computer software industry is
         A
one of most competitive markets in today's
    B   C
technologically advanced society.
       D

PART VII

Directions: Questions 161-174 are based on a selection of reading materials, such as notices, letters, forms, newspaper and magazine articles, and advertisements. You are to choose the **one** best answer (A), (B), (C), or (D), to each question. Then, on your answer sheet, find the number of the question and mark your answer. Answer all questions following each reading selection on the basis of what is **stated** or **implied** in that selection.

Read the following example.

> The Museum of Technology is a "hands-on" museum, designed for people to experience science at work. Visitors are encouraged to use, test, and handle the objects on display. Special demonstrations are scheduled for the first and second Wednesdays of each month at 13:30. Open Tuesday-Friday 12:00-16:30, Saturday 10:00-17:30, and Sunday 11:00-16:30.
>
> When during the month can visitors see special demonstrations?

(A) Every weekend
(B) The first two Wednesdays
(C) One afternoon a week
(D) Every other Wednesday

Sample Answer

The reading selection says that the demonstrations are scheduled for the first and second Wednesdays of the month. Therefore, you should choose answer (B).

Now begin work on the questions.

GO ON TO THE NEXT PAGE

On June 7 the company will hold its first worldwide videoconference. All twenty facilities will be linked by a satellite broadcasting system so that employees can see and speak with each other. Officials of the Zurich head office will begin the conference by telling us about their goals for the next ten years. Next, each facility manager will speak about current challenges. The last hour will be devoted to questions from the floor at all locations. Due to time differences, employees in Asia and South America will have to come to their broadcast facilities outside of regular business hours. Additional pay will be provided for them for this inconvenience. If this format proves productive, we hope to schedule worldwide and regional videoconferences periodically.

161. What will be the first agenda item at the conference?

(A) Plans for a decade
(B) Twenty-year goals
(C) Present challenges
(D) Questions from employees

162. Why will some employees receive extra pay?

(A) They must speak at the conference.
(B) The conference will take place before or after work.
(C) They must travel to other offices to attend.
(D) Their departments have met certain goals.

Questions 163-164 refer to the following newspaper article.

WASHINGTON—A government study released yesterday said that businesses should implement widespread commercial use of encryption, mathematical formulas to scramble electronic data, to curb the theft of computer data, wireless communications, and other electronic information. A committee of the government research council, which gives science and technology advice, said a broad use of encryption would help industries in many ways, including by making banking and telecommunications networks more secure and by giving people greater privacy. The committee also recommended that export controls on encryption technologies be progressively relaxed but not eliminated.

163. What does the study suggest businesses do?

(A) Curb electronic information sharing
(B) Use special technology to scramble electronic data
(C) Progressively relax government export controls
(D) Invest in government research

164. According to the article, how will the committee's recommendations benefit businesses?

(A) Science and technology advice will be available.
(B) Computer data will be processed more quickly.
(C) Government resources will be shared.
(D) Telecommunications networks will be more secure.

GO ON TO THE NEXT PAGE

Questions 165-168 refer to the following job advertisement.

 CHIEF INFORMATION OFFICER

We are one of the fastest-growing major health-care facilities in the country, with an immediate need for a Chief Information Officer. Our CIO is responsible for all information-systems activities, including systems analysis, management reporting, and computer functions. This person sets information-systems policies, procedures, and technical standards and acts as a liaison between Information Services and other management departments. The ideal candidate has an advanced degree and 7 years' experience in health-care information systems, including at least 4 years of supervisory experience. Programming experience is not necessary, but experience with systems conversions is beneficial.

We offer a competitive salary and excellent benefits, along with the opportunity to work in a dynamic, growing organization. Please send resume with cover letter and salary history to:

University Medical Center
P.O. Box 1234
Dubai, UAE
ATTN: Human Resources

Phone, fax, and e-mail applications will not be processed.

165. Who placed the advertisement?

(A) A secretarial school
(B) The Dubai chief information officer
(C) A computer company
(D) A hospital

166. Which of these is required?

(A) Programming experience
(B) Ten years of work experience
(C) Supervisory experience
(D) A medical degree

167. What must an applicant submit?

(A) An employment history
(B) An application fee
(C) Personal references
(D) Medical records

168. How should one apply?

(A) In person
(B) By fax
(C) By mail
(D) By e-mail

Mach
Motors Company, Inc.

Fredriksdalsgatan 100 412 GS Göteborg, Sweden

Dear Customer:

The satisfaction and safety of all our customers is of prime concern to us. We are therefore contacting all owners of this year's Spectra to alert them to improvements in the design of one of the car's features. You may have noticed that the rear seat belts have a tendency to remain locked inside the retractors when the car is parked at a sharp angle, such as on a steep hill. Once the car is back on level ground, the seat belts unlock and the rear-seat passengers are able to put on their seat belts.

Our engineers have developed new parts for the retractors that significantly reduce this problem. It would be our pleasure to have new retractors installed for you at no charge. Simply bring your Spectra to the nearest Mach dealer and allow twenty-four hours for installation. Once the improvement has been made, we are confident that your car's seat belts will meet the highest standards for safety.

If you have any questions, please contact your local dealer.

Sincerely yours,

Gunnar Widengren

Gunnar Widengren
Vice President

169. To whom is the letter addressed?

(A) Mach Spectra owners
(B) Mach service technicians
(C) Mach parts department staff
(D) Mach dealers

170. What is the purpose of the letter?

(A) To recommend seat belt use
(B) To announce a parts improvement
(C) To offer tips on parking
(D) To advertise a new car model

171. What is the company offering for free?

(A) An improved parking brake
(B) A car seat cover
(C) Front seat belts
(D) A better retractor

GO ON TO THE NEXT PAGE

Questions 172-174 refer to the following E-mail message.

```
*E-mail*

To:       Robert O'Neill <oneill@shannon.com.ie>
From:     Georges Bemanajara <beman@les.dts.mg>
Subject:  Europe Trip
Date:     Tues, 07 Sept 11:53:05
```

Just want to leave my phone number in the Netherlands with you: 23-319501. I'll be in Amsterdam until the 15th but want to keep in touch. I plan to be in London the 16th-19th before returning home. Will try to contact Stacie Drese and Amy Little at the engineering firm in London as soon as I arrive; however, I am worried about rumors of an upcoming air-traffic controller's strike. If that were to occur, could the seminar be postponed? Please give me a call at your earliest convenience.

172. Who is traveling to Amsterdam?

(A) Stacie Drese
(B) Amy Little
(C) Georges Bemanajara
(D) Robert O'Neill

173. What is the last day of the business trip in Amsterdam?

(A) 7th
(B) 15th
(C) 16th
(D) 19th

174. What might cause the seminar to be delayed?

(A) An airport strike
(B) Adverse weather conditions
(C) A high priority meeting
(D) Rumors of a cancellation

Stop! This is the end of the mini-test. Now check your answers with the answer key in Appendix A.

CHAPTER 2

第2章

TOEICテストを受けるに
当たってのアドバイス

- TOEICテストを受けるための準備
- テスト当日の準備
- 総合的な英語力を伸ばす

第2章

TOEICテストを受けるための準備

アドバイス　各パートの問題形式を知る

テスト形式を知れば、個々の問題の内容に集中して取り組むことができます。

■ TOEICテストはSection I のListeningとSection II のReadingからなる試験時間2時間の多肢選択式テストです。各セクションには100問の設問があり、全体で200問になります。

■ Section I のListeningが始めに行われます。試験時間は45分間で、次のように4つの問題形式（パート）で構成されています。

　Part Ⅰ　写真描写問題
　Part Ⅱ　応答問題
　Part Ⅲ　会話問題
　Part Ⅳ　説明文問題

Listeningでは、一人あるいは数人の録音された音声で100問それぞれの問題が流れます。この音声は一度しか流れません。

■ Section II のReadingはSection I のListeningに続いて行われます。試験時間は75分間で、次の3つの問題形式（パート）で構成されています。

　Part Ⅴ　文法・語彙問題
　Part Ⅵ　誤文訂正問題
　Part Ⅶ　読解問題

Readingの各パートの間には音声の案内はありませんので、時間内にすべての設問に答えられるよう時間配分に注意してください。

アドバイス　特殊な分野のスキルや知識は問われないことに注意する

TOEICテストは英語能力を測定します。言いかえれば、言語の運用能力を測定するものです。以下に挙げる事項や状況がテストに現れても、その分野についての知識はテストされません。

■ 地理について。国の場所、国や首都の名称

■ 歴史的事実や出来事

■ 英語を公用語とする国または他の国の祝日の名称と日付

■ 時事的な話題や政治的指導者の名前

■ 特殊なビジネス用語と専門用語。たとえば、株式指標の名称、機器の名称など

■ 数学

■ 重さと長さの単位。たとえば、フィートとインチ、マイルとキロメートル、ポンドとキログラムの換算など

■ 文学と芸術に関する事柄

TOEICテストに出題される一般的な内容のリストが本書のイントロダクションにあります。

アドバイス 以下の受験方法に留意する

■ **最初に質問を読んでおく**： ListeningのPart ⅢやPart Ⅳでは、それぞれの音声を聞く前になるべく質問を読んでおきます。ReadingのPart Ⅶでも質問を先に読んでおけば、解答に必要な情報を見つけられます。

■ **解答する前に設問全体を聞く、または読んでおく**：複数の選択肢が正解に思われることもあるでしょう。あわてずに解答を選びましょう。

■ **知らない単語があってもあわてない**：必ずしもすべての単語の意味を知っておく必要はありません。質問されていることが全体の要点についてだけであり、知らない単語とは何の関係もないこともあるでしょう。

■ **要点を頭の中でまとめてみる**：そうすることで質問に対する答えがわかることもあるでしょう。

■ **確信が持てなければ推測する**：TOEICテストでは推測で解答しても罰則はありません。もっとも正解らしく思われる解答を選んでください。解答しないよりは推測で解答したほうが有利です。

■ **Listeningでは音声に遅れないようにする**：各設問に時間を使いすぎないように注意してください。5秒から8秒のポーズの後に次の設問の音声が流れてきます。解答が決まったらすぐに解答用紙にマークするようにしましょう。前の設問に戻ってはいけません。後続の設問に答えられなくなることがあります。

■ **Readingでは時間が余れば見直しをする**：自分の解答をチェックし、解答用紙にマークしてない設問がないようにします。このセクションでの受験方法はListeningとは異なります。

アドバイス　テストに備えて体調を整える

■ **食事**：テスト会場へ行く前にきちんと食事をとりましょう。食べすぎると眠くなりますが、体力が持続するように十分な食事を取りましょう。

■ **睡眠**：TOEICテストを受験する前の晩は十分休むようにしましょう。テストの前の晩に十分な睡眠をとることは、徹夜で勉強するより効果があります。

■ **リラックス**：本書をよく読んで、練習問題を全部終えたら、自信を持ってテストに臨めるでしょう。テストの出来映えを心配せずに、自信を持ってテストを受けましょう。

アドバイス　TOEICテストを受ける時に注意すること

■ **必要な事項をもれなく記入する**：氏名などを解答用紙に記入したか確認しましょう。第6章に解答用紙のサンプルが掲載されています。

■ **問題の指示を注意深く読む**：本書の練習問題でも問題の指示を読む練習ができます。テストを受ける時にも、各パートの前の指示を読むようにしましょう。

■ **答えを1つだけ選んで、解答用紙にマークする**：2つ以上の答えをマークすると、両方とも不正解となります。

■ **テスト会場に持参できるものとできないもの**：

　持参するもの：受験票、身分証明書、筆記用具、腕時計。
　持参できないもの：録音機、カメラ、辞書。これらのものは試験会場に持ち込むことはできません。

アドバイス　英語環境をつくる

TOEICテストは英語能力テストです。英語の運用能力を測定します。TOEICテストに備えるには、できるだけ多く英語を聞いたり読んだりする環境をつくると良いでしょう。英語の教科書や文法書も有効ですが、本物の英語のコミュニケーションを欠いている嫌いがあります。TOEICテストはグローバルな職場で使われる実際の話し言葉や書き言葉に重点を置いて出題します。以下に、生きた英語に触れるのに役立つ資料や方法を挙げます。

・ＣＤやオーディオカセット

書籍、講演、歌、詩などを英語で録音したものを聞きましょう。話者は誰なのか、何の話題か、主な内容は何かなどがわかるまで、何回か聞いてみましょう。

・同僚や友達

英語力を伸ばそうという仲間と英語のディスカッショングループをつくりましょう。

・英語の先生／ネイティブ・スピーカー

先生や英語のネイティブ・スピーカーと話す機会をつくりましょう。

・ラジオ

英語放送を聞いてみましょう。リスニングの練習には最適です。全部の単語がわからなくても大丈夫です。話題は何なのか、話者は誰なのか、討論のテーマは何かなどを理解するようにしましょう。

・ビデオ／テレビ

英語のビデオやテレビ番組を見ましょう。テープを止めて、あらすじを要約し、次にどうなるかを予測しましょう。ビデオやテレビ番組を友達と一緒に見た後で、英語でそれについてディスカッションしましょう。

・書籍

いちいち辞書をひかないでも読める本を見つけましょう。小説などを読むと語彙が増え、色々な種類のフォーマルな英語とインフォーマルな英語を知ることができます。機器などの取扱説明書やビジネス文書も語彙力増強に役立ちます。

・パンフレット

英語圏の観光局や、旅行代理店、民間団体、大学、大企業などに行ったり手紙を書いて問い合わせてみましょう。こうした機関では、パンフレットや良い英語教材になるものを入手できます。

・雑誌

多くの航空会社は機内誌を配布しています。こうした雑誌には、しばしば職場に関連した面白い記事が載っています。また、様々な話題を短い記事にまとめた週刊ニュース誌もたくさんあります。ファッション、食事、スポーツ雑誌も実際の書き言葉を学習するツールとなります。

・通信販売のカタログ

英語でビジネスをしている会社のなかには通信販売で製品を売っているところもあります。英語のカタログや製品情報を請求しましょう。

・メニュー

メニューを持ち帰ることができるレストランもたくさんあります。英語版のメニューをもらいましょう。

・新聞

英字新聞を読みましょう。英語学習者用に発行されている新聞もあります。

・ワールド・ワイド・ウェブとインターネット

ESL (English as a second language) のウェブ・サイトを見てみましょう。英語の記事がオンラインで読める新聞や雑誌もたくさんあります。また友人や同僚と英語で電子メールをやり取りしましょう。

CHAPTER 3

第3章

TOEIC
Section I Listening

■Section I Listening の概要

■Section I Listening のための全体的な受験方法

■Section I Listening パート別の受験方法

■第3章のまとめ

3 第3章

Section I　Listeningの概要

・Section I Listeningは、TOEICテストの第1問から第100問までです。カセット・テープで音声が流れます。このセクションは4つのパートに分かれます。

　　Part I　　写真描写問題
　　Part II　　応答問題
　　Part III　　会話問題
　　Part IV　　説明文問題

・英語で録音された音声で、様々なコメント、質問、短い会話、短いアナウンスがなされます。その音声の理解に基づいて、質問に答えていきます。

・音声を止めることはできませんが、各質問の間に5秒から8秒のポーズがありますので、その間に解答します。

・録音された音声はすべて1度しか流れません。

・Section I Listeningは全部で45分です。

アドバイス　強く発音された単語に注意する

Listening では、強く発音された単語に注意を払いましょう。英語の話し言葉では、文中のある単語が強く発音されます。つまり、話される文中のある部分は他の部分よりも強勢が置かれて発音されるということです。強く発音される単語には通常もっとも重要な情報が含まれており、そうしたものに名詞、動詞、形容詞があります。文中の他の単語はほとんど、またはまったく強勢が置かれません。たいていの場合、これらはあまり重要な意味を持たない単語ですが、文法上必要なものです。そうしたものに冠詞の a と the, 代名詞、前置詞、接続詞、助動詞があります。

CD1　No.5

Example 1

The doctor and a nurse are talking with a patient.

話し言葉の英語では、上の文は 4 つの個所に強勢が置かれます。すなわち、名詞の doctor, nurse, patient と動詞の talking です。矢印はこの文が話されるときに強勢が置かれる単語を示しています。

↓   ↓   ↓   ↓

The <u>doctor</u> and a <u>nurse</u> are <u>talking</u> with a <u>patient</u>.

ほとんどあるいはまったく強勢が置かれない単語は、冠詞の the と a, 接続詞の and, be 動詞の are, そして前置詞の with です。この文で強勢が置かれた単語だけを聞けば、何を言っているのかだいたいわかるはずです。強く発音された単語で要点がわかります。

3

アドバイス　英語の実際の話し言葉に慣れる

Listeningでは、英語のネイティブ・スピーカーである男性と女性の声が流れます。自然なスピードで話され、インフォーマルな話し言葉とフォーマルな話し言葉があります。

インフォーマルな英語とフォーマルな英語の例をいくつか挙げます。

	インフォーマルな英語		フォーマルな英語
短縮	*I'll*	➜	*I will*
	he's	➜	*he is or he has*
発音省略	*gonna*	➜	*going to*
	wanna	➜	*want to*
語彙	*lots of*	➜	*many*
	boss	➜	*director or supervisor*
	get in touch with	➜	*contact*
	yeah	➜	*yes*
文法	*Who are you talking to?*	➜	*To whom are you speaking?*

Listeningで聞く会話とコメントは、世界中の職場、レクリエーションの場、プライベートな場で話されるような英語の例です。

実際に話される英語のリスニング練習方法については第2章を読んで下さい。

アドバイス　解答を選ぶ前に録音された音声を注意深く聞く

Listeningで正しい解答を選ぶには、普通は問題全体を聞いてみる必要があります。正解の手がかりは音声の始めにあったり、中ほどにあったり、終わりの部分にあったりします。

3

Part I：写真描写問題

このパートでは動作、もの、場所、人々などの写真を見ながら、テープから各々の写真に対して4つのコメントを聞きます。4つの選択肢のすべてが写真について正しい描写をしているように聞こえるかもしれませんが、正解は1つだけです。写真描写問題は全部で20問あります。各問の間には5秒の間隔があります。

正解する実力をつけるためのアドバイスをいくつか挙げます。

アドバイス　4つのコメントを聞く前に写真をさっとながめておく

各々の写真に対して次のような質問を自分でしてみましょう。

どこで撮影されたか？
主題は何か？
何が起きているか？
写真の人々は誰か？

アドバイス 同じように聞こえる、異なる意味を持つ単語に注意する

4つの選択肢を聞くときは、発音が同じように聞こえても、意味の異なる単語である場合があるので注意しましょう。

CD1 No.6

Example 2

They're *walking* in a garden.
They're *working* in a garden.

They're working in a garden.

She's *setting* the table.
She's *sitting* at the table.

She's sitting at the table.

---

working と walking, sitting と setting は同じように聞こえますが意味はまったく違います。写真を見ながら注意深く聞いて、このような似た音の単語に惑わされないようにしましょう。

アドバイス　写真についてのコメント全体をよく聞く

写真についてのコメントは部分的に正しいことがあります。コメント全体が正しいのか、ある部分だけが正しいのか、注意して聞きましょう。

CD1　No.7

Example 3

He's adjusting the dials on a television set.

男性がダイヤルを調整しているのは正しいですが、写真にはテレビは写っていません。よって上のコメントは、写真を全体的に正しく言い表わしていないことになります。

実力強化　Skill Building

Exercise A

下の3枚の写真を見てください。各々の写真についてのコメントを聞き、正しいコメントのアルファベットに〇をつけましょう。各々の写真について、正解は2つ以上あります。このページの一番下に正解があります。

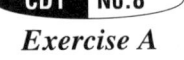

CD1　No.8

Exercise A

1.

1. A. They're putting the violins away.
   B. The performance has begun.
   C. They're standing on a stage.
   D. The concert is taking place outdoors.
   E. The curtain is beginning to rise.
   F. They're drawing bows across the strings.
   G. They're giving a concert.

2.

2. A. There are buildings near a lake.
   B. The land in this area is very flat.
   C. Buildings are reflected in the water.
   D. There are houses on the hillside.
   E. The water is very calm.
   F. Factory chimneys rise above the village.
   G. People are boating on the river.

3.

3. A. The men are wiring an appliance.
   B. The men are all wearing hats.
   C. Wiring is being placed underground.
   D. A man is opening a window.
   E. The men are setting a table.
   F. The men are laying wheels on the ground.
   G. A man is pulling a cable.

解答

1. B, F and G　　　2. A, C, D, and E　　　3. B, C, and G

Exercise B

例に従って下の写真についてできるだけ多くの単語や文を書いてみましょう。答えとして考えられるものがこのページの一番下に挙げてあります。他に異なる答えもあり得ます。

写真に何が写っているか　　　　　　**写真についての文**

a large table　　　　　　　　　　　People are sitting around a large table

men

women

_____　　　　_____

_____　　　　_____

_____　　　　_____

_____　　　　_____

_____　　　　_____

_____　　　　_____

自己学習

■ 本や雑誌の写真に目を通しましょう。色々な場面や状況を見つけ出すようにします。各々の写真に対して、写真に関連する単語を書きとめ、写っている内容を言い表わす文を書いてみます。書いた文がTOEICテストの選択肢にとても似ていることもあるでしょう。

写真に何が写っているか　　　　　**写真についての文**

_____　　_____
_____　　_____
_____　　_____
_____　　_____
_____　　_____
_____　　_____
_____　　_____
_____　　_____

■ 写真や絵を友達や同僚と交換しましょう。自分で書いた文を見せずに友達に写真を描写してもらいましょう。そしてどちらの文がその写真をより正確に言い表わしているか、自分のものと比べましょう。

Part II：応答問題

このパートでは、一人の話し手が質問をして、それにもう一人の話し手が3種類の応答をします。問題用紙には何も印刷されていません。3つの応答はすべて正しい英語ですが、質問に対する応答としては1つだけが適切です。応答問題は全部で30問です。各問の間に5秒の間隔があります。

このパートで正解する実力をつけるためのアドバイスをいくつか挙げます。

アドバイス　質問の目的に焦点を合わせる

質問の目的を理解することが重要です。他の多くの言語と同じく英語でも、質問に対する応答文は質問文と同じ文法構造であるとはかぎりません。

CD1　No.9

Example 4

Who's going to be in charge of processing paychecks now?

(A) Yes, I have a credit card.
(B) The assistant accountant.
(C) It's a complicated process.

質問文と同じ文法構造の応答文を想定すれば、応答文は "is going to be in charge." というフレーズを含んでいると思うかもしれません。しかし選択肢Bはこのフレーズを含んでいなくても "Who?" という質問に対する適切な答えになっています。

CD1　No.10

Example 5

Where is the employee cafeteria?

(A) He's out sick today.
(B) Yes, I'm really hungry.
(C) I'm not sure; I just started here.

質問文と同じ文法構造の応答文を想定すれば、応答文は"It is located" というフレーズを含んでいると思うかもしれません。しかし、このフレーズを含んでいなくても選択肢Cは場所を聞く質問に対して現実にあり得る答えになっています。いつも質問に即した答えが返ってくるとはかぎりません。TOEICテストの問題は、実際の英語の話し言葉を扱っているということに注意してください。

3

アドバイス　疑問詞に注意して聞く

疑問詞や疑問文の語順に注意して聞きましょう。そうした文はどのような応答が期待されるかを示しているのが普通です。次に挙げる質問と応答を考えてみましょう。

CD1　No.11

Example 6

How are we going to the party?	→	*We're taking a taxi.*
When is the party?	→	*Thursday, at 4 P.M.*
Where is the party?	→	*In the director's lounge.*
Are we going to the party?	→	*Yes, we are.*

---

how, when, where のような疑問詞の用法をしっかりと頭に入れ、それぞれの疑問詞が求める情報を簡単に予想できるようにしましょう。疑問文の語順にも注意しましょう。yes や no の答えを求める質問文は疑問詞で始まりません。例えば、"Are we going to the party?" という問いに対しては、"Yes, we are." または、"No, we aren't." あるいは、"I'm not sure."という答えが返ってくるでしょう。

アドバイス　似た発音の単語に注意を払う

このパートのいくつかの選択肢では、似た発音の単語の意味の違いを聞き分ける必要があります。

CD1　No.12

Example 7

What is the fare to the airport?

Incorrect	→	*That's a fair price.*
Correct	→	*About 12 dollars.*

---

fair と fare は同じ発音ですが、意味はまったく異なります。この質問では空港まで行くのにかかる金額を尋ねています。

実力強化　Skill Building

3

Exercise C

次の質問を聞いて各々の質問の目的にもっともよく対応するアルファベットを選んでみましょう。この練習で話し手が実際に何を尋ねているのかがわかるようになります。正解はこのページの一番下にあります。

CD1 No.13

Exercise C

Sample Question: Where is the nearest post office?
　　Purpose: Asking for information (location)

質問

1. *Who's coming to the reception?*
2. *When are you taking your vacation?*
3. *Is it okay if I change the air filter?*
4. *Do you know why they built the new museum so far from the old one?*
5. *The play starts at 7:30, doesn't it?*
6. *You're not really taking a new job, are you?*
7. *Shouldn't we hire a new designer?*
8. *Would you like to join us for lunch?*

質問の目的

A. Asking for information (person)
B. Making a suggestion or request
C. Asking for confirmation (time)
D. Asking for information (time)
E. Extending an invitation
F. Expressing disbelief
G. Asking for information (reason)
H. Asking for permission (action)

解答

1.A　2.D　3.H　4.G　5.C　6.F　7.B　8.E

Exercise D

Exercise Cの質問を聞きましょう。質問文をTOEICルーラーで隠し、右側にある返答のなかから適切なものを選んでください。正解はこのページの一番下にあります。

CD1 No.14

Exercise D

Sample Question: Where is the nearest post office?
    Answer: There's one across from the city park.

質問

1. Who's coming to the reception?

2. When are you taking your vacation?

3. Is it okay if I change the air filter?

4. Do you know why they built the new museum so far from the old one?

5. The play starts at 7:30, doesn't it?

6. You're not really taking a new job, are you?

7. Shouldn't we hire a new designer?

8. Would you like to join us for lunch?

応答

1. _____   A. Nothing closer was available.

2. _____   B. Yes, I start in two weeks.

3. _____   C. The entire department is invited.

4. _____   D. Yes, we should.

5. _____   E. I thought it was at eight.

6. _____   F. I haven't decided yet.

7. _____   G. Sorry, but I have a noon meeting.

8. _____   H. Only if it's really dirty.

解答

1.C 2.F 3.H 4.A 5.E 6.B 7.D 8.G

自己学習

■ 質問文のカード集を作りましょう。カードや小さい紙の表に質問文を英語で書きます。その下に質問の目的を書きます。下の例を参照してください。

■ カードの裏側には質問に対して思いつく限りの応答をいくつも書きとめます。職場、テレビ、ラジオ、映画で聞いた実際の例を使いましょう。

■ これらのカードを何枚か作って友達や同僚と練習してみましょう。声を出して質問を読み、友達に適切な答えをいくつかしてもらいます。友達の答えと自分が裏に書いた答えを比べてみましょう。

> *Where is Mr. Davidson going?*
>
> asking for information
> (location)

> He's going to a café.
>
> He's going to go home.
>
> He's starting a new job at Bailey Incorporated.

> *Do you know what time the plant opens?*
>
> asking for information
> (time)

> It's open 24 hours.
>
> I'm not sure.
>
> Ask Ms. Chang.

Part Ⅲ：会話問題

このパートでは、二人の間の短い会話が流れます。その会話文自体は問題用紙には書いてありません。会話は実際に話される英語で構成されています。問題用紙にはその会話についての質問とその質問に対する4つの選択肢が書かれています。この4つの選択肢から正解を1つ選びます。各々の会話の間には8秒間のポーズがあります。会話問題は全部で30問あります。

このパートで正解する実力をつけるためのアドバイスを次にいくつか挙げてみましょう。

アドバイス　質問を先に読む

会話を聞く前に質問を読むように努めましょう。時間があれば、選択肢もざっと読んでおきましょう。質問を先に読むことによって何を聞けばよいかがわかり、何についての会話なのか見当がつきます。

次の質問を考えてみましょう。

Where are the speakers?

この質問を読むことにより、話し手がどこにいるのかがわかればよいという判断がつきます。話し手のいる場所についての手がかりを見つけるように会話を聞き取ればよいのです。

CD1　No.15

Example 8

On the recording, you will hear:

　　Man 1: *Are you ready to order, sir?*

　　Man 2: *I just need a few more minutes to read the menu.*

　　Man 1: *No problem. I'll be back in a moment to tell you the daily specials.*

In your test book, you will read:

Where are the speakers?

　(A)　At a library.
　(B)　At a supermarket.
　(C)　At a restaurant.
　(D)　At a movie theater.

答えの手がかりに的を絞って聞けば、次のような単語や表現を聞き取れるでしょう。

ready to order （最初の話し手は何か注文を聞こうとしている）
menu （メニューはレストランにあるものである）
daily specials （レストランではよくその日のおすすめ料理を出すことがある）

話し手がどこにいるかという手がかりに的を絞って聞けば、選択肢A，B，Dを除外することができます。

では次の質問を読んでみましょう。

What does the woman want to do?

会話を聞く前にこの質問を読むことによって、女性が何を求めているかに的を絞って聞くことができるわけです。話し手がどこにいるか、彼らが誰か、女性が何をしているかということを知る必要はありません。

CD1 No.16

Example 9

On the recording, you will hear:

Woman: *Is that today's paper? I want to see if our advertisement is in it.*

Man : *No, this is yesterday's. Today's hasn't come in yet.*

Woman: *Oh, I'll call downstairs and see if they have a copy.*

In your test book, you will read:

What does the woman want to do?

(A) Put an advertisement in the paper.
(B) Order a newspaper subscription.
(C) Have some photocopies made.
(D) Check the paper for an advertisement.

最初のせりふで、女性は "I want to see ..." と言っています。これにより彼女が望んでいること——広告が新聞に載っているかどうか——がわかります。この場合、see と check は同じ意味になります。よって選択肢Dが正解です。

アドバイス 会話の場面と話し手が誰なのかを想像してみる

会話を聞きながら次のような質問を自分でしてみます。

　　話し手はどこにいるか？
　　話し手は何をしているか？
　　話し手は誰か？
　　話し手の関係は何か？

さらに、問題用紙に書かれている質問から、会話の場面がわかることもよくあります。次の質問を例にとってみましょう。

　　Who mailed the reports?

話し手たちはオフィスで働いていることが想像されます。

会話の中のある語句から設定状況がわかることもあります。例えば会話で次のような語句が聞こえたとします。

assembly line	plant supervisor
shift	foreman
technicians	production line

工場か生産施設の場面であることが想像できるでしょう。

次の単語を例にとってみましょう。

patient	x-ray
doctor	exam
appointment	medicine

その会話は病院か診療所でなされていると想像できます。会話の場面を想像したり、会話の光景を頭のなかに描ければ、質問に答えることが容易になります。

アドバイス 解答する前にすべての選択肢を注意深く読む

会話の中で話される単語が4つの選択肢のなかに出てくることがよくあります。繰り返して出てくるこれらの単語が質問の答えに関係するかどうかを判断する必要があります。次の例を見てください。

CD1 No.17

Example 10

On the recording, you will hear:

> Man: *Brenda, can you give me a hand with this marketing project this afternoon?*
>
> Woman: *Well, I need to finish this product proposal today, then I'm going to catch a train at 5:15.*
>
> Man: *OK. Could we start on it first thing tomorrow morning, then?*

In your test book, you will read:

What does the man want Brenda to do?

(A) Postpone the proposal.
(B) Hand him some papers.
(C) Tell him what time the train leaves.
(D) Help him with a project.

選択肢Aは女性の提案書について述べています。彼女が提案書を作成していることは事実ですが、男性は彼女にそれを遅らせるようには言っていません。

選択肢Bでは男性は「手」(a hand)を求めています。すなわち「手伝ってくれ」ということです。しかし彼は自分に何か手渡す(to hand)ようにとか、くれるようにとは頼んでいません。

選択肢Cは電車の発車時刻について述べています。女性は確かに電車の時刻を言っていますが、これは男性が知りたいことではありません。

男性はプロジェクトに手助け(a hand)を必要としています。したがって、選択肢Dが正解となります。

実力強化　　Skill Building

Exercise E

TOEICルーラーで次の会話を隠し、会話を聞きながら下の質問に合う適切な解答を選びましょう。このページの一番下に正解があります。

CD1 **No.18**

Exercise E

Woman:　Didn't you just come back from a trip to Colombia?

Man:　Yes, just yesterday. I really enjoyed my tour of the coffee farms. I brought back samples, and I just brewed a pot for everyone in the office.

Woman:　Great! I can't wait to have some.

---

1. _D_ What does the woman want to do?

2. _H_ Where did the man go?

3. _G_ When did the man return from his trip?

4. _B_ Where is this conversation probably taking place?

A. To a coffee shop.

B. In an office.

C. Tour a farm.

D. Drink some coffee.

E. Today.

F. At home.

G. Yesterday.

H. To Colombia.

解答

1.D　2.H　3.G　4.B

Exercise F

次の会話を聞いて、与えられている答えに対する質問を書いてみましょう。考えられる質問がこのページの一番下にあります。あなたの解答とは少し違うかもしれません。

CD1 **No.19**

Exercise F

Man: *I'm calling to let you know that your credit card payment is several weeks overdue.*

Woman: *Hmm... I thought I'd paid that. Perhaps it was delivered to the wrong address.*

Man: *Well... please check your records to see if you've already paid.*

A. First of all what should I do? _____?

B. Have you noticed your credit card payment is overdue _____?

C. How many days are for overdue? _____?

D. _____ _____?

E. _____ _____?

F. _____ _____?

A. To check her records.

B. She thought she had already made the payment.

C. Several weeks

D. The woman has missed a payment.

E. A credit card payment.

F. In a billing office.

想定される解答

A. What does the man tell the woman to do?
B. What does the woman say about the payment?
C. How late is the woman's payment?
D. Why did the man call?
E. What is the man calling about?
F. Where does the man probably work?

自己学習

■ 下の例を参考にして、短い会話を書き込んだカードを何枚か作ります。カードまたは小さい紙の表に、この章か、この本の他のセクションからの短い会話を一つ書きます。音声スクリプトは付録に載っています。

■ カードの裏には会話についての質問を書きます。声を出して会話を読み、次にカードを裏返して、会話を見ずに質問に答えてみましょう。

■ 何枚かのカードを作って友達や同僚と練習してみましょう。声を出して短い会話を読み、友達に自分で作った質問に答えてもらいます。次に友達が作ったカードで同じことを練習します。

Woman: *We should think about finding another hotel for staff meetings.*

Man: *Why? The food and service are great here, and there's plenty of space!*

Woman: *Yes, but the prices go up every week.*

Why is the woman NOT happy with the hotel?

How does the man feel about the food and service?

Where is this conversation probably taking place?

Who are the speakers?

Part Ⅳ：説明文問題

このパートではいくつかの短いアナウンスが流れます。それぞれのアナウンスは一人の話し手が1度だけ読みます。これらのアナウンスは職場、旅行、レクリエーションなどの場面で実際に話される英語で構成されています。フォーマルさの程度には違いがあり、アナウンス、短いスピーチ、広告などを含みます。問題用紙にアナウンスのテキストは印刷されていませんが、アナウンスについての質問と各質問に対する4つの応答が書かれています。この4つの選択肢の中から正解を1つだけ選びます。Part Ⅳは全部で20問あり、1つの質問に答えるのに8秒間の時間が与えられます。

正解する実力をつけるためのアドバイスをいくつか挙げてみましょう。

アドバイス 質問を先に読む

アナウンスを聞く前に質問を読むようにします。質問を先に読んでおけば何を聞き取ればよいのかがわかり、アナウンスが何についてのものかというおおよその見当がつきます。

また、見当をつけることで、おおまかな情報を得ればよいのか、細かいところまで聞く必要があるのかといった判断をすることもできます。

Example 11のアナウンスに対する次の質問を考えてみましょう。

おおまかな情報についての質問

What is the purpose of this talk?
Where is this talk being given?
Who is the speaker?

おおまかな情報に関する質問に答えるには、アナウンスの要点に的を絞って聞くようにします。

Example 11のアナウンスについて細かい情報を聞く質問を考えてみましょう。

細かい情報についての質問

What is the final destination of the flight?
How long is the flight to Dubai?
Where will the plane stop first?

細かい情報についての質問に対してはアナウンスのなかに出てくる特定の事実、時間、日付などを注意して聞く必要があります。

3

ではサンプルのアナウンスを聞いてみましょう。

CD1 No.20

Example 11

Good afternoon and welcome aboard Global Air Flight 875 from Copenhagen to Bangkok, with intermediate stops in Dubai and Calcutta. We are preparing to depart in a few minutes. At this time, your seat back should be returned to its full upright position and your seat belt should be fastened. Our anticipated flying time to Dubai is six hours and twenty-five minutes. We hope you enjoy the flight.

何を聞き取ればいいのかがわかれば、正しく質問に答えることが容易になります。

注　推測が必要とされる問題

質問に答えるために必要な情報がいつもはっきりと述べられているとはかぎりません。アナウンスのなかの情報から推測したり、結論を導かなければならないこともあります。こうして得られた結論には、おおまかな情報や細かい情報が含まれます。

Example 11 で、大まかな情報である "Who is the speaker?" という質問に答えるには推測が必要となります。全体のアナウンスから推測すると、話し手は客室乗務員であるとわかります。細かい情報についての質問でも推測が必要となることがあります。たとえば、"Where will the plane stop first?" という質問の答えは説明文の中で直接的には述べられていません。しかし、最初の着陸地は Dubai であると推測できます。なぜならば、話し手がその都市までの飛行時間を述べているからです。

アドバイス　質問に答える前にアナウンス全体を聞く

アナウンスを聞く前に質問を読むのは良いことですが、アナウンス全体を聞き終わるまで解答しないようにしましょう。アナウンスの最後に重要な情報があるかもしれません。すべての情報を考慮して要点を理解したり推測したりする必要がある場合もあります。

前のページのアドバイスに従って、次の例題のアナウンスを聞きましょう。質問を先に読み、要点と詳細を聞き取り、推測し、すべての情報を考慮してから解答する練習をしましょう。

CD1　No.21

Example 12

Questions 1 and 2 refer to the following report.

The Eastern Gas Company has been given permission to increase the charges for natural gas service. The revised rate for natural gas service will not be effective until March first of next year. The overall increase will amount to 20 cents per cubic meter. Details of this change are available at the gas company billing office.

---

1. What will increase, according to the report?

    (A) The area serviced by the company.

    (B) The number of company offices.

    (C) The length of the billing cycles.

    (D) The price of natural gas service.

正解はDです。アナウンスの1行目と2行目に "increase the charges for natural gas service" というフレーズがあるからです。この部分を聞き逃しても、"The revised rate" とか "overall increase ... to 20 cents" というフレーズが聞こえるでしょう。これらの細かい情報から、要点は天然ガスサービスの価格の値上げについてであるとわかります。

2. When will the increase go into effect?

    (A) March 1.

    (B) March 8.

    (C) March 20.

    (D) March 30.

正解はAです。アナウンスの3行目に "March first of next year." というフレーズがあるからです。このなかで聞こえた他の数字に惑わされないようにしましょう。

アドバイス　アナウンスの導入部分と最初の部分に特に注意する

説明文が読まれる前に次のようなアナウンスが聞こえます。

Questions 3 and 4 refer to the following announcement ...(or talk, advertisement, speech, etc.)

導入部分でどのようなアナウンスであるかを聞き取った後で、アナウンスの冒頭の1～2文を特に注意して聞きます。これらの文から話し手が誰か、どこでこのアナウンスがなされているかということがわかることがあります。場面がわかれば、アナウンスの続きを理解しやすくなります。

例えば、次のような音声が流れます。

CD1 No.22

Example 13

Questions 3 and 4 refer to the following announcement.
I'd like to take this opportunity to welcome you all to our seventh annual electronics sales convention. This year we are proud to announce ...

この情報を聞けば、次のような質問に答えることができます。

Where is this talk probably being given?	➜	(at a sales convention)
What is the speaker's job?	➜	(an electronics salesperson or conference organizer)
How often are the conventions held?	➜	(annually, or once a year)
What type of products might be presented at this convention?	➜	(cameras, VCRs, electronic parts, etc.)

Exercise G

TOEICルーラーで次のスクリプトを隠し、音声を聞きながら下の質問に対する適切な解答を選びましょう。

Pawl.   5   violin

CD1 No.23

Exercise G

Welcome to Hoffberg Fine Instrument Company. I'm Paul York and I'll be conducting the tour today. Our facility here, one of the five operated by Hoffberg, is where the company's famous violins are manufactured. To start, we'll tour the production area, where we'll observe skilled craftsmen completing the assembly process. Then we'll visit the audiovisual room, where we'll see a short film on the history of Hoffberg Fine Instruments. Before we begin, are there any questions?

1.___F___ Who is probably speaking?

2.___e D___ What will the visitors do first?

3.___C___ How is the history of the company presented?

4.___G___ What does Hoffberg Company produce?

A. Medical instruments

B. A tourist

C. With a videotaped film

D. Take a tour of production

E. With a slide presentation

F. A company employee

G. Violins

解答

1.F   2.D   3.C   4.G

3

TOEIC ルーラーで次のスクリプトを隠しましょう。下記の人々のそれぞれにもっともふさわしいと思われる休暇を選んでください。

Vacation Package

(A) A family with two young children _Southern Italy_

(B) A couple who enjoy sporting adventures _Greece scuba diving_

(C) A university student with limited finances _Beach resort_

CD1 No.24

Exercise H

Happy Travel is pleased to announce three new vacation packages. First, come out on a grape-picking holiday in Southern Italy. We offer reasonably priced room and board and a discounted round-trip airline ticket. Make friends and enjoy the beautiful scenery. Our second package is a fun-for-all beach-resort vacation. Shopping, snorkeling, and bike rentals are all available, and there are supervised activities for the young. Thrill seekers will want to try our luxury scuba diving package off the coast of Greece. Our top-class diving instructors will make sure you have an underwater experience that's out of this world! Call now for details on all three packages.

---

3 - Italy Airline
- Beach shoop - Scuba Greece
B Dying

想定される解答

A. Beach resort vacation (because there are activities for children)
B. Scuba diving (because it's an adventurous sport, is expensive, and cannot be done with children)
C. Italy grape picking (because it's inexpensive)

自己学習

■短いアナウンスが放送される英語のラジオ番組やテレビ番組を聞きましょう。たとえばニュース、天気予報、広告、インタビューなどがあります。できれば録音しましょう。アナウンスが終わった後で、次のような質問について考えてみましょう。

話し手は誰か？
話しの要点は何か？
話し手の目的は何か？
そのアナウンスはどこで行われているか？
誰を聞き手に想定しているか？

また、他の聞き取った情報も書きとめ、アナウンスの細かい情報についての質問を書いてみましょう。

■友達や同僚と細かい情報を交換し、お互いの質問に答えて練習しましょう。

■本章や本書の他の章からの短いアナウンスを聞いて、メモを取り、質問をしてみましょう。自分のメモを付録にある音声スクリプトを見てチェックします。以下に一例を挙げます。

According to our current production process, units can come off the assembly line and be packaged even if they have been incorrectly assembled. To test units, our inspectors must manually examine the packaging contents and pull any faulty units off the line in the event of a failed inspection. I personally think we can revise this procedure to avoid packaging incorrectly assembled units. But first, I'd like to hear from you all to verify that I have correctly summarized our current procedures. Does anyone have any comments on this?

Where is this talk probably being given?	(at a factory)
What is the speaker concerned about?	(a production process)
What does the speaker recommend?	(revising procedures)
How do inspectors examine units?	(by hand)
What does the speaker want to do first?	(take comments from listeners)
What does the speaker ask for?	(comments from listeners)

第3章のまとめ

Section I Listening のための全体的な受験方法

■ 強く発音された単語に注意する

■ 英語の実際の話し言葉に慣れる

■ 解答を選ぶ前に録音された音声を注意深く聞く

Section I Listening パート別の受験方法

Part I：写真描写問題

■ 4つのコメントを聞く前に写真をさっとながめておく

■ 同じように聞こえる、異なる意味を持つ単語に注意する

■ 写真についてのコメント全体をよく聞く

Part II：応答問題

■ 質問の目的に焦点を合わせる

■ 疑問詞に注意して聞く

■ 似た発音の単語に注意を払う

Part III：会話問題

■ 質問を先に読む

■ 会話の場面と話し手が誰なのかを想像してみる

■ 解答する前にすべての選択肢を注意深く読む

Part IV：説明文問題

■ 質問を先に読む

■ 質問に答える前にアナウンス全体を聞く

■ アナウンスの導入部分と最初の部分に特に注意する

CHAPTER **4**

第4章

TOEIC
Section II Reading

- ■ Section II Reading の概要
- ■ Section II Reading のための全体的な受験方法
- ■ Section II Reading パート別の受験方法
- ■ 第4章のまとめ

第4章

Section II Reading の概要

・Section II Reading は、TOEIC テストの第101問から第200問までです。このセクションは3つのパートに分かれています。

    Part V　　文法・語彙問題
    Part VI　　誤文訂正問題
    Part VII　　読解問題

・問題用紙に印刷されている問題には独立した文および長文問題があります。質問に答えるには、英語の文法、語法、語彙の知識とともに総合的な読解力が必要となります。

・Section II Reading は全部で75分です。その間に自分のペースで3つのパートを解答していきます。

アドバイス　フォーマルな英語の書き言葉に慣れる

Readingで使われる英語はフォーマルな英語の書き言葉であり、Listeningで出てきたような縮約形やインフォーマルな英語は普通使われません。

フォーマルさの程度の違いを次の例で見てみましょう。

インフォーマルな英語		フォーマルな英語
I'm sorry, I can't come.	➜	I regret that I will be unable to attend.
Please call back.	➜	I look forward to your reply.
Can you give me a hand with this?	➜	I would appreciate your assistance in this matter.

次の2つの例で言葉の違いを見てみましょう。一方は話し言葉で、他方は書き言葉の例です。

スタッフ会議からの抜粋（話し言葉）
↓

There aren't enough parking spaces for everyone going to the party at the hotel on Wednesday night, so they're arranging a shuttle bus to pick us up and drop us off there. Please use the bus so that the hotel has enough room for their own guests.

ホテルからの通知（書き言葉）
↓

Because the hotel does not have sufficient parking spaces for everyone attending the reception on Wednesday evening, we have arranged a shuttle bus to bring guests to the hotel entrance. We ask that you take advantage of this service so that we may accommodate our overnight guests.

ホテルからの通知では、文の構造がより複雑で使われている単語もよりフォーマルです。たとえば、スタッフ会議のplease use はホテルからの通知ではwe ask that you take advantage of になり、同様にparty は reception に、enough は sufficient になっています。

実際に使われるフォーマルな英語の書き言葉を何から学ぶかについてのアドバイスが第2章に載っています。

アドバイス　知識と関連付けて読む

文や文章を読むときは、すでに持っている知識を使ってその文章の意味を理解するようにしましょう。読みながらテキストについての概念をまとめていきます。そして、その概念を発展させていくにしろ、変えるにしろ、その裏付けとなるものをテキストのなかに見出すように努めます。

Example 1

Billing Date: January 2	Policy: Automobile	Policy #: A34 9256681
Due Date: January 25	Minimum Due: $58.28	In full: $524.52

Original premium: $582.80
Last payment:　$58.28 CR

This bill offers you a choice of convenient payment plans to meet your individual needs. You may pay "in full" and avoid incurring a finance charge. Or you may pay the "minimum due" now and the balance in future monthly payments. A periodic rate of 4% per month will be applied to the outstanding balance.

上のテキストで読者がどのように考えていくかを調べてみましょう。

「これは請求書だろう。billing date って書いてある。policy というのはよく保険で使う言葉だ。だから保険請求書に違いない。自動車？　そうだ、自動車保険は多くの国にある。premium というのも保険請求書で使われる。これは自動車保険に対する請求書に違いない」

「CRって何の略だろう？　last payment と書いてあるからすでに支払われたお金に違いない。たぶんcreditの略だろう。支払いがすでになされたのなら、どうして支払いプランが提示されるのだろう？　この最後の支払いは前年のものに違いない」

アドバイス　文や文章に先に目を通しておいてから質問を読む

文章をさっと読んで、その内容や目的をおおまかにつかみましょう。この方法はReadingのどのパートでも役立ちます。

さっと目を通して大まかな概念をつかんだら、質問と選択肢を読み、再度、文や文章を読み返します。

Part V：文法・語彙問題

このパートには、単語やフレーズが1箇所抜けたセンテンスが40あります。そのセンテンスの下に(A), (B), (C), (D) と符号を付けた4つの単語またはフレーズがあります。もっとも適切なものを選んでセンテンスを完成させます。

センテンスに最も適した単語またはフレーズを見つける実力を養成するためのアドバイスをいくつか挙げてみましょう。

アドバイス	問題が語彙についての知識か、あるいは文法についての知識を要求しているのかを判断する

すべての選択肢を注意して読みます。いくつかの、またはすべての選択肢が同じ品詞であれば、正しい単語を選びます。また、同じ単語の異なる形が選択肢になっているときは、文法的に正しい形を選ぶべきです。

次の例を考えてみましょう。

Example 2

Everyone should have periodic eye examinations to make sure any problems are quickly -------.

(A) produced
(B) responded
(C) discovered
(D) prepared

Example 3

Everyone should have periodic eye examinations to make sure any problems are quickly -------.

(A) discovering
(B) discover
(C) discovered
(D) to discover

Example 2では、センテンスの意味に適した単語を選ばなければなりません。身体の異常は早期発見につとめ、治療すべきです。

Example 3では、文法的に正しい単語の形を選ばなければなりません。この文は受動態です。過去分詞のdiscoveredを選べば、受動態の文(any problems are quickly discovered.)が完成します。

アドバイス　センテンス全体の意味を考慮して抜けている単語を選ぶ

問題のセンテンス全体の、あるいはおおまかな意味を理解すれば、抜けている単語を選ぶのが容易になります。

次の例を考えてみましょう。

Example 4

The firm ------- Mr. Morrison as its accountant after it was learned that he had not been mishandling funds.

(A) reinstated
(B) distracted
(C) determined
(D) reprimanded

このセンテンスの最後の部分から、モリソン氏は何も間違ったことはしていなかったことがわかります。「こういう場合、会社はどうするか？」と考えてみれば、選択肢(A) reinstated のみが意味の通じる答えであるとわかります。モリソン氏は復職したのです。

アドバイス　接頭辞、語幹、接尾辞の知識を利用して最も適した単語を選ぶ

接頭辞(prefix)：単語の始めにある文字またはその一群

語幹(stem)：単語の主要な部分

接尾辞(suffix)：単語の最後にある文字またはその一群

単語の色々な部分の知識を利用して正しい解答を選びます。たとえば、接頭辞pre- がbefore を意味し、re- がagain を意味することを知っていれば、prearrange, preseason, preflight そして reappear, reattach, reinstall などの単語の意味を特定できます。

語幹view がsee を意味することを知っていれば、preview がsee beforeという意味であり、review がview again であるとわかります。

一般的な接頭辞、語幹、接尾辞とその意味、実例を挙げておきます。

接頭辞		語幹		接尾辞	
anti-	against	**bio**	life	**-er**	a person who does something
auto-	self	**biblio**	book	**-ful**	full of
bi-	two	**cycle**	circle, round	**-less**	without
ex-	out, or former	**demo**	people	**-ly**	forms an adverb from an adjective
mono-	one	**dict**	say	**-ness**	forms a noun from an adjective
multi-	many	**dorm**	sleep		
pre-	before	**duct**	lead		
syn-	with	**flect**	bend		
tri-	three	**graph**	writing		
re-	again	**labor**	work		
un-	not	**lingua**	language		
		temp	time		
		vis	see		

例

biographer	a person who writes a story of a life
reflection	light bent back
monolingual	speaking one language
dormitory	a place to sleep
laboratory	a place to work
laborer	a person who works

注意：単語を接頭辞と語幹に分解することによって、多くの単語の意味を推測するのに役に立ちますが、接頭辞を持っているように見えても、実は持っていない単語もあります。たとえば、precious, premier, pressure というような単語では、pre- は before（以前）を意味する接頭辞ではなくて、単語の語幹の一部です。単語の構成要素を探すことは大切ですが、単語がいつも接頭辞や接尾辞を含んでいるとはかぎらないということに注意しましょう。

アドバイス 抜けている品詞を特定して文法的に正しい形を決定する

抜けている品詞（名詞、動詞、形容詞、副詞、前置詞、接続詞など）がわかれば、除外できる選択肢もあります。たとえば、抜けている単語が動詞なら、動詞でない選択肢は除外できます。

次の例で考えてみましょう。

Example 5

Please ------- your face with a mask when using welding materials.

(A) protection
(B) protect
(C) protecting
(D) protective

この例では命令を表わす動詞形、すなわち命令形の動詞を入れればセンテンスは文法的に正しくなります。

選択肢(A)と(D)は動詞ではないのですぐに除外できます。(B)と(C)はともに動詞ですが、(C) protecting は命令形ではないので、(B) protect が正しい答えになります。

注意：接尾辞を理解していれば品詞の識別が容易になります。例えば、silent、persistent のように -ent で終わる形容詞の名詞形の多くは、silence, persistence のように-ence で終わるなどといったことも覚えておきましょう。

アドバイス 単語によっては他の単語との組み合わせで 使われることが多いものがあるので注意する

英語にはある一定の単語の組み合わせがよく見られます。たとえば、make という動詞はan appointment, a date, a mistake などと一緒に使うことができ、do という動詞はa job, homework, an errand などと一緒に使われることがよくあります。例：I made a mistake when I was doing my homework.

ここではどの選択肢でも意味が通じるように思えるかもしれません。つまり英語の語法についての知識を問う問題となっています。

次の例を考えてみましょう。

Example 6

Mr. Dupré has asked me to send his -------
regards to you and your staff.

(A) warm
(B) firm
(C) close
(D) good

regards という単語はwarm やbest という単語と一緒によく使われます。close と good もふさわしいように思えますが、これらはregards を修飾する場合には使われません。

Example 7

He has ------- a great deal of time on this
project.

(A) passed
(B) spent
(C) cost
(D) paid

time という単語はpassed やspent と一緒に使われますが、この2つの表現の意味は異なります。pass time というのは、リラックスしていたり、待っていたりするときに時間が過ぎていくことを意味するので、この用法は上のセンテンスでは意味をなしません。spend a lot of time on something は、何か特別な目的のために時間を費やすことを意味します。

アドバイス　センテンスの各部分間の文法的関係に注意する

センテンスを完成させるのに文法的に正しい形を選ぶ際は、そのセンテンスの各部分が他の部分と一緒になって正しいセンテンスを構成するように注意しましょう。1つのフレーズがセンテンスの他の箇所での解答のヒントとなることがよくあります。

次の例を考えてみましょう。

Example 8

The notebook computer is the -------
profitable of all the products that are
presently on sale.

(A) as
(B) so
(C) more
(D) most

of all the products というフレーズから、このノートパソコンは他の2台以上の製品と比較されているということがわかります。よって最上級の形容詞が必要です。選択肢(D) は形容詞の最上級なのでこれが正解になります。

Example 9

Mrs. Hayashi ------- from her trip to Jakarta
late yesterday evening.

(A) return
(B) returned
(C) returns
(D) be returned

ここでの手がかりはlate yesterday evening というフレーズで、これは行動が過去のことであることを示しています。選択肢(B) は単純過去時制なのでこれが正解です。

実力強化　Skill Building

Exercise A　　抜けている品詞の特定

次のセンテンスを読んで、各々で抜けている品詞を特定してみましょう。下に挙げられた品詞の中から選んで、カッコの中に書きましょう。最初のセンテンスは例として解答してあります。

noun	preposition	verb	adverb	conjunction	adjective

1. In order for the conference to run smoothly, we will need hundreds ------- volunteers.
   (preposition)

2. The need for skilled workers in the manufacturing trade will ------- dramatically over the next decade. (verb)

3. West Street has the city's ------- concentration of art galleries, museums, and restaurants.
   (adjective)

4. The RBI Corporation has ------- maintained that its greatest growth potential lies overseas.
   (adverb)

5. The airline industry announced yesterday that it had canceled a $3.5 billion ------- for jet airplanes. (noun)

6. The audience is reminded that neither cameras ------- recording equipment will be permitted in the auditorium. (preposition)

解答

1. preposition　2. verb　3. adjective　4. adverb　5. noun　6. conjunction

4

Exercise B   センテンスの完成

ここではExercise Aと同じセンテンスを使って、あなたが思いついた単語を書きこんで文を完成させ
ましょう。

1. In order for the conference to run smoothly, we will need hundreds --of-- volunteers.

2. The need for skilled workers in the manufacturing trade will --increase-- dramatically over the next decade.

3. West Street has the city's --finest-- concentration of art galleries, museums, and restaurants.

4. The RBI Corporation has ------- maintained that its greatest growth potential lies overseas.

5. The airline industry announced yesterday that it had canceled a $3.5 billion ------- for jet airplanes.

6. The audience is reminded that neither cameras ------- recording equipment will be permitted in the auditorium.

想定される解答

1. of (only possible answer)	2. increase, decrease, rise, fall 3. highest, largest, finest
4. always, recently, predictably	5. contract, proposal, plan, agreement
6. nor (only possible answer)	

Exercise C   最も適した答えの選択

語群のなかの単語を使ってセンテンスの空所を埋めましょう。使わない単語もあります。

increase	increasingly	largest	strongest	of	for	always	once	or	nor
agreement	agreeable								

1. In order for the conference to run smoothly, we will need hundreds ---*of*--- volunteers.

2. The need for skilled workers in the manufacturing trade will *increase* ------- dramatically over the next decade.

3. West Street has the city's *largest* ------- concentration of art galleries, museums and restaurants.

4. The RBI Corporation has *alwas* ------- maintained that its greatest growth potential lies overseas.

5. The airline industry announced yesterday that it had canceled a $3.5 billion *agreement* ------- for jet airplanes.

6. The audience is reminded that neither cameras *nor* ------- recording equipment will be permitted in the auditorium.

自己学習

・単語帳を作る

読解力の増強に最適な方法の一つとして、頻繁に辞書を引かずに読めるやさしい文章を探すことが挙げられます。英文法の理解力と語彙を増やすのに、以下に挙げることをしてみるのも良いでしょう。

■ 読むのを止めてその都度辞書を引いたりせずに簡単に読める文章を探しましょう。

■ 読みながら未知の単語に下線を引き、文章の前後関係からその意味を推測しましょう。この時点では辞書はまだひきません。

■ 読み終えたら、文章の前後関係から理解したと思われる単語を5個から10個選びましょう。

■ そして、単語帳（下の例を参照のこと）にその5個の単語を書いて辞書を引き、品詞とその文のなかでの意味を書きましょう。

■ 次に、それらの単語を使って自分でセンテンスを書いてみましょう。できれば先生か英語のネイティブ・スピーカーに自分のセンテンスを見てもらい、単語を正しく使えたか調べましょう。

新出単語	品詞	意味	例文
Draft	Verb	draw or write the first version of	Mr. Ito has drafted the proposal, but it has not yet been reviewed.
Recipient	Noun	a person who receives	The recipient of the award gave a speech of thanks.

Part VI ： 誤文訂正問題

このパートは20のセンテンスで構成されています。各センテンスには単語か文法、または語法に1箇所間違いがあります。1つのセンテンスには4つの単語またはフレーズに下線が引かれており、その下線を引かれた単語やフレーズのなかから間違ったものを1つ選びます。

このパートで間違いを見つける実力をつけるためのアドバイスをいくつか挙げてみましょう。

アドバイス 下線を引かれていない単語は正しいことに注意する

文法・語彙問題の項で指摘したように、センテンスの正しい部分が解答の手がかりを与えてくれることがあります。たとえば、動詞に下線が引かれていれば、それが主語に合った形かどうかを調べます。代名詞に下線が引かれていれば、それが指す名詞に合った形かどうかを調べます。

次のセンテンスを考えてみましょう。

Example 10

Three colleagues from China, who will be

conducting research in this country, needs
‾‾‾‾‾‾‾‾‾‾‾‾‾‾‾‾‾‾‾   ‾‾‾‾‾
        A   **B**

 housing in the downtown area from June 7
        ‾‾‾‾‾‾‾‾‾‾‾‾‾‾‾‾‾
                 C

to July 31.
‾‾‾‾‾‾
  D

このセンテンスの主語、three colleagues は複数なので、動詞も複数形に合った形でなければなりません。よって選択肢(B) needs は誤りです。

Example 11

Because there were only a few applicants
                     ‾‾‾‾‾‾‾‾‾‾‾
                         A

for the position, it is expected that
             ‾‾‾‾‾‾‾‾‾‾
               B

Mr. Da Silva will be able to do all the
                    ‾‾
                     C

interviewing by itself.
            ‾‾‾‾‾
             D

このセンテンスの下線が引かれていない部分には代名詞itself が指すような中性の名詞はありません。よって選択肢(D) が誤りです。

アドバイス 下線を引かれた部分のなかに誤りが含まれていないか調べる

下線が引かれた単語またはフレーズのなかに誤りがあるかどうかを調べます。

次のセンテンスを考えてみましょう。

Example 12

> Because <u>some of our</u> existing clients
> A
> <u>will not requiring</u> our services <u>this season</u>,
> B   C
> we <u>must increase</u> our marketing efforts.
> D

このセンテンスでは、助動詞will の後にはrequire かbe required ，be requiring またはhave required などの動詞形が続いて文法的に正しい文となります。よって選択肢(B) に誤りがあることになります。

Example 13

> The executive department's plans to move
>
> the offices <u>from downtown</u> to a suburban
> A
> area <u>met with</u> little resistance; <u>indeed</u>, most
> B   C
> employees look <u>forward to move</u>.
> D

このセンテンスでは、選択肢(D) に誤りがあります。look forward to という表現のあとには動名詞（動詞＋〜ing）が来なければならず、look forward to moving とするべきです。

Example 14

> We <u>recognize that</u> <u>many of you</u> have had to
> A   B
> <u>put up occasional</u> disruptions in the
> C
> workplace <u>during</u> our recent renovations.
> D

このセンテンスでは、選択肢(C) に前置詞が抜けています。put up with something で「何かに耐える」という意味になります。これは動詞句の例で、一つないし複数の前置詞または副詞と組み合わされて個々の単語の意味と異なる意味になります。

動詞句を覚え、正しく使えるようになれば、英語力が高まり、誤文訂正問題に対処できるようになります。

よく使われる動詞句とその意味を挙げます。

動詞句	
get through with	finish
get on with	continue
get over	recover from
look into	investigate
look forward to	anticipate gladly
look over	examine
put in for	request formally
put off.	postpone
put up with.	tolerate

アドバイス　複文の構造に注意する

複文の構造に注意しましょう。複文は独立した主節と、独立しては使えない1つないし複数の従属節から成ります。主節と従属節の関係を示す単語に注目しましょう。

複文の例を見てみましょう。

■ *Although* replacement work on gas lines will begin on Monday, employees will not be affected.

■ Replacement work on gas lines, *which* will begin on Monday, will not affect employees.

このような複文の構造を分析すれば、文どうしのつなぎ方の誤りを見つけることができるでしょう。

例題を見てみましょう。

Example 15

However we normally close the theater
 A
doors after the show begins, latecomers will
           B
be seated during the intermission.
  C   **D**

however という単語は第2節の文頭に来たときに2つの節をつなぐ役目を果たします。

We normally close the theater doors after the show begins; *however*, latecomers will be seated during the intermissions.

したがって、問題文は、(A) の However を Although に置きかえれば適切な文となります。

Example 16

ABC Textiles realized a profit of approximately
                A   **B**
DM 95 million last year, so makes them
                        C
one of the industry leaders in Germany.
 D

この文では第2節は関係詞節で、関係代名詞 which を用いて節を導かなければなりません。

ABC Textiles realized a profit of approximately DM 95 million last year, *which* makes them one of the industry leaders in Germany.

アドバイス　時間や場所を示す単語に注意して文を読む

センテンスの中の単語やフレーズから、正しい動詞の時制がわかることがあります。次の時間表現を考えてみましょう。

last month	today	tomorrow
yesterday	now	in two weeks
since Tuesday	always	next July

これらの表現は、過去、現在、未来の時制を示します。これらが文の中で使われているとき、動詞の時制が適当であるか調べましょう。

次のセンテンスを考えてみましょう。

Example 17

The new brochures describing all our
                                A   B

services were delivered to us late yesterday
                                             C

and were shipped out early tomorrow
                  D

morning.

この文中で時間を表わしているのは、late yesterday（過去）と early tomorrow morning（未来）です。文の始めの部分はパンフレットが送られた過去のことを述べており、2番目の部分では tomorrow morning という句が「発送する」という未来のことを示しています。パンフレットは明朝早く will be shipped out（発送される）というわけです。よって選択肢(D)に間違いがあります。

空間や場所を示す単語も正しく使われているか注意しましょう。次の場所を示す前置詞と副詞を考えてみましょう。

above	across	down	near	through
away	outside	opposite	toward	underneath

では次のセンテンスを考えてみましょう。

Example 18

The fastest way to get to England from
          A   B

France by car is over the tunnel linking
                            C

the two countries.
      D

この文では、tunnel という単語が誤りを見つける手がかりとなります。drive over a bridge と言うことはできますが、トンネルの場合 drive through a tunnel と言わなければなりません。よって選択肢(C)には誤りがあります。

実力強化　Skill Building

Exercise D

次に挙げる各々2つの文のうちで間違っている文の符号に○をつけましょう。正解はこのページの一番下にあります。

1. a. The airline has slowly built up service to ten European and Asian destinations.
   b. The airline has slowly build up service to ten European and Asian destinations.

2. a. The new factory will located south of the town and will employ workers from the entire province.
   b. The new factory will be located south of the town and will employ workers from the entire province.

3. a. Investors in the fund stand to made substantial profits.
   b. Investors in the fund stand to make substantial profits.

4. a. To request vacation time, employees should receive advance approval from their supervisors.
   b. To request vacation time, employees should receive advancing approval from their supervisors.

5. a. Experience shows that preparation the key to the negotiation of any settlement.
   b. Experience shows that preparation is the key to the negotiation of any settlement.

6. a. There are much more reasons to analyze this economic theory than have been stated.
   b. There are many more reasons to analyze this economic theory than have been stated.

7. a. All and every company car must be returned to the central parking lot after use.
   b. Each and every company car must be returned to the central parking lot after use.

8. a. Wages have never been as high as they are now.
   b. Wages have never been as higher as they are now.

9. a. Despite a late start, Mrs. Cho was eventually able to achieve competent in the French language.
   b. Despite a late start, Mrs. Cho was eventually able to achieve competence in the French language.

10. a. Advertising agencies sometimes ask customers to pay their bills in advance.
    b. Advertising agencies sometimes ask customers to pay its bills in advance.

解答

1.B	2.A	3.A	4.B	5.A	6.A	7.A	8.B	9.A	10.B

自己学習

次のような条件作文をすると、英語の書き言葉の重要な構造的側面を集中的に練習することができます。

■ 本、雑誌、新聞などから記事を選びます。簡単に読めて理解できるものがよいでしょう。その記事から1つか2つのパラグラフ（約100 語から200語くらいのもの）を取り出して次の指示の一つにしたがって書き換えます。異なる番号の指示に従うごとに、その文章全体を書き換えることになります。意味が通じるようにするには、他にも修正をしなければならないこともあります。次ページのExample 19を参照してください。

■ 次の指示のいずれかにしたがって文章を書き換えてください。

1. 文章を現在時制から過去時制に変える。
2. 文章を現在時制から未来時制に変える。
3. 複文があれば、可能な場合、短く簡潔な単文に分ける。
4. 可能な場合、単文を複文に統合する。
5. テキスト中の形容詞の同義語を見つける。同義語を使っても文章の意味が通るようにすること。
6. 可能な場合、単数の主語を複数形にする。その新しい主語に合うように各文の動詞形や代名詞を変える。
7. 可能な場合、複数形の主語を単数形に変える。その新しい主語に合うように各文の動詞形や代名詞を変える。
8. 女性の主語を男性の主語に変えて、必要に応じて代名詞を変える。
9. 男性の主語を女性の主語に変えて、必要に応じて代名詞を変える。
10. 時間や場所を表す前置詞および前置詞句を見つける。

次は 1，3，7 の指示に従った作文例です

Example 19

オリジナルの文章

> Currently, all work sites within the company have safety rules that every worker is expected to follow. Many of the rules concern special clothes or other safety items that must be worn, the safe way to perform work tasks, and the use of equipment while working.

1．文章を現在時制から過去時制に変える。

In the past, all work sites within the company had safety rules that every worker was expected to follow. Many of the rules concerned special clothes, etc.

3．複文があれば、可能な場合、短く簡潔な単文に分ける。

Currently, all work sites within the company have safety rules. Every worker is expected to follow these rules. Many of the rules concern special clothes or other safety items. These items must be worn ... etc.

7．可能な場合、複数形の主語を単数形に変える。

Currently, one work site in the company has a safety rule that a worker is expected to follow. The rule concerns a special piece of clothing or a safety item that must be worn, etc.

Part VII : 読解問題

このパートは多くの英文テキストからなり、各々に一連の質問が続きます。全部で40問あります。文章の形式はさまざまで、旅行、レクリエーション、職場などの状況でよく見かける種類のものです。

このパートの質問では次のようなことが要求されます。

■ 本文の要点やそれが書かれた目的を見出す
■ 細かい情報を探す（本文とは違う単語が使われることがある）
■ 本文について推論する

このパートで正解する実力を養成するためのアドバイスをいくつか挙げてみましょう。

アドバイス　必要に応じて文章を読んだり読み直すのに十分な時間を確保する

このパートは前の2つのパートよりも時間がかかります。75分間の半分以上を読解問題に費やさなければならないかもしれません。本書の第6章にある全200問の練習問題を解答すれば、Readingの3つのパートにどのように時間を配分すればよいかがわかるでしょう。

アドバイス　職場で使われる文書のレイアウトに慣れる

文書のレイアウト、あるいは形式に慣れれば、その文書の内容について予想することができ、もっとも重要な情報をすばやく見つけられるでしょう。

たとえば、手紙の受取人、または書き手の名前または肩書きを質問されるかもしれません。手紙の送り手、すなわち書き手の名前はビジネス・レターでは手紙の最後に来て、受取人の名前と肩書きは手紙の最初に来るのが普通です。しかし、オフィスでのメモでは、送り手と受取人の名前は両方ともページの一番上の日付の下に来ます。こういうことを知っていると必要な情報をすばやく得るのに役立ちます。

4

Example 20

Questions 161-162 refer to the following memorandum.

Date:	July 31
To:	Marketing Division
From:	Stephen Schneider, Director - Planning & Research
Re:	The Market Monthly Newsletter

Attached is a copy of the *Market Monthly*, a newsletter published by the Marketing Division, designed to keep you updated on competitors, trends, and events that impact the markets of interest to this company.

If there are individuals in your area who do not receive the newsletter and should be added to the distribution list, please contact the *Monthly's* managing editor, Maria Lopez, at ext. 240.

I would appreciate receiving any comments or suggestions you have regarding the *Market Monthly*. Please feel free to contact me at ext. 167.

161. Whom should readers contact with suggestions?

(A) The company director
(B) The marketing manager
(C) Mr. Schneider
(D) Ms. Lopez

このメモの最後で書き手は提案を求めています。オフィス・メモに慣れていれば、書き手の名前はメモの一番上のFrom という単語の次に来ることがわかるでしょう。よって読み手は(C) Mr. Schneider に連絡すべきです。

ビジネスの通信でよく使われるさまざまな形式の文書を挙げます。

- advertisement
- business letter
- chart
- e-mail
- evaluation
- fax or facsimile
- graph
- informal note
- invitation

- itinerary
- memo or memorandum
- notice
- schedule
- table
- telephone message
- ticket
- voucher

余暇、旅行、職場など、日常生活の多くの場面で見かけるテキストに慣れましょう。TOEICテストで出題される文章はさまざまな場面で実際に使われる英語の書き言葉の例に基づいています。

アドバイス　本文の上にある導入のセンテンスを読む

本文の上にある導入文を読むと、どういう種類の文章をこれから読むのかがわかります。

Example 21

Questions 163-164 refer to the following instructions.

> Our FAX machine is easy to use.
>
> First, place the document on the feeder tray, face down.
>
> Next, enter the recipient's fax number.
>
> Finally, press the start button.

本文の上にある導入文中のinstructions という単語により、一連の手順、または使用法について読むということがわかります。こうしたことを知ることが情報を探すのに役立つ場合がよくあります。たとえば、指示における手順の一つを見つけたければ、そうした手順はたいてい実行される順番に書かれていると想定できます。

アドバイス　始めに文章全体を未知の単語にとらわれずにさっと読む

スキャニング、あるいは、すばやく読むことにより、その文章が何についてであるのか、なぜ書かれたかということがわかります。自分の知っているキーワードやフレーズを拾い読みし、未知の単語にはとらわれないようにしましょう。この方法は要点についての質問に答えるのに役立ちます。

次の例を考えてみましょう。右側をTOEICルーラーで隠し、左側の文章を読んでください。いくつかの単語が黒く塗りつぶされていますが、その記事の要点を理解するにはある部分のみを読解できればいいことを示しています。次にページの下にある問題165を読んで解答しましょう。

Example 22

Questions 165-167 refer to the following article.

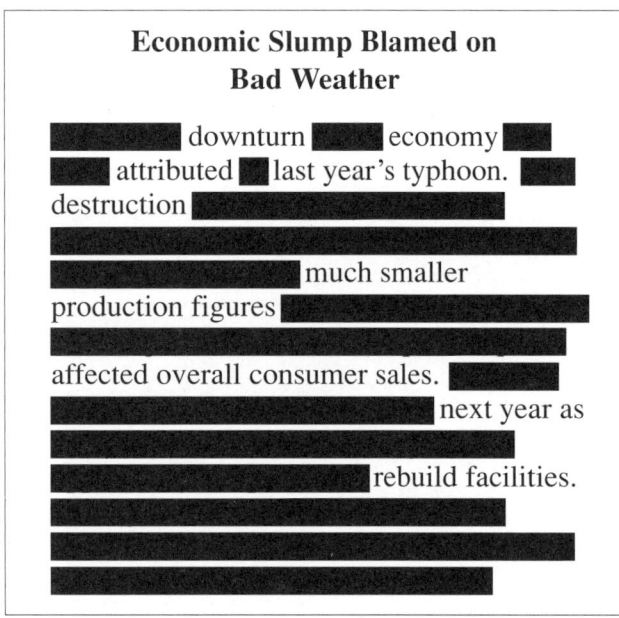

Economic Slump Blamed on Bad Weather

The recent downturn in the economy has been attributed to last year's typhoon. The destruction of several key electronics manufacturing plants on the eastern side of the nation has led to much smaller production figures in that key industry. The resulting demand has driven prices up and affected overall consumer sales. Industry experts predict a sharp rebound next year as many industries take advantage of the opportunity to update and rebuild facilities. Damage to residential areas was also significant, and housing reconstruction has been strong throughout the last year.

165. What is the main idea of the article?

(A) A major storm is approaching the area.
(B) New manufacturing plants have been constructed.
(C) A large company is going out of business.
(D) A major storm has affected businesses.

Economic Slump, blamed, downturn, typhoon, destruction, affected overall consumer sales などの語句を読むだけで、台風が企業活動に影響を与えたということがわかります。

本文を読み直す前に質問を読んでおくことは良い方法です。たとえば、実際の広告、メモ、議題など
を読むとき、たいていは何か目的を持って読むはずです。ある物の価格を知りたいとか、会議が始ま
る時間とか、手続きの変更についての詳細とか、あるいは単に電話番号を知りたいだけかもしれませ
ん。文章の後にある質問にさっと目を通しておけば、何を目的に読むかがはっきりします。

Example 23

Questions 168-169 refer to the following card.

Welcome **Ms. Martelli**

to the Star Plaza Hotel. We hope you have a pleasant stay.
Please present this card when enjoying our restaurant, coffee
shop, and sporting facilities and when signing charges to your
room account.

Check Out Date: **10th December**

Room No. **635**　　　　　　　　**P. Angelo**

　　　　　　　　　　　　　　　Desk Clerk

---

168. When did the guest receive the card?

(A) When checking into the hotel
(B) When ordering a meal at the restaurant
(C) When paying the bill
(D) When making a room reservation

169. Who issued this card to the guest?

(A) Ms. Martelli
(B) P. Angelo.
(C) The restaurant cashier
(D) The accounts manager

問題168はこの文書の1行目を読むだけで答えられます。welcome という単語は、客がたった今着い
たところであることを示しています。次の行の、We hope you have a pleasant stay. もそのことを裏
付けています。問題168の正解が選択肢(A)であることを理解するのに以下の文章を読み続ける必要は
ありません。

問題169も文書の最後の行を読むだけで答えられます。質問を読めば、このカードを発行した人の名
前を見つければよいことがわかります。よってテキストの最後の部分に目をやり、このカードに署名
したか、あるいはカードを発行したdesk clerk の名前をつきとめればよいのです。選択肢(B)がdesk
clerk の名前です。

アドバイス　要点を知りたいときは、題名と各パラグラフの最初の文を読む

キーポイントは英語で書かれたテキストのある特定の部分にあることがよくあります。各パラグラフの最初の文を読むことにより、いくつかのパラグラフから構成される文章の概要がわかります。広告または通知のような短いテキストでは、その文章の始めにある単語またはフレーズを読めば、「これは何の文章ですか」とか、「これは誰に宛てたものですか」あるいは「これはなぜ書かれましたか」というような質問に答えることができます。

Example 24

Questions 170-173 refer to the following advertisement.

SEARCHING FOR AN APARTMENT?

Apartments Fast, Inc. makes it quick and simple!

We offer up-to-date availability on the type of rental you are searching

for:

• Apartments, Studios, Duplexes, Corporate Suites
• All Price Ranges
• Short- and Long-Term Leases
• Furnished or Unfurnished

Specializing in Corporate Apartments

We specialize in completely furnished apartments with all the necessities and comforts of home. Whether you wish to entertain clients in a corporate apartment or secure temporary housing, we will make all the necessary arrangements.

Our service is tailored to your needs while working within your budget. You'll find that our prices are much less than what you would pay at a regular or extended-stay hotel. And we have a wide variety of apartments conveniently located throughout the city for you to choose from.

CALL NOW: 123-4321

For your free apartment search

---

170. What service does *Apartments Fast, Inc.* offer?

(A) Cleaning people's homes and
     apartments
(B) Helping people to find places to rent
(C) Buying and selling apartments and
     homes
(D) Moving furniture and appliances for people

問題170に答えるには、この広告の目的を知る必要があります。広告の各段落の初めには次のように書いてあります。

We offer up-to-date availability on the type of rental you are searching for ...,

We specialize in completely furnished apartments with all the necessities and comforts of home ...,

Our service is tailored to meet your needs while working within your budget.

これらのキーフレーズにより選択肢(B) が正しいことがわかります。

実力強化　　Skill Building

Exercise E　　　文脈から意味を推測する

次の文章で灰色で覆われていない単語を読んで、文章の全体的な意味を理解してみましょう。それから、後にあるコメントの内容が正しいかどうか答えてみましょう。正解はこのページの一番下にあります。

Ms. Rose Kemper
Kemper Garments Ltd.
EDGEWARE
Middlesex HA8 9XG
ENGLAND

Paul Timmerman
Het Overloon 1
Postbut 6500
NL-6401 JH Heerlen
The Netherlands

Dear Mr. Timmerman:

Thank you for your inquiry regarding our wool sweaters. We do have the model numbers you requested. These garments can be shipped directly from here or from our main office in Manchester. The cost per garment is £18, plus £15 shipping per crate of 40 garments.

In your letter you indicated that you would like to have 60 garments shipped to your business location. Delivery of this size usually takes two to three weeks, unless you prefer the shipment to arrive by air. I should mention that the cost of shipping will be higher in this case.

Finally, I have enclosed a copy of this year's catalog with our new patterns as well as a copy of last year's catalog, for which we have limited product availability.

Once you decide how you would like to have the garments shipped to you, please contact me directly and I will make the necessary arrangements. We look forward to filling your order.

Yours truly,
Rose Kemper
Rose Kemper

---

1. Rose Kemper works in the garment industry.　　　　　　　　Yes　No
2. Rose Kemper is requesting a shipment.　　　　　　　　　　Yes　No
3. Paul Timmerman lives in England.　　　　　　　　　　　　Yes　No
4. The requested garments are available.　　　　　　　　　　Yes　No
5. Kemper Ltd. has two locations.　　　　　　　　　　　　　Yes　No
6. Paul Timmerman has indicated how the goods should be shipped.　Yes　No
7. Two catalogues are enclosed with the letter.　　　　　　　Yes　No

解答

1. Yes　2. No　3. No　4. Yes　5. Yes　6. No　7. Yes

Exercise F　　　文脈から意味を推測する

次の文章を読んで、単語が抜けたまま文章の意味を理解してみましょう。それから、後にあるコメントの内容が正しいかどうか答えてみましょう。正解はこのページの一番下にあります。

Slogan Effort Underway at TagCorp

As part of its ☐ strategy for promoting the ☐ and ☐ image and visibility, ☐ executives have ☐ working ☐ the past ☐ months to develop a ☐ slogan and ☐ logo. This ☐ will ☐ company letterhead ☐ merchandise and ☐ recognizable as ☐ TagCorp symbol. ☐ president Linda Ortiz ☐ yesterday, "☐ really don't have the ☐ of recognition ☐ need to ☐ us a strong ☐ identity ☐ provide a ☐ of what ☐ company is ☐ about."

The ☐ effort ☐ headed ☐ Gene Dupré, associate vice-president ☐ marketing, ☐ has been ☐ with a number of ☐ consultants to develop ☐ by testing proposals ☐ focus groups ☐ ☐ , outside ☐ professionals, and ☐ . Dupré ☐ that last year a company task force came up ☐ suggestions ☐ enhancing and ☐ the company's image, and he ☐ subsequently hired, in ☐ to conduct ☐ he calls a 'research-based' ☐ and marketing plan. "We ☐ to convey, in a ☐ way, ☐ distinctive about TagCorp. We're ☐ on the excellent value we offer and ☐ breadth of products ☐ develop here."

---

1. The company has worked on this project for several years.   Yes   No
2. The company is trying to increase product recognition.   Yes   No
3. Linda Ortiz was hired to lead the project.   Yes   No
4. Proposals have been tested on outside professionals.   Yes   No
5. TagCorp produces many different products.   Yes   No

解答

As part of its overall strategy for promoting the company and improving the company image and visibility, TagCorp executives have been working for the past few months to develop a company slogan and a new logo. This logo will adorn company letterhead and merchandise and be immediately recognizable as the TagCorp symbol. TagCorp president Linda Ortiz said yesterday, "We really don't have the kind of recognition we need to give us a strong visual identity and to provide a sense of what the company is all about."

The slogan effort is being headed by Gene Dupré, associate vice-president for marketing, who has been working with a number of marketing consultants to develop slogans by testing proposals on focus groups such as buyers, outside sales professionals, and retailers. Dupré said that last year a company task force came up with suggestions on enhancing and managing the company's image, and he was subsequently hired, in part to conduct what he calls a 'research-based' communications and marketing plan. "We want to convey, in a succinct way, what's distinctive about TagCorp. We're focusing on the excellent value we offer and the breadth of products we develop here."

1. No 　 2. Yes 　 3. No 　 4. Yes 　 5. Yes

4

Exercise G　テーマを理解する

次の各々のリストの中から、他の単語の属性を示す単語を見つけてみましょう。第1問は例としてすでに解答してあります。

1. cat　lion　rabbit　(animal)　dog　cow

2. receptionist　employee　manager　executive　assistant　director

3. desk　cabinet　bookcase　table　furniture　chair　stool

4. rain　snow　weather　wind　fog　ice

5. cement　steel　wood　glass　material　brick

6. kitchen　room　basement　closet　parlor　bathroom

7. circle　square　triangle　shape　rectangle

8. emotion　anger　love　boredom　fear　pleasure

9. painting　sports　music　hobby　cooking　gardening

10. hammer　wrench　sander　drill　tool　saw

解答

1. animal　2. employee　3. furniture　4. weather　5. material　6. room　7. shape　8. emotion　9. hobby　10. tool

自己学習

■ 普通の手紙やＥメールで英語の文通ができる友達を作りましょう。何度も英語で読んだり書いたりすれば英語を自由に使いこなせる力が向上します。

■ 日記をつけましょう。その日の自分を振り返ったりとか、職場で何をしたとか、英語のクラスで何を学んでいるとか、あるいは全部含めて書いてみましょう。日記を書いたら友達や同僚と日記を交換しましょう。そして友達の日記を読んだら感想を書き、友達にも同じように書いてもらうようにしましょう。

■ 週に１回、同僚と英語を学習するためにお昼休みを利用しましょう。英語の新聞や雑誌から記事を選んで、前の晩に読んでおきます。辞書を引いたりせず、文脈から意味を理解するように努めましょう。同僚と同じ記事を読んでおき、その記事に関連した質問をいくつかお互いにしてみましょう。その記事について英語または日本語で議論してもよいでしょう。

第４章のまとめ

Section II Reading のための全体的な受験方法

■ フォーマルな英語の書き言葉に慣れる

■ 知識と関連付けて読む

■ 文や文章に先に目を通しておいてから質問を読む

Section II Reading パート別の受験方法

Part V：文法・語彙問題

■ 問題が語彙についての知識か、あるいは文法についての知識を要求しているのかを判断する

■ センテンス全体の意味を考慮して抜けている単語を選ぶ

■ 接頭辞、語幹、接尾辞の知識を利用して最も適した単語を選ぶ

■ 抜けている品詞を特定して文法的に正しい形を決定する

■ 単語によっては他の単語との組み合わせで使われることが多いものがあるので注意する

■ センテンスの各部分間の文法的関係に注意する

Part VI：誤文訂正問題

■ 下線を引かれていない単語は正しいことに注意する

■ 下線を引かれた部分の中に誤りが含まれていないか調べる

■ 複文の構造に注意する

■ 時間や場所を示す単語に注意して文を読む

Part Ⅶ：読解問題

■ 必要に応じて文章を読んだり読み直すのに十分な時間を確保する

■ 職場で使われる文書のレイアウトに慣れる

■ 本文の上にある導入のセンテンスを読む

■ 始めに文章全体を未知の単語にとらわれずにさっと読む

■ 本文を読み直す前に質問を読む

■ 要点を知りたいときは、題名と各パラグラフの最初の文を読む

CHAPTER **5**

第5章

TOEIC サンプル・テスト問題と解説

■ 本章のもっとも効果的な活用法

■ 解答用紙

■ TOEICサンプル・テスト問題（70問）と解説

第5章

本章のもっとも効果的な活用法

この章にはTOEICテスト各パートからのサンプル問題と、正解（➡）、不正解についてそれぞれの詳細な解説が収められています。問題を解き進めていく際には、TOEICルーラーを使って解説をかくすようにします。

Listeningのサンプル問題の聞き取りには、付属のCDをお使いください。各ページの左側にある音声スクリプトと右側にある解説をTOEICルーラーで隠します。そして、音声を聞いて正しいと思う解答を解答用紙にマークしましょう。一度にすべてのListening問題を聞いてもよいですし、問題ごとにCDを止めてもよいでしょう。音声スクリプトと解説からTOEICルーラーを外して解答をチェックし、解説をよく読んで、なぜ正解だったのか、または不正解だったのかを確認しましょう。

Listeningの問題については、第3章に詳しい説明がありますので、参照してください。

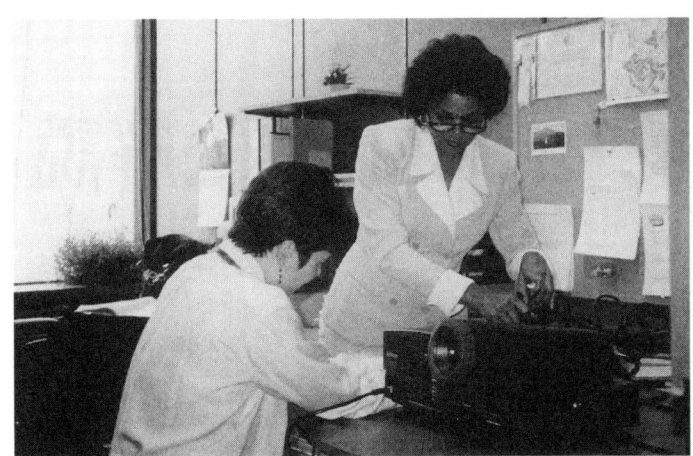

Example Question 1 (not recorded)

On the recording, you will hear:

(A) They're leaving the office.

Example Question 1　解説

(A) 人々は待っているように見えるが、ホテルの中にいる。

(B) 人々はまだ部屋の中にいる。

Readingのサンプル問題を進めるときは、ページの右側にある解説をTOEICルーラーで隠します。そして左側にあるテキストを読み、正しいと思う解答を解答用紙にマークします。一度にすべての問題を解答してもよいですし、各問ごとに確認してもよいでしょう。ページの右側にある解説からTOEICルーラーを外して解答をチェック、解説をよく読んで、なぜ正解だったのか、または不正解だったのかを確認しましょう。

Readingの問題については、第4章に詳しい説明がありますので、参照してください。

Example Question 2

Please note that customs regulations do not permit the shipment of ------- items.
(A) perishable
(B) compatible
(C) sustainable
(D) incredible

Example Question 2　解説

➡ (A) perishableはいたみやすく腐りやすい食べ物を形容する言葉で、その種の食品には税関規定が適用される。

解答用紙

1.	Ⓐ	Ⓑ	Ⓒ	Ⓓ
2.	Ⓐ	Ⓑ	Ⓒ	Ⓓ
3.	Ⓐ	Ⓑ	Ⓒ	Ⓓ
4.	Ⓐ	Ⓑ	Ⓒ	Ⓓ
5.	Ⓐ	Ⓑ	Ⓒ	Ⓓ
6.	Ⓐ	Ⓑ	Ⓒ	Ⓓ
7.	Ⓐ	Ⓑ	Ⓒ	Ⓓ

8.	Ⓐ	Ⓑ	Ⓒ
9.	Ⓐ	Ⓑ	Ⓒ
10.	Ⓐ	Ⓑ	Ⓒ
11.	Ⓐ	Ⓑ	Ⓒ
12.	Ⓐ	Ⓑ	Ⓒ
13.	Ⓐ	Ⓑ	Ⓒ
14.	Ⓐ	Ⓑ	Ⓒ
15.	Ⓐ	Ⓑ	Ⓒ
16.	Ⓐ	Ⓑ	Ⓒ
17.	Ⓐ	Ⓑ	Ⓒ

18.	Ⓐ	Ⓑ	Ⓒ	Ⓓ
19.	Ⓐ	Ⓑ	Ⓒ	Ⓓ
20.	Ⓐ	Ⓑ	Ⓒ	Ⓓ
21.	Ⓐ	Ⓑ	Ⓒ	Ⓓ
22.	Ⓐ	Ⓑ	Ⓒ	Ⓓ
23.	Ⓐ	Ⓑ	Ⓒ	Ⓓ
24.	Ⓐ	Ⓑ	Ⓒ	Ⓓ
25.	Ⓐ	Ⓑ	Ⓒ	Ⓓ
26.	Ⓐ	Ⓑ	Ⓒ	Ⓓ
27.	Ⓐ	Ⓑ	Ⓒ	Ⓓ

28.	Ⓐ	Ⓑ	Ⓒ	Ⓓ
29.	Ⓐ	Ⓑ	Ⓒ	Ⓓ
30.	Ⓐ	Ⓑ	Ⓒ	Ⓓ
31.	Ⓐ	Ⓑ	Ⓒ	Ⓓ
32.	Ⓐ	Ⓑ	Ⓒ	Ⓓ
33.	Ⓐ	Ⓑ	Ⓒ	Ⓓ
34.	Ⓐ	Ⓑ	Ⓒ	Ⓓ

35.	Ⓐ	Ⓑ	Ⓒ	Ⓓ
36.	Ⓐ	Ⓑ	Ⓒ	Ⓓ
37.	Ⓐ	Ⓑ	Ⓒ	Ⓓ
38.	Ⓐ	Ⓑ	Ⓒ	Ⓓ
39.	Ⓐ	Ⓑ	Ⓒ	Ⓓ
40.	Ⓐ	Ⓑ	Ⓒ	Ⓓ
41.	Ⓐ	Ⓑ	Ⓒ	Ⓓ
42.	Ⓐ	Ⓑ	Ⓒ	Ⓓ
43.	Ⓐ	Ⓑ	Ⓒ	Ⓓ
44.	Ⓐ	Ⓑ	Ⓒ	Ⓓ
45.	Ⓐ	Ⓑ	Ⓒ	Ⓓ
46.	Ⓐ	Ⓑ	Ⓒ	Ⓓ
47.	Ⓐ	Ⓑ	Ⓒ	Ⓓ
48.	Ⓐ	Ⓑ	Ⓒ	Ⓓ

49.	Ⓐ	Ⓑ	Ⓒ	Ⓓ
50.	Ⓐ	Ⓑ	Ⓒ	Ⓓ
51.	Ⓐ	Ⓑ	Ⓒ	Ⓓ
52.	Ⓐ	Ⓑ	Ⓒ	Ⓓ
53.	Ⓐ	Ⓑ	Ⓒ	Ⓓ
54.	Ⓐ	Ⓑ	Ⓒ	Ⓓ
55.	Ⓐ	Ⓑ	Ⓒ	Ⓓ
56.	Ⓐ	Ⓑ	Ⓒ	Ⓓ

57.	Ⓐ	Ⓑ	Ⓒ	Ⓓ
58.	Ⓐ	Ⓑ	Ⓒ	Ⓓ
59.	Ⓐ	Ⓑ	Ⓒ	Ⓓ
60.	Ⓐ	Ⓑ	Ⓒ	Ⓓ
61.	Ⓐ	Ⓑ	Ⓒ	Ⓓ
62.	Ⓐ	Ⓑ	Ⓒ	Ⓓ
63.	Ⓐ	Ⓑ	Ⓒ	Ⓓ
64.	Ⓐ	Ⓑ	Ⓒ	Ⓓ
65.	Ⓐ	Ⓑ	Ⓒ	Ⓓ
66.	Ⓐ	Ⓑ	Ⓒ	Ⓓ
67.	Ⓐ	Ⓑ	Ⓒ	Ⓓ
68.	Ⓐ	Ⓑ	Ⓒ	Ⓓ
69.	Ⓐ	Ⓑ	Ⓒ	Ⓓ
70.	Ⓐ	Ⓑ	Ⓒ	Ⓓ

Part I：写真描写問題

Sample Question 1

CD1 No.25 On the recording, you will hear:

(A) The people are waiting outside a hotel.
(B) All the people have left the room.
(C) Several people are gathered near a table.
(D) Two women are drinking coffee.

Question 1　解説

(A) 人々は待っているように見えるが、ホテルの中にいる。
(B) 人々はまだ部屋の中にいる。
➡ (C) ４人の男性がテーブルの前に立ち、並んで順番を待っているように見える。
(D) コーヒーカップがテーブルの上にあるが、女性達はコーヒーを飲んではいない。

Sample Question 2

CD1 No.26 On the recording, you will hear:

(A) She's talking on the telephone.
(B) She's reading a newspaper.
(C) She's copying a document.
(D) She's standing in a telephone booth.

Question 2　解説

➡ (A) 女性は受話器を耳に当てて会話をしているように見える。
(B) 女性は紙を見ているが、新聞紙ではない。
(C) 女性は書類（何か書かれたもの）を持っているが、それをコピーしてはいない。
(D) 女性はオフィスの仕事場に座ってはいるが、立ってはいない。

Sample Question 3

CD1 **No.27** On the recording, you will hear:

(A) *The drivers are leaning against the trucks.*
(B) *The trucks are lined up along the road.*
(C) *The engines are being repaired.*
(D) *The workers are unloading the trucks.*

Question 3　解説

(A) 写真の中にトラックが写ってはいるが、人の姿は見えない。

➡ (B) 4台のトラックが道路に沿って一列に駐車されている。

(C) トラックが修理中であることを示すものは何もない。

(D) (A)と同じく、写真の中に人の姿は見えない。

Sample Question 4

CD1 **No.28** On the recording, you will hear:

(A) *He's filling in a form.*
(B) *He's using a keyboard.*
(C) *He's signing a contract.*
(D) *He's writing on a board.*

Question 4　解説

(A) 男性は何か書いているが、書式のような印刷した用紙に記入しているのではない。

(B) 男性は壁のボードに書いている。コンピュータのキーボードを叩いているのではない。

(C) 契約書は紙に印刷されるものである。男性は何か書いているが、法律関係の書類に署名をしているのではない。

➡ (D) 男性は他の人が読めるように大きなボードに文字を書いている。

Sample Question 5

CD1 No.29 On the recording, you will hear:

(A) A crane is moving material to the top of a building.
(B) The frame of a building is exposed.
(C) The construction of a building is completed.
(D) People are attending a groundbreaking ceremony.

Question 5 解説

(A) 工事現場の写真だが、クレーンはない。ク
　　レーンは大きな物を上げ下ろしする大型機
　　械である。

➡ (B) ビルが建設中である。今のところ、支柱、
　　すなわち骨組しかない。

(C) 壁や屋根がまだ取り付けられていないので、
　　ビルは完成していない。

(D) 着工セレモニーは建設プロジェクトの開始
　　時に催されるが、このプロジェクトはすで
　　に進行中である。ブルドーザーが土を運ん
　　でいるが、セレモニーに参加している人の
　　姿は見えない。

Sample Question 6

CD1 No.30 On the recording, you will hear:

(A) A lion is stepping down from a platform.
(B) Some birds are perched on a lion's head.
(C) Tourists are inside a museum.
(D) Statues are located in an outdoor area.

Question 6 解説

(A) 銅像のライオンは歩いて降りてくることは
　　できない。

(B) ライオンの頭上で止まっていたり羽を休め
　　ている鳥はいない。

(C) 写真の中に観光客はいるようだが、場所は
　　屋外で、博物館の中ではない。

➡ (D) ライオンも含め、屋外には複数の銅像があ
　　る。

Sample Question 7

CD1 **No.31** On the recording, you will hear:

(A) He's walking through a factory.
(B) He's supervising a team of mechanics.
(C) He's ordering new parts for an engine.
(D) He's repairing a tractor part.

Question 7 　解説

(A) 男性は作業中であるが、工場とは断定できない。彼は定位置で作業をしており、歩き回ってはいない。

(B) 男性は機械作業をしているのでメカニックかもしれないが、彼1人しか写っていないのでグループの監督をしているとは言えない。

(C) 彼はエンジンのような機械の部品を扱っているが、新しい部品を注文しているのではない。

➡ (D) 彼は作業台でトラクター（農耕機の一種）の部品を修理している。

写真には人物が含まれている場合とそうでない場合があります。しかしいずれにしても、各センテンスのメッセージと写真の内容とを照合すればよいわけです。聞き取れない語句が出てきてもあわてないでください。たとえばSample Question 5の選択肢(D) People are attending a groundbreaking ceremony. の groundbreaking ceremonyの意味はすぐには理解できなかったかもしれません。それでも、写真のなかに人々 (people)が見当たらないことから、この選択肢が正解でないと判断することができます。

Part Ⅱ：応答問題

Sample Question 8

CD1 No.32 On the recording, you will hear:

(Man) *Would you mind changing seats with me?*
(Woman) *(A) No, I don't mind at all.*
   (B) Sorry, I don't have change.
   (C) There are no more seats available.

Question 8　解説

➡ (A) 女性は席を替わることを気にしていない。むしろ進んでそうしようとしている。

   (B) 質問文のchangeという単語は「替わる」という意味の動詞で、「硬貨」や「お金」を意味する名詞ではない。

   (C) 男性も女性もすでに席に座っている。男性が尋ねているのは他に席が空いているかどうかではなく、女性と席を替わってもらえるかどうかである。

Sample Question 9

CD1 No.33 On the recording, you will hear:

(Woman 1) *Why don't you let me leave the tip?*
(Woman 2) *(A) Because I need you here.*
   (B) It's not too far.
   (C) I've already taken care of it.

Question 9　解説

   (A) 最初の女性はチップ（心付け）を置いていきたかったのであり、leave on a trip（旅行に行く）とは言っていない。

   (B) ここでのleave the tipは「チップを置いていく」という意味で、距離については話していない。

➡ (C) 二人目の女性はすでにチップをあげた（taken care of）と言っている。

Sample Question 10

CD1 No.34 On the recording, you will hear:

(Man 1) *Haven't you worked here longer than Mrs. Kim?*
(Man 2) *(A) No, it's very close to the office.*
   (B) No, we were hired at the same time.
   (C) No, she won't have to wait much longer.

Question 10　解説

   (A) longerという単語はここでは時間のことで、距離のことではない。

➡ (B) 二人目の男性はMrs. Kimと同時期に雇われた(hired at the same time)ので、二人は同じ期間ここで働いている。

   (C) この会話ではMrs. Kimがどのくらいの期間働いているかについて話しており、彼女がどのくらい待たなければならないかについては話していない。

ある一定の表現が会話の方向性を示す場合があります。Sample Question 8の“Would you mind …?”や9の“Why don't you …?”などがそのよい例です。

Sample Question 11

CD1 No.35 On the recording, you will hear:

(Woman) *The leadership training with Mr. García begins at ten o'clock, doesn't it?*

(Man) *(A) No, it leaves at eleven.*
(B) It's not raining now.
(C) I thought it was at nine.

Question 11　解説

(A) 女性はtraining（トレーニング）と言っているのに、この返答はtrain（電車）のことを話題にしている。

(B) この返答は天気（raining）のことを話題にしている。

➡ (C) 女性はいつトレーニングが始まるのかを尋ねている。「10時でしょう」と付加疑問文を用いて、それが正しいかどうか確かめようとしている。これに対し、男性は「9時」という正しい時間を女性に教えている。

Sample Question 12

CD1 No.36 On the recording, you will hear:

(Man 1) *Should I turn off these lights?*

(Man 2) *(A) Just keep driving straight along this road.*
(B) No, only the ones in your office.
(C) Yes, it's too heavy for me.

Question 12　解説

(A) 最初の男性はどこで曲がったらいいかと道順を聞いているのではない。

➡ (B) 最初の男性は電気を消してよいかと尋ねており、その答えは「自分のオフィスの電気だけ消して下さい」となっている。

(C) lightsは名詞として使われており、形容詞ではない。

Sample Question 13

CD1 No.37 On the recording, you will hear:

(Woman 1) *Do you like this hot weather, or do you prefer the cold?*

(Woman 2) *(A) I have trouble with the heat.*
(B) It's just an allergy.
(C) Yes, I'm feeling much better, thanks.

Question 13　解説

➡ (A) coldは気温のことである。

(B) ここでのcoldは病気ではなく、女性が風邪をひいていたり、アレルギーを持っているかを話題にしているのではない。

(C) 女性の健康について話しているのではない。

Sample Question 14

CD1 No.38 On the recording, you will hear:

(Man) *Where should I hand in this application?*

(Woman) *(A) By the end of the month.*
(B) At window number five.
(C) Sorry, I don't have one.

Question 14　解説

(A) 質問は「時間」ではなく「場所」に関してである。

➡ (B) この選択肢が「どこ」へ申込書を持って行けばいいのかという質問の答えになっている。

(C) 男性は申込書をすでに持っており、欲しがってはない。

会話はキャッチボールのようなものです。1つひとつの単語をすべてとらえようとするのではなく、話し手が互いに何を伝えようとしているか、その要点をつかむよう心がけましょう。また、TOEICのPart IIでは質問文の趣旨を理解することがポイントになります。

Sample Question 15

CD1 No.39 On the recording, you will hear:

(Woman) *What's the most popular sightseeing spot in this area?*

(Man) *(A) Nearly three million people.*
(B) Taking a tour by bus.
(C) The national art gallery.

Question 15　解説

(A) 女性は「数」を尋ねているのではないので、数字は答えにならない。

(B) 女性は「何をするか」ではなく、「場所」を尋ねている。

➡ (C) 「一番人気のあるスポットは？」という問いに対して、「美術館」が正しい答えになる。ここでのspotは「場所」を意味している。

Sample Question 16

CD1 No.40 On the recording, you will hear:

(Woman 1) *How many factories does your company have?*

(Woman 2) *(A) Just one, but it's very large.*
(B) That's one of the factors.
(C) We're working on it at the moment.

Question 16　解説

➡ (A) 質問は「数」を尋ねているので、数字が答えになる。

(B) 最初の女性はfactorではなくfactoryという単語を使っている。factorは「条件」や、「結果を導く要因」という意味である。

(C) 工場は仕事をするところだが、質問はそこでの仕事についてではない。

Sample Question 17

CD1 No.41 On the recording, you will hear:

(Man 1) *When did the theft take place?*

(Man 2) *(A) From the living room.*
(B) In the middle of the day.
(C) Some video equipment was taken.

Question 17　解説

(A) take placeは「起こる」という意味である。男性は「いつ」窃盗が起こったかを尋ねているのであり、「どこで」起こったかを尋ねているのではない。

➡ (B) この選択肢は時間を答えていて、「いつ」という質問に正しく対応している。

(C) 質問は窃盗についてだが、何が盗まれたかについては尋ねていない。

ふつうwhereで始まる質問文は場所について、whenであれば時間、how manyであれば数について尋ねることになります。こうした疑問詞をしっかりと聞き取ってこそ、正解が得られるのです。

Sample Question 10の "Haven't you …?" のような否定疑問文、11のような付加疑問文は瞬時の理解が困難な表現のひとつでしょう。文法知識があっても実際の会話に出てくると思ったより難しくなります。「習うより慣れろ」です。日本語に訳さず、直接英語で理解する訓練から始めましょう。たとえば、映画やビデオなどを字幕を見ずに鑑賞してみるとよいでしょう。否定疑問文や付加疑問文など、英語コミュニケーションの生きいきとした実例が体感できます。

Part III : 会話問題

Sample Question 18

In the test book, you will read:

18. What is the man's problem?
    (A) His folder is missing.
    (B) The woman gave him the wrong paper.
    (C) He forgot to hand in the folder.
    (D) He is late for a meeting.

CD1 No.42 On the recording, you will hear:

(Woman) *Here's the schedule. Do you have everything you need?*

(Man) *I can't find my folder with the guidelines in it.*

(Woman) *You just had it in your hand a minute ago!*

Question 18 解説

➡ (A) 男性はフォルダーがないと言っている。すなわちフォルダーが見当たらないである。

(B) 女性は男性に間違った書類を渡しているのではない。予定表を渡しているのである。

(C) 男性はフォルダーがないと言ってはいるが、それを提出し忘れたのではない。

(D) ミーティングについては何も述べられていない。

Sample Question 19

In the test book, you will read:

19. When should the patient return to the doctor's office?
    (A) Today.
    (B) Tomorrow.
    (C) After one week.
    (D) After two weeks.

CD1 No.43 On the recording, you will hear:

(Man) *Before I leave, is there anything else I need to know, doctor?*

(Woman) *Well, you should start your medication this evening, and take it for two weeks. I'll need to see you here again after that.*

(Man) *OK. I'll make an appointment on my way out.*

Question 19 解説

(A) 男性は今日これから薬を服用するのである。

(B) 男性は to know と言っているのであり、tomorrow とは言っていない。医者は彼にまた来るように言ってはいるが、すぐにとは言っていない。

(C) 1週間とは言っていない。

➡ (D) 薬の服用期間は2週間である。医者はそのあと再診すると言っている。

TOEIC の Part III では、音声を聞きながら、会話がどういう場面で行われているかを想像することが正解への鍵になります。場面を思い浮かべることは、会話の内容をより正確に理解する大きな手がかりになるのです。

Sample Question 20

In the test book, you will read:

20. Where does this conversation probably take place?
    (A) At the man's house.
    (B) At the man's office.
    (C) At a jewelry store.
    (D) At a clothing store.

CD1 No.44 On the recording, you will hear:

(Man) *Excuse me, I think I dropped my watch in the fitting room when I was trying on a suit here this morning. Has anyone found it?*

(Woman) *I don't see it here, but if you leave your name and phone number, I'll call you if it turns up.*

(Man) *Thanks. I'll give you my office number and my home number.*

Question 20 解説

(A) 男性は自宅の電話番号を残していくと言っているのである。また、試着室は個人の家の中にあるものではない。

(B) 男性はオフィスの電話番号も残していくと言っており、オフィスにいるのではない。

(C) 時計は確かに貴金属だが、男性は時計を落としたと言っており、時計を買おうとしているのではない。

➡ (D) 男性は試着室とスーツの試着について述べているので、衣料品店にいると考えられる。

Sample Question 21

In the test book, you will read:

21. What will happen three months from now?
    (A) Road repairs will begin.
    (B) The trip downtown will take over an hour.
    (C) The trip downtown will become shorter.
    (D) Main Street will be closed.

CD1 No.45 On the recording, you will hear:

(Woman) *They've started the road repairs on Main Street.*

(Man) *I know. For the next three months, it'll take over an hour to get downtown.*

(Woman) *Yes, but after that we'll be able to get there much faster.*

Question 21 解説

(A) 道路の修復はすでに始まっている。

(B) 修復が行われている間だけ、ダウンタウンまで1時間ほどかかるのである。

➡ (C) 3カ月後には道路の修復は終了し、ダウンタウンまでの所要時間は短縮される。

(D) 男性の「これから3カ月間は〜」という言葉から、道路の修復にそれだけ時間がかかることがわかるが、3カ月間後Main Streetは元の状態に戻るはずである。

Sample Question 22

In the test book, you will read:

22. Who is the woman talking to?
    (A) A hotel clerk.
    (B) A flight attendant.
    (C) A taxi driver.
    (D) A long-distance operator.

CD1 **No.46** ▷ On the recording, you will hear:

(Man) *Good evening, front desk. May I help you?*

(Woman) *Yes, I have a 7:45 flight tomorrow morning, so I'll need a wake-up call. How long does it take to get to the airport?*

(Man) *If you get a cab from here by 6:30, it should only take15 minutes. Should I call you at 5:45?*

Question 22　解説

➡ (A) 女性はモーニングコールを頼むためにフロントに電話をかけたので、ホテルのフロント係と話をしていると考えられる。

(B) 女性は翌朝、空港に行く予定だが、客室乗務員と話しているのではない。

(C) 女性は翌朝、タクシーに乗る予定だが、運転手と話しているのではない。

(D) 女性はモーニングコールを頼んでいるのであり、長距離電話をかけたいのではない。

Sample Question 23

In the test book, you will read:

23. Why doesn't the man move to an apartment near the university?
    (A) The rent is too high.
    (B) He doesn't want to live there.
    (C) The apartments are all currently occupied.
    (D) There are no nice apartments in that area.

CD1 **No.47** ▷ On the recording, you will hear:

(Man) *It's so hard to find an apartment in this city. They're either too small or too expensive.*

(Woman) *Have you looked over by the university? Rents are low around there, and some of the apartments are really nice.*

(Man) *I tried that area, but there's nothing available until summer.*

Question 23　解説

(A) 市内の家賃は高いが、大学付近では比較的安い。

(B) 男性は大学付近でアパートを探してみたが、空室はひとつもなかった。

➡ (C) 大学近くのアパートはすべて夏まで賃貸済みである。

(D) 女性は「あの地域のアパートは良い」と言っている。

Sample Question 24

In the test book, you will read:

24. What will Mr. Miyoshi probably do?
    (A) Employ more people to work for him.
    (B) Talk to the new head of finance.
    (C) Apply for a position in accounting.
    (D) Ask for a promotion.

CD1 No.48 On the recording, you will hear:

(Woman 1) *Did you hear that Mr. Miyoshi in accounting was just promoted to head of finance?*

(Woman 2) *I did. Do you know if he'll be hiring any new staff?*

(Woman 1) *Yes, he'll need three more people.*

Question 24 解説

➡ (A) ミヨシ氏は 3 人をスタッフに加えるつもりである。
(B) ミヨシ氏自身が新任の財務部長である。
(C) ミヨシ氏は以前、経理部に属していた。
(D) ミヨシ氏は昇進したばかりである。

Sample Question 25

In the test book, you will read:

25. Where does this conversation probably take place?
    (A) In a pharmacy.
    (B) In a hotel.
    (C) In a dentist's office.
    (D) In a supermarket.

CD1 No.49 On the recording, you will hear:

(Man 1) *I didn't pack any toothpaste. Can you tell me if there's a pharmacy nearby?*

(Man 2) *There's a shop downstairs in the lobby where you can buy some.*

(Man 1) *Good. Then I won't have to go out of the building in this rain.*

Question 25 解説

(A) 男性は近くに薬局があるかと聞いているのであり、まだ薬局にはいない。
➡ (B) 二人の男性はロビーと店のある建物にいる。ホテルにはロビーがあり、多くの場合店もある。また、男性は「歯磨き粉を荷物に入れてくるのを忘れた」と言っているので、旅行中であることがわかる。
(C) 男性は歯磨き粉を買う必要はあるが、歯医者については何も触れられていない。
(D) スーパーマーケットでは歯磨き粉は売っているが、通常ロビーはない。

5

Sample Question 26

In the test book, you will read:

26. How will the woman spend her vacation?
    (A) By taking a camping trip.
    (B) By going to the mountains.
    (C) By looking for a new home.
    (D) By relaxing on the beach.

CD1 No.50 On the recording, you will hear:

(Man) *Lisa, are you going to the beach again for your vacation this summer?*

(Woman) *No, this year we're renting a house in the mountains with my sister and her family. How about you, Bill?*

(Man) *We're going on a camping trip up north by Lake Hudson.*

Question 26 解説

(A) Billという男性がキャンプに行くのであって、Lisaという女性ではない。

➥ (B) 女性は姉の家族と一緒に山へ行く予定である。

(C) 女性は別荘を借りようとしているのであり、新しい家を探そうとしているのではない。

(D) BillはLisaに「今年の夏もまた海に行くのか」と尋ねているが、Lisaは「行かない」と答えている。

Sample Question 27

In the test book, you will read:

27. What does the woman want Mr. Kim to do?
    (A) Wait for Mrs. Wagner to finish her call.
    (B) Reschedule his appointment.
    (C) Meet with Mrs. Wagner's customers.
    (D) Come back after lunch.

CD1 No.51 On the recording, you will hear:

(Man) *My name is Sung-hi Kim. I have an appointment with Mrs. Wagner.*

(Woman) *She's talking to a customer on the phone right now, but she'll see you as soon as she finishes the call. Would you like a cup of coffee?*

(Man) *No, thanks. I've just come from lunch.*

Question 27 解説

➥ (A) Mrs. Wagnerは電話中だが、受付の女性はMr. Kimに「待っている間にコーヒーはどうですか」と勧めている。つまり電話が終わるまで待っていて欲しいのである。

(B) 受付の女性はMr. Kimにあらためて来ることを求めてはいない。

(C) 受付の女性はMr. KimにMrs. Wagnerの顧客に会ってくれとは頼んでいない。

(D) Mr. Kimはちょうど昼食を終えたところであるし、女性も昼食後に戻って来るようにとは言っていない。

音声を聞く前に質問文だけでもさっと読むようにしましょう。少しでも聞き取りのポイントをつかめば、それだけ集中して聞くことができるからです。

Part IV ：説明文問題

Sample Questions 28 and 29

In the test book, you will read:

28. Who is Elena Pappas?
    (A) A front desk clerk.
    (B) A physician.
    (C) A tour guide.
    (D) A dance teacher.

29. Where is the announcement being made?
    (A) At a trade fair.
    (B) At a health club.
    (C) At a language school.
    (D) At a folk festival.

Question 28　解説

(A) フロント係は Maria Sandor である。
(B) physical conditioning（体調を整えること）については述べられているが、physician (医師) については述べられていない。
(C) international と around the world という言葉はフォークダンスに関して使われており、観光に関してではない。
➡ (D) Elena Pappas はダンスレッスンのインストラクターである。

Question 29　解説

(A) trade fair（展示会）については述べられていない。
➡ (B) 冒頭部分から、このアナウンスはヘルスクラブのメンバーに向けられていることがわかる。
(C) international という単語は使われているが、language school については触れていない。
(D) アナウンスはフォークダンスについてであり、フォークフェスティバルについてではない。

CD1 No.52　On the recording, you will hear:

Questions 28 and 29 refer to the following announcement:

Attention health club members. Back by popular demand, our expert instructor, Elena Pappas, will again offer her International Folk Dancing sessions beginning January 15. Enjoy the fun of moving to music, gain the benefits of physical conditioning, and meet new people while you learn the basics of folk dances from around the world. Enrollment is limited to sixteen. See Maria Sandor at the front desk for details.

TOEIC の Part IV では、ひとつのアナウンスに対して２つあるいはそれ以上の質問に答えなければなりません。Part III と同じく、できれば、音声を聞く前に質問だけでもさっと目を通しておきましょう。速やかに解答をすませ、次のアナウンスへ移る準備をしておくことも大切です。

Sample Questions 30-32

In the test book, you will read:

30. What is the celebration for?
    (A) To officially open Oak Park.
    (B) To welcome a new president.
    (C) To mark an anniversary.
    (D) To salute future association leaders.

31. If it rains, when will the celebration take place?
    (A) April 25.
    (B) April 29.
    (C) June 2.
    (D) June 9.

32. Which activity will be included in the celebration?
    (A) Reports on the year's achievements.
    (B) Speeches by new association officers.
    (C) Planning for future children's activities.
    (D) Dedication of commemorative trees.

Question 30　解説
(A) Oak Park は祝賀会が開催される場所として出てくるが、開催の理由ではない。Oak Park の開園については述べられていない。
(B) 過去の歴代会長の栄誉が称えられるが、新会長に関しては何も述べていない。
➡ (C) キーワードは anniversary で、祝賀会は協会25周年を記念して開催されようとしている。
(D) 将来の会長ではなく、歴代の会長について述べている。

Question 31　解説
(A) 協会は25周年を迎えようとしているのであって、4月25日はアナウンスに出てこない。
(B) 4月29日は委員会を手伝いたい人々が Tom Suzuki に連絡する締切日である。
(C) 6月2日土曜日は天候が良ければ祝賀会を催す日である。
➡ (D) 6月2日が雨天ならば、祝賀会は6月9日に開催される。

Question 32　解説
(A) 協会の業績については述べていない。
(B) スピーチをするのは visiting dignitaries（来賓）であり、協会のメンバーではない。
(C) 子供向けの催しが計画されているのは今回の祝賀会であり、将来の祝賀会ではない。
➡ (D) 協会の歴代会長の栄誉を称えるために二本の桜が贈呈される。

CD1 No.53 On the recording, you will hear:

Questions 30 through 32 refer to the following announcement:

The anniversary committee is finalizing plans for the celebration of our twenty-fifth anniversary on Saturday, June second. In the event of rain, the celebration will be held on June ninth. The official ceremonies are scheduled to begin at five o'clock in Oak Park and will include speeches by visiting dignitaries and the dedication of two cherry trees as a salute to past presidents of the association. Special events for children are also being planned. Anyone who would like to assist the anniversary committee should contact Tom Suzuki before April twenty-ninth.

Sample Questions 33 and 34

In the test book, you will read:

33. What are the workers concerned about?
    (A) Payroll costs.
    (B) Job security.
    (C) Salary cuts.
    (D) Factory security.

34. What is Mr. Singh's attitude toward the workers' complaints?
    (A) He insists on hiring only full-time workers.
    (B) He supports the workers' strike.
    (C) He rejects the company policy.
    (D) He maintains that expenses must be cut.

Question 33　解説

(A) 社長の Mr. Singh が賃金の支払いについて懸念している。

➡ (B) 従業員が懸念しているのは、付加手当や雇用の保証もなく、常勤従業員の業務が臨時従業員に取って代わられることである。

(C) salary cuts とは賃金削減であるが、使われている non-salaried という語は、雇用形態を指し、賃金削減を意味しているのではない。

(D) Gemini Industries は工場の名前のようである。しかし、従業員は工場の安全性についてではなく、雇用について心配しているのである。

Question 34　解説

(A) 会社は正社員ではなく、臨時従業員をより多く雇おうとしている。

(B) 従業員は会社に対してストライキを行っている。しかし社長の Mr. Singh は会社と同じ考えではあるが、従業員とは意見が一致していない。

(C) Mr. Singh は会社の方針を擁護しており、拒絶しているのではない。

➡ (D) 彼は賃金削減による会社の経費削減を主張している。

CD1　No.54　On the recording, you will hear:

Questions 33 and 34 refer to the following report:

Union workers at Gemini Industries are in their fifth day of a strike in protest of the growing use of temporary workers. More and more workers are seeing their full-time jobs replaced by non-salaried, short-term positions without benefits or job security. Gemini President Raymond Singh insists that the company reduce payroll costs to remain competitive.

Part Ⅳ では、複数の質問に答えなければなりませんが、それはアナウンスの内容に沿ったものです。したがって、質問と選択肢を見ながらその答えに相当する情報をつかむという、さらに積極的なリスニングになります。文字を見ながら音声を聞く、文字情報と音声情報を結びつける。このトレーニングを積み重ねればリスニング力が強化され、Part Ⅳ の問題も楽に解答できるようになります。

Part V：文法・語彙問題

Sample Question 35

35. Please note that customs regulations do not permit the shipment of ------- items.
    (A) perishable
    (B) compatible
    (C) sustainable
    (D) incredible

Question 35　解説

➡ (A) perishable はいたみやすく腐りやすい食べ物を形容する言葉で、その種の食品には税関規定が適用される。
  (B) compatible は他人とうまくやっていける人、または問題なく一緒に使える物を修飾する語である。
  (C) sustainable は「（長い間）維持できる」という意味の形容詞である。
  (D) incredible は「信じられない」という意味で、輸送貨物を修飾する語ではない。

Sample Question 36

36. Brencorp has demonstrated a strong ------- to employee development through its many incentive programs.
    (A) committing
    (B) committed
    (C) committee
    (D) commitment

Question 36　解説

  (A) ing で終わる動詞の多くは名詞としても使われるが、committing が名詞として使われることはまずない。
  (B) 動詞の原形に ed をつけた形の committed は形容詞としても使われるが、名詞にはなり得ない。
  (C) committee は名詞なので、語形としてはあてはまるが、示す(demonstrate)対象にはならない。
➡ (D) commitment は「何かをしようという意思(promise)」を意味する名詞で、示す(demonstrate)ことができ、形容詞 strong で修飾される。

Sample Question 37

37. Prolonged ------- to moisture can adversely affect the proper functioning of this audio unit.
    (A) enclosure
    (B) exposure
    (C) exclusion
    (D) exertion

Question 37　解説

  (A) enclosure は何かを囲むものである。正解の単語に似ているが、綴りと意味が異なる。
➡ (B) exposure to moisture は湿気を与えるという意味になり、オーディオ・セットに損傷を与えかねないということ。
  (C) exclusion の後には to ではなく of が続くのがふつう。また、湿気を除くことはオーディオセットを守ることであって損傷を与えることではない。
  (D) exertion は「努力、作業」という意味で、後には of が続くのが正しく、意味上でも不適切。

Sample Question 38

38. Despite an exceptionally low rice harvest, analysts predict that the Tarvo Republic will not need to rely on ------- staple foods this year.
    (A) import
    (B) imports
    (C) imported
    (D) importer

Question 38　解説

  (A) import は通常、動詞または名詞として使われる。形容詞として使われることもあるが、ここでは不可。
  (B) imports は動詞または名詞としてのみ使われる。ここでは形容詞が必要。
➡ (C) imported は「主食」を修飾する形容詞である（動詞の原形に ed をつけた形）。
  (D) importer は輸入をする人または会社を意味する名詞である。

Section Ⅱ Reading は Section Ⅰ Listening と違って時間配分を自分でコントロールできます。しかし、100問を75分で解答しなければならないので、全問解答するためには、1つの問題に時間をかけすぎないようにしましょう。

Sample Question 39

39. Warning! This strap must be fastened ------- around the crates in order to hold the load in place.
    - (A) minutely
    - (B) securely
    - (C) portably
    - (D) thickly

Question 39　解説

- (A) minutelyは「詳細に、綿密に」という意味の副詞で、皮ひもの結び方を形容するのには使われない。
- ➡ (B) 文意から、「しっかりと」という意味のsecurelyがあてはまる。
- (C) portablyは「移動できるように」という副詞で、fasten, hold...in placeという表現とは逆の意味になる。
- (D) thickは「太い」という意味の形容詞なので、その副詞形thicklyはここでは不適切。

Sample Question 40

40. Construction engineers ------- that damage from last week's flood will exceed £ 50,000.
    - (A) estimates
    - (B) is estimating
    - (C) have estimated
    - (D) have been estimated

Question 40　解説

- (A) 現在形を使うことはできるが、主語engineersが複数形なので、後に続く動詞に三・単・現のsはつかない。
- (B) 文意から現在進行形も可能だが、is estimatingは単数形の主語に対応するので誤り。
- ➡ (C) 現在完了形を使えば「エンジニアは見積もりを終えた」という意味になる。have estimatedは複数形の主語に正しく対応する。
- (D) have been estimatedは受動態だが、エンジニアが何かを「行った」のであるから、不適切である。

Sample Question 41

41. When changing jobs, it is important to consider ------- salary and benefits.
    - (A) both
    - (B) either
    - (C) yet
    - (D) or

Question 41　解説

- ➡ (A) 転職を考えている人は、給与と付加手当の両方(both)を含むすべての重要項目について考慮するものである。
- (B) eitherは二つのもののいずれか一つを選択する場合に使われる。
- (C) yetはhoweverと同じく対照を示す。給与と付加手当はどちらも考慮すべきものとして取り上げられているのであって、比較対照として扱われているのではない。
- (D) 接続詞orは二つのものの比較あるいは選択を示し、両方を含むという意味にはならない。

Sample Question 42

42. The train station is ------- located near museums, monuments, and other tourist attractions in the city.
    - (A) conditionally
    - (B) conveniently
    - (C) affordably
    - (D) belatedly

Question 42　解説

- (A) 駅の場所は特定の条件に左右されるものではないので、conditionallyは誤り。
- ➡ (B) 駅は観光スポットの近くの便利な(convenient)良い場所にあるという意味になる。
- (C) 駅から近くの観光スポットに行くのにそれほどお金はかからないかもしれないが、この文は費用についてではなく場所について述べている。
- (D) belatedlyは「遅すぎて」という意味。駅は当初の予定よりも遅れて建てられたかもしれないが、この文は時間についてではなく、場所について述べている。

文脈に要注意です。文脈、つまり前後関係を意味と文法（用法）の両面から正確に把握するようにしてください。そして、文脈から答えを選び、選択した語句が適当かどうかを文脈で確認するようにしましょう。Part Vは文脈と正しい選択肢との組み合わせの問題です。

Sample Question 43

43. Last year, requisition orders for children's clothes increased more than orders for all other types of -------.

(A) apparel
(B) appearances
(C) apparatus
(D) appliances

Question 43　解説

➡ (A) 洋服について述べているので、clothingの同意語apparelが正解。
(B) appearancesはこの文の主題に関係がなく、あてはまる名詞ではない。
(C) apparatusは「機具、機械」という意味。この文は機械について述べていない。
(D) applianceはapparatusと同様に「機具、機械」という意味なので、(C)と同じ理由で誤り。

Sample Question 44

44. Check ------- that information on the bill and the receipt match exactly before submitting your records.

(A) care
(B) careful
(C) carefully
(D) carefulness

Question 44　解説

(A) チェックの仕方を形容する副詞が必要だが、careは名詞なので誤り。
(B) 名詞を修飾するcarefulは形容詞なので、読み手に何かをするように伝える動詞の命令形checkを修飾できない。
➡ (C) carefullyは請求書と領収書のチェックの仕方を形容する副詞なので、正解である。
(D) 動詞checkの目的語はinformationで、carefulness（注意深さ）が目的語になっては意味をなさない。

Sample Question 45

45. Lifelong learning is the only way to remain ------- in today's job market, according to economist Chun Ho Suk.

(A) competitor
(B) competition
(C) competitive
(D) competed

Question 45　解説

(A) a competitor であれば正しいが、不定冠詞aがないので誤り。
(B) in competitionとすれば正しいが、competitionだけでは誤り。
➡ (C) 形容詞competitiveは生涯学習に参加する人を言い表わすので正解。
(D) 形容詞を入れるべきだが、competedは通常、動詞としてのみ使われる。

選択肢の違いに要注意です。意味の違い、品詞、時制、単数複数、語の組み合わせなどの違いをできるだけ明確にしてください。そのうえで、文脈にもっとも適した選択肢を選ぶようにしましょう。また、文脈は文全体だけではなく、文の各部分にもあります。必要に応じてどちらも活用できるようにしてください。

Sample Question 46

46. Not only ------- the suppliers send the wrong components, but they also sent them to the wrong department.
    (A) had
    (B) did
    (C) were
    (D) have

Sample Question 47

47. Even when two parties seem radically opposed to one -------, an effective negotiator can help find common ground.
    (A) other
    (B) the other
    (C) another
    (D) others

Sample Question 48

48. The Trade Ministry's report ------- that the growing scarcity of skilled labor is limiting business expansion.
    (A) asserts
    (B) refers
    (C) recites
    (D) calls

Question 46 解説

(A) had + send の形は「ある人が別の人に何かをさせる」という意味の使役動詞の過去形として使うことはできる。たとえば Jane had Mary send a check to the phone company.「ジェインはメアリーに電話会社に小切手を送らせた」のような形で使われるが、ここでは文意に合わない。

➡ (B) 文の後半から判断して、時制は単純過去であり、文頭に否定の副詞句not only がある倒置形となっている。ゆえに did ...send という倒置形が適切である。

(C) 述部動詞が一般動詞の原形send なので、were という be 動詞は文法的に誤り。

(D) have + 動詞の原形は使役の意味を表わすが、文意とは合わないし、文法的にも誤り。

Question 47 解説

(A) one other は one more とほぼ同じ意味で、名詞を修飾することが多く、二者間の関係を示すものではない。

(B) one other, the other, the other one の形はあるが、one the other という形はない。

➡ (C) one another は「互いに」という意味で、二者間の関係を表わし、適切である。

(D) one others は単数形one と複数形others が混在するので文法的に誤り。

Question 48 解説

➡ (A) 主語report に対応するthat 以下の節を目的語とし説明する動詞が入るべきである。assert は state, declare と同意で、「断言する」という意味。

(B) 動詞refer はその直後にto が必要となる。

(C) recite は「大きな声で暗唱する」という意味なので、文意に合わない。

(D) calls that という形は文法的に誤りである。

語彙を増やしましょう。語彙が豊かなほど、単語や語句の意味・用法の違いが区別できます。ふだんから多くの英文に接し、英文のなかで単語の意味と用法を身につけるといった積み重ねが大切であることは言うまでもありません。多聞多読です。

Part VI：誤文訂正問題

Sample Question 49

49. The machinery <u>we sell</u> <u>is assembling</u> in this
   　　　　　　A　　　　　B

   country, but <u>most of the parts</u> come <u>from abroad</u>.
   　　　　　　　C　　　　　　　　　　D

Question 49　解説

(A) 関係代名詞thatが省略されている。この文ではthatは省略可能。

➡ (B) 機械はこの国で「組み立てられている」ので、is assembledという受動態が正しい形である。

(C) most ofの後に直接名詞が続く場合は、定冠詞theが必要となるが、省略される誤りがよく見られる。

(D) abroadは前置詞などを伴わず単独で用いられることが多いが、この場合は「海外から」という意味を表わす正しい形である。

Sample Question 50

50. The applicants <u>who</u> meet <u>the requirements</u> for the
   　　　　　　　　A　　　　B

   position <u>they will be contacted</u> in order
   　　　　　　　C

   <u>to schedule</u> an on-site interview.
   　　　D

Question 50　解説

(A) 関係代名詞whoの先行詞はapplicants「申請者」で、who以下が面接の連絡を受ける申請者がどういう人なのかを説明する節を作っている。

(B) 満たされるべきrequirements（必須条件）は特定のものなので、requirementsの前には定冠詞theが必要。

➡ (C) この文にはすでにthe applicantsという主語があるので、theyは不要。

(D) in orderという句の後にはto scheduleという不定詞が来る（「in order to ＋ 動詞の原形」で「～するために」という意味）。

Sample Question 51

51. <u>Because</u> rising incomes and falling mortgage rates,
   　　A

   sales <u>of residences</u> and <u>commercial buildings</u>
   　　　　　B　　　　　　　　　　C

   reached another <u>monthly high</u> last week.
   　　　　　　　　　　D

Question 51　解説

➡ (A) rising incomes以下の名詞句が後に続くので、becauseの後にofが必要。because of はよく使われる句である。

(B) of residencesはsalesを説明する前置詞句なので正しい。

(C) 商用またはビジネスの目的で使われている建物のことをcommercial buildingsという。

(D) 販売額が月間の最高額に達したということ。つまり月間の新記録を作ったということである。

Sample Question 52

52. An important factor <u>should be considered</u> is Mr.
   　　　　　　　　　　　A

   Lopez's <u>ability</u> to keep the new restaurant going
   　　　　　B

   <u>for several months</u> <u>with limited revenue</u>.
   　　　C　　　　　　　　　　D

Question 52　解説

➡ (A) to be またはthat should be とすれば正しいが、関係代名詞thatを省略したshould be のみでは誤り。

(B) ability to keep the new restaurant goingは「ロペス氏が新しいレストランを運営していく知識と能力を持っている」という意味。

(C) for several monthsは「数カ月の間」という意味で、ロペス氏がレストランを運営し得る期間を表している。

(D) with limited revenueは「限られた収入で」という意味で、レストランの収入があまり多くないことを示している。

TOEICのPart VIは下線を引いた4つの語句から間違っているものを1つだけ指摘（選択）する問題です。指摘するだけでどう訂正するかまでは問われていません。しかし、自分の解答が正しいかどうかを確認するためには、どこがどう間違っているのかについても理解できている方がよいでしょう。間違いの種類は大きく分けると、「余分な語の削除」、「不足語の補充」、「語句の一部訂正」、「語句の全面入れ替え」の4つになります。参考にしてください。

Sample Question 53

53. This year, the judges had the difficult yet enjoyable
                                              A
    task of selecting twelve winning photos from the
                              B   C
    many who were entered.
             D

Question 53　解説

(A) この文では yet は but と同意。この仕事は難しいけれども楽しいという意味。

(B) コンテストに入賞した12枚の写真を winning photos と言っている。ここでの winning は形容詞である。

(C) 応募されたたくさんの写真の中から12枚の写真が選ばれたということを示している。

➡ (D) 関係代名詞 who の先行詞はものではなく、人である。the many は the many photographs を指すので、この文では who を使うことができない。

Sample Question 54

54. While he worked as a travel agency, Mr. Nakamura
       A   B
    specialized in arranging tours of the Middle East.
                   C   D

Question 54　解説

(A) while は二つの物事が同時に起こっていることを表現する時に使われる。ナカムラ氏は旅行代理店に勤めていた時にツアーをアレンジしていたのである。

➡ (B) ナカムラ氏は人間なので agency ではなく agent である。agency は会社またはオフィスのことである。

(C) specialize in は「を専門とする」という意味。後には名詞または動名詞が続くので arranging は正しい形。ナカムラ氏は中東ツアーを専門にアレンジしていたのである。

(D) 定冠詞 the は the Middle East, the Southwest のように地域名の前に置かれることがある。

Sample Question 55

55. The accounting supervisor was displeased to learn
                              A
    that the budget report would not be finished
             B   C
    by time.
      D

Question 55　解説

(A) displeased はここでは感情を表わす形容詞として使われている。動詞 was の時制は that 以下の節の時制と合っているので正しい。He felt displeased. という言い方もある。

(B) budget は report を修飾しており、「予算報告書」という意味になる。

(C) that 以下の主語は report で、報告書を完成する責任者が主語ではないので、動詞は受動態となる。

➡ (D) 正しい形は on time である。by を使うのであれば by the time とし、後に time を説明する節が必要となる。

Sample Question 56

56. Electronics Superstore has announced that it will
                          A
    have closed early for the upcoming
       B   C
    holiday next week.
          D

Question 56　解説

(A) 現在完了形 has announced はこの文では正しい時制で、主語 Superstore（単数形の名詞）に正しく対応する。

➡ (B) 文意から判断して、来週の祝日に早めに閉店するものと考えられるので、will be closed または will close とすれば正しい。

(C) for the upcoming holiday は時間を表わす前置詞句である。

(D) holiday next week で「来週の祝日」という意味になり、holiday の後には前置詞は不要。next week は祝日が始まる時を示している。

間違いに気付くためには、文の意味内容と構造の両方に注意を払う必要があります。特に下線部前後の意味と構造、修飾と被修飾の関係をよく吟味してください。

Part VII：読解問題

Questions 57-58 refer to the following notice.

```
JWS TRAVEL SERVICES
8 NORTH MAIN STREET
BOSTON, MA 01731


    MS. REBECCA JOHANNSON
    52 ELM STREET
    CAMBRIDGE, MA 02138


We are pleased to confirm your travel plans as follows:

WE  20 MAR   LV BOSTON           505P   EUROPEAN AIRWAYS   EA 832   WORLD TRAVELER
TH  21 MAR   AR LONDON-HEATH     455A

                                 SEAT 20-F

TH  21 MAR   LV LONDON-HEATH     720A   EUROPEAN AIRWAYS   EA 435   EURO TRAVELER
TH  21 MAR   AR STOCKHOLM        1057A

                                 SEAT 13-A

Thank you for your business.
```

Sample Question 57

57. For what kind of travel is this notice intended?
    (A) airplane
    (B) train
    (C) luxury bus
    (D) cruise ship

Question 57　解説

➡ (A) European Airways に予約が入っているので、この通知は飛行機の旅行についてである。

(B) Airways は列車の旅行には使われない。

(C) 旅行日程の書式が典型的な航空券の予約確認の書式である。Airways はバス会社を指す言葉ではない。

(D) 船旅会社にも Airways という語は使われないし、船旅の乗客には通常、座席番号は与えられない。

Sample Question 58

58. What is Ms. Johannson's final destination?
    (A) London
    (B) Stockholm
    (C) Cambridge
    (D) Boston

Question 58　解説

(A) Ms. Johannson はボストンからストックホルムへ行く途中にロンドンで飛行機を乗り換える予定である。

➡ (B) Ms. Johannson の最終目的地はストックホルムで、3月21日木曜日の午前10時57分に到着する。

(C) Ms. Johannson は現在 Cambridge に住んでいる。これは書面にある彼女の住所からわかる。

(D) ボストンはこの通知を送った旅行会社の所在地である。

Questions 59-60 refer to the following notice.

Message for: *Mr. Ibrahim*

From: *Michel LeBlanc*

Taken by: *Henri*

Time: *2:15 p.m., Thurs.*

Message:

Michel LeBlanc at Batir Construction called. Has finished updating the contract but can't meet you on Friday at 3. Wanted to know when he can reach you to reschedule. Will be at home this evening, but will try to contact you before then. If he doesn't get in touch with you, call him after 8 p.m. at home at 24-55-5123.

Sample Question 59

59. Why did Mr. LeBlanc call Mr. Ibrahim?
   (A) To rearrange a meeting
   (B) To ask for some building work to be done
   (C) To find out when a meeting will end
   (D) To request a work schedule

Question 59　解説

➡ (A) このメッセージは Mr. LeBlanc がミーティングのスケジュールを変更したいということを伝えている。reschedule は arrange for another time（別の日時に予定を立て直す）という意味。

(B) building work については何も書かれていない。

(C) ミーティングの時間を変更することについて書かれているが、新たなミーティングの開始、あるいは終了時刻については書かれていない。

(D) reschedule は予定などを変更するという意味の動詞として使われている。work schedule という表現は使われていない。

Sample Question 60

60. What is Mr. LeBlanc going to do?
   (A) Meet Mr. Ibrahim on Friday.
   (B) Revise the contract.
   (C) Go out for the evening.
   (D) Telephone again this afternoon.

Question 60　解説

(A) Mr. LeBlanc が金曜日に会うことができないので予定を変更してくれるようにというメッセージである。

(B) Mr. LeBlanc はすでに契約の更新を終えたと述べてある。

(C) Mr. LeBlanc は今晩家にいると述べてある。

➡ (D) you は Mr. Ibrahim を指す。つまり Mr. LeBlanc が Mr. Ibrahim にもう一度連絡を取るようにするのである。

TOEIC の Part VII では英文の内容に関して具体的な質問をしています。オフィスメモやビジネスレター、広告、さらには時刻表やグラフなどさまざまな内容です。ふだんから、英字新聞はもとより、機器の取り扱い説明書、食品のパッケージなどの英文も読み、多種多様な英語表現に慣れておきましょう。

Information About Your New Furniture Upholstery

Upholstery Characteristics

Leather: Leather hides can be treated in a number of different ways. This may include sanding or buffing, depending on the style of furniture. Leather hides may have characteristics referred to as "hallmarks of the trail." These characteristics include scarring from barbed wire, insect bite marks, or even branding marks that are used on ranches. Leather may also have shade variations. They can go from lighter colorations to darker colorations on the same piece of furniture. Leather may also have a natural aroma similar to that found on leather apparel when first unpacked. This aroma may dissipate after a short period of time.

General Upholstery: Striped or plaid fabrics that are designed to match may appear unmatched at delivery. In this case, try turning over or repositioning the cushions first. Many times, this alleviates the problem.

Skirting: The skirting located along the bottom of the sofa may be wrinkled or folded from the shipping process. These wrinkles will fall out with time. Wrinkles in fabric or skirting are quickly remedied with the use of steam.

Sample Question 61

61. For whom is this information intended?
    (A) Upholstery repairers
    (B) Manufacturers of leather furniture
    (C) Delivery personnel
    (D) Purchasers of new furniture

Question 61　解説

(A) この情報はupholstery（室内装飾材料）について良く知らない人へ向けたものである。upholstery repairers（室内装飾修理業者）はupholsteryのいろいろな種類やそれぞれの場合に何をすべきかについてすでによく知っている。

(B) furniture manufacturers（家具製造者）はすでにこの情報を知っている。製造者だったらこういう手紙を顧客に情報として提供するために書くだろうと考えられる。

(C) delivery personnel（配送業者）は新しい家具の取り扱いについて知っているべきだが、この通知は配送業者に向けられたものではない。

➡ (D) この書面はpurchasers of new furniture（新しい家具の購入者）に対し、家具に関する情報や取り扱い方の説明をするためのものである。

Question 62-63 refer to the information on the previous page.

5

Sample Question 62

62. What is NOT mentioned as the source of a
   characteristic mark?
   (A) Barbed wire fences
   (B) Insect bites
   (C) Branding
   (D) Sanding

Question 62　解説

(A) 加工前の皮の状態の特徴として、フェンス
として利用されているbarbed wire（有刺鉄
線）の傷跡、虫食いの跡、烙印を押された
跡が挙げられている。

(B) insect bite（昆虫の噛んだ跡）も加工前の特
徴の1つとして挙げられている。

(C) branding marks（烙印）はその家畜の所有者
を示すものである。

➡ (D) 皮製品を仕上げるために施す方法の1つと
して sanding(サンドペーパーをかけること)
が述べられている。

Sample Question 63

63. What should be done if fabric patterns do not match?
   (A) The furniture should be returned to the
      manufacturer.
   (B) The cushions should be rearranged.
   (C) Steam should be applied to the material.
   (D) The material should be unfolded carefully.

Question 63　解説

(A) 家具の返品については述べられていない。

➡ (B) 書面では、クッションをひっくり返したり、
位置を変えることを提案している。これは
rearrangeと同意。

(C) steam(蒸気をあてること)は、すその部分の
しわを直す方法として述べられており、柄
が合わない生地の直し方ではない。

(D) Fold（折りたたむ）という単語がSkirting
（ソファのすそにある部分）の説明文に出て
くるが、柄が合わない生地の直し方として
は、何かをunfold（折ったものを広げること）
するようにとは述べられていない。

TOEICのPart VIIの質問のなかには詳細な内容に関するものもあります。先に質問文と選択肢に目を通してから、本文の内容と一致する選択肢
を選ぶようにするとよいでしょう。

5

Annual School-to-Work Career Conference Survives a Storm

The eighth annual School-to-Work Career Conference was held in Peterstown last Sunday, despite a major ice storm over the weekend that made travel in the area a considerable challenge.

More than 400 attendees came to the Jefferson Convention Center in downtown Peterstown. Students from local high schools, many of them accompanied by their families, received a variety of career information. Volunteers from the Peterstown Business Center helped students complete aptitude questionnaires and explore possible career paths. Presentations and workshops were given by local business leaders, and a large number of professionals were available to answer students' questions about careers.

The conference was sponsored by the Peterstown Business Association and the Peterstown school system. An association spokesperson commented that the willingness of people to come out in the poor weather was a good sign for the future of businesses in the area. He added that he hoped blue skies and a strong economy would be in the forecast for next year's conference.

Sample Question 64

64. For whom was the conference planned?
    (A) High school teachers
    (B) Community volunteers
    (C) High school students
    (D) New business owners

Question 64　解説

(A) high school という言葉は出てくるが、teachers は出てこない。

(B) community volunteers（地区のボランティア）は会議を手伝ったが、会議は彼らのために計画されたものではない。

➡ (C) この記事は students について何度か述べており、彼らは地元の高校から来たとも書いてある。

(D) 地元の会社経営者らが大会運営を手伝った。ビジネスの将来については述べているが、new business owners（新たな会社経営者）については述べていない。

Sample Question 65

65. What was the purpose of the questionnaires?
    (A) To recruit volunteers
    (B) To provide family entertainment
    (C) To solicit funds
    (D) To help determine skills

Question 65　解説

(A) ボランティアはすでに雇われている。彼らは学生の調査票記入を手伝った。

(B) たくさんの家族がこのイベントに出席し、楽しんだかもしれないが、この調査票の目的は楽しませることではない。

(C) 記事に business と economy という単語が出てくるが、solicit funds（基金を募る）ことについては何も書かれていない。

➡ (D) 学生はボランティアに手伝ってもらって調査票を記入し、適職を見つけるとある。つまり調査票に記入することで自分の aptitudes（適性）を見出すのだと考えられる。

Question 66 refers to the article on the previous page.

5

Sample Question 66

66. What was an obstacle to the success of the conference?
   (A) The economy was weak.
   (B) The weather was unfavorable.
   (C) There were not enough volunteers.
   (D) Local business leaders were not available.

Question 66　解説

(A) 協会の広報担当者は来年の景気が良くなることを望むとは述べたが、今年の会議では不景気についての言及はない。

➡ (B) 第一段落で、強い雪嵐のため、会議当日の交通が困難だったと述べている。

(C) 参加したボランティアの数については何も述べられていない。

(D) 地元の会社経営者らはワークショップやプレゼンテーションを行うために会議に参加した。

Part Ⅶの質問に答えるには少なくとも 3 つのリーディング・スキルが必要です。全体をさっと通して読む(Skimming)、特定の情報を求めて読む(Scanning)、一字一句をていねいに読む(Careful Reading)という読み方です。これらを本文と質問文の内容に合わせて、うまく切り換えたり、組み合わせるようにトレーニングしましょう。

5

Bristol Motor Company
1 Gray Drive
Canberra ACT 0201

12 June

Vera Hsu, Director
Canberra Transit System
15 Central Street
Canberra ACT 0216

Dear Ms. Hsu:

I am writing to your office regarding the widening of the Centura Highway, due to begin this year. This important roadway passes the Bristol Motor Company. Many of our 2,000 employees use the Canberra public transportation system and access the bus station located opposite our facilities on Centura Highway.

Between the hours of 7:30 a.m. and 8:00 a.m., and 4:30 p.m. and 5:30 p.m., a considerable number of our employees cross Centura Highway as they go to and from work. To date we have not heard of any plan to provide a traffic signal, a walkway overpass, or the services of a traffic officer to ensure the safety of our employees. We believe that steps need to be taken to reduce the possibility of accidents both during the construction phase and beyond.

I would like to arrange a meeting with you as soon as possible to discuss the above options. We at Bristol Motor Company are willing to cooperate with your office to the fullest extent and would appreciate your immediate attention to this matter.

Sincerely,

Jeff Hall

Assistant Vice President
Bristol Motor Company

Sample Question 67

67. Which issue is discussed in the letter?
    (A) The modernization of a public transportation system
    (B) The expansion of a motor company
    (C) The promotion of safety awareness training
    (D) The widening of a major road

Question 67 　解説

(A) 多くの従業員が公共交通機関を利用するが、それが近代化されるわけではない。
(B) Bristol Motor Company が事業拡大計画を発表しているわけではない。
(C) この書状において安全が大きな関心事ではあるが、安全認識向上トレーニングは解決策としてはあげられていない。
➡ (D) Centura Highway の拡張は安全に関する問題を提起している。

Questions 68-70 refer to the letter on the previous page.

5

Sample Question 68

68. Which group of people is Mr. Hall concerned about?
    (A) Construction engineers
    (B) Bus and train operators
    (C) Motor company employees
    (D) City traffic officers

Question 68　解説

(A) 工事技術者は幹線道路の拡張に従事しているが、Mr. Hall は書状のなかで彼らについては何も述べていない。

(B) Mr. Hall はバスや電車の運転手について心配しておらず、彼らについて何も述べていない。

➡ (C) Mr. Hall は拡張された幹線道路を横断しなければならない Bristol Motor Company の従業員について心配している。

(D) 市の交通担当官の派遣が安全問題の解決策として述べられているが、心配の理由ではない。

Sample Question 69

69. What is NOT mentioned as a possible solution?
    (A) Adding bus routes
    (B) Hiring a traffic officer
    (C) Building a walkway
    (D) Installing a traffic signal

Question 69　解説

➡ (A) バス路線を増やすことが幹線道路を横切ってバス乗り場へ向かう従業員の危険を減らすことにはならない。Mr. Hall はこれを解決策として提案してはいない。

(B) 人々が道路を横切る地点に交通担当官を派遣するようにと Mr. Hall の書状には書かれている。

(C) Mr. Hall の提案には歩道橋の設置案が含まれている。

(D) Mr. Hall は事故を防ぐ1つの方法として交通信号の設置を提案している。

Sample Question 70

70. How can Vera Hsu assist Bristol Motors?
    (A) By reducing bus fares
    (B) By decreasing work hours
    (C) By speeding up construction
    (D) By addressing traffic concerns

Question 70　解説

(A) Mr. Hall の書状にはバス料金については述べられていない。

(B) Mr. Hall は多くの従業員が幹線道路を横断する時間帯を挙げているが、Ms. Hsu に労働時間を短縮することを頼んではいない。

(C) 工事は今年始まる予定である。Mr. Hall は Ms. Hsu にスケジュールを早めるように頼んではおらず、工事中および工事後の安全を確保することを頼んでいる。

➡ (D) Mr. Hall は Ms. Hsu に会って、幹線道路の交通によって引き起こされる事故を防ぐ方法について話し合うことを望んでいる。

Section II Reading では、Section I Listening と違い、前に解答した問題を見直すことができます。ひととおり解答したあとで、時間に余裕があればぜひ見直すようにしましょう。

CHAPTER 6

第6章

TOEIC練習テスト(200問)

■ TOEIC練習テストのもっとも効果的な活用法

■ 解答用紙

■ TOEIC練習テスト（200問）

6 第6章

TOEIC練習テストのもっとも効果的な活用法

本書の前章までは、TOEICテストに関する詳しい説明と、英語能力を高めるための例題と練習問題でした。この章にはTOEIC練習テスト（200問）が収められています。このテストをもっとも効果的に活用するために、実際のTOEICテストと同じように取り組んでください。以下にTOEIC練習テストを受ける際の注意点を挙げます。

■ サンプルの解答用紙を使いましょう

次のページには、実際のTOEICテストに使用されるのと同様の解答用紙（サンプル）があります。練習テストに取り組む際には、実際のテストを受ける時と同じように解答用紙に正確にマークする時間を取りましょう（**249ページに切り取り用のTOEIC練習テスト用の解答用紙がありますので使いましょう**）。

■ 静かな場所で練習テストを受けましょう

2時間と少々の間、集中を妨げられない場所で受けましょう。

■ 一度に全問解答しましょう

Section I Listening と Section II Reading の間や、各パートの間で休憩を取ったりしないようにしましょう。実際のテストでも休憩を取ることはできません。疲れてもそのまま続けて解答しましょう。

■ 時間を計るために時計を使いましょう

練習テストを受ける際は、必ず時間を計りましょう。アラーム機能が付いていれば利用しましょう。ただし、実際のTOEICテスト受験会場ではアラーム機能は使用できません。

■ 制限時間を守りましょう

Section I Listening は音声を聞いて解答します。Listening の解答時間は45分間です。Section II Reading を始める前に、テストの終了時刻を確認するか、あるいはアラームを75分後にセットしましょう。実際のTOEICテストでも Reading の3つのパートに解答する時間は75分間です。75分を過ぎたら解答をやめてください。制限時間内でできるだけ多くの問題に解答できるようにしましょう。実際のテストでのスコア予測がより正確になります。

■ 練習テストのスコアを計算するためにスコア換算表を使いましょう

付録Bには、スコア換算表、正解、正解・不正解それぞれの選択肢の解説があります。練習テストのスコアを算出したい時は、付録Bを見てください。解説を注意深く読んで、自分の解答の正誤理由を理解しましょう。

TOEIC 練習テスト
（149ページ）

ANSWER SHEET

REGISTRATION NO.
受験番号

フリガナ
NAME　氏名

LISTENING (Part Ⅰ～Ⅳ)

NO.	A B C D	NO.	A B C D	NO.	A B C	NO.	A B C	NO.	A B C D	NO.	A B C D	NO.	A B C D	NO.	A B C D	NO.	A B C D
1	Ⓐ Ⓑ Ⓒ Ⓓ	11	Ⓐ Ⓑ Ⓒ Ⓓ	21	Ⓐ Ⓑ Ⓒ Ⓓ	31	Ⓐ Ⓑ Ⓒ Ⓓ	41	Ⓐ Ⓑ Ⓒ	51	Ⓐ Ⓑ Ⓒ	61	Ⓐ Ⓑ Ⓒ Ⓓ	71	Ⓐ Ⓑ Ⓒ Ⓓ	81	Ⓐ Ⓑ Ⓒ Ⓓ	91	Ⓐ Ⓑ Ⓒ Ⓓ
2	Ⓐ Ⓑ Ⓒ Ⓓ	12	Ⓐ Ⓑ Ⓒ Ⓓ	22	Ⓐ Ⓑ Ⓒ Ⓓ	32	Ⓐ Ⓑ Ⓒ Ⓓ	42	Ⓐ Ⓑ Ⓒ	52	Ⓐ Ⓑ Ⓒ	62	Ⓐ Ⓑ Ⓒ Ⓓ	72	Ⓐ Ⓑ Ⓒ Ⓓ	82	Ⓐ Ⓑ Ⓒ Ⓓ	92	Ⓐ Ⓑ Ⓒ Ⓓ
3	Ⓐ Ⓑ Ⓒ Ⓓ	13	Ⓐ Ⓑ Ⓒ Ⓓ	23	Ⓐ Ⓑ Ⓒ Ⓓ	33	Ⓐ Ⓑ Ⓒ Ⓓ	43	Ⓐ Ⓑ Ⓒ	53	Ⓐ Ⓑ Ⓒ	63	Ⓐ Ⓑ Ⓒ Ⓓ	73	Ⓐ Ⓑ Ⓒ Ⓓ	83	Ⓐ Ⓑ Ⓒ Ⓓ	93	Ⓐ Ⓑ Ⓒ Ⓓ
4	Ⓐ Ⓑ Ⓒ Ⓓ	14	Ⓐ Ⓑ Ⓒ Ⓓ	24	Ⓐ Ⓑ Ⓒ Ⓓ	34	Ⓐ Ⓑ Ⓒ Ⓓ	44	Ⓐ Ⓑ Ⓒ	54	Ⓐ Ⓑ Ⓒ	64	Ⓐ Ⓑ Ⓒ Ⓓ	74	Ⓐ Ⓑ Ⓒ Ⓓ	84	Ⓐ Ⓑ Ⓒ Ⓓ	94	Ⓐ Ⓑ Ⓒ Ⓓ
5	Ⓐ Ⓑ Ⓒ Ⓓ	15	Ⓐ Ⓑ Ⓒ Ⓓ	25	Ⓐ Ⓑ Ⓒ Ⓓ	35	Ⓐ Ⓑ Ⓒ Ⓓ	45	Ⓐ Ⓑ Ⓒ	55	Ⓐ Ⓑ Ⓒ	65	Ⓐ Ⓑ Ⓒ Ⓓ	75	Ⓐ Ⓑ Ⓒ Ⓓ	85	Ⓐ Ⓑ Ⓒ Ⓓ	95	Ⓐ Ⓑ Ⓒ Ⓓ
6	Ⓐ Ⓑ Ⓒ Ⓓ	16	Ⓐ Ⓑ Ⓒ Ⓓ	26	Ⓐ Ⓑ Ⓒ Ⓓ	36	Ⓐ Ⓑ Ⓒ Ⓓ	46	Ⓐ Ⓑ Ⓒ	56	Ⓐ Ⓑ Ⓒ	66	Ⓐ Ⓑ Ⓒ Ⓓ	76	Ⓐ Ⓑ Ⓒ Ⓓ	86	Ⓐ Ⓑ Ⓒ Ⓓ	96	Ⓐ Ⓑ Ⓒ Ⓓ
7	Ⓐ Ⓑ Ⓒ Ⓓ	17	Ⓐ Ⓑ Ⓒ Ⓓ	27	Ⓐ Ⓑ Ⓒ Ⓓ	37	Ⓐ Ⓑ Ⓒ Ⓓ	47	Ⓐ Ⓑ Ⓒ	57	Ⓐ Ⓑ Ⓒ	67	Ⓐ Ⓑ Ⓒ Ⓓ	77	Ⓐ Ⓑ Ⓒ Ⓓ	87	Ⓐ Ⓑ Ⓒ Ⓓ	97	Ⓐ Ⓑ Ⓒ Ⓓ
8	Ⓐ Ⓑ Ⓒ Ⓓ	18	Ⓐ Ⓑ Ⓒ Ⓓ	28	Ⓐ Ⓑ Ⓒ Ⓓ	38	Ⓐ Ⓑ Ⓒ Ⓓ	48	Ⓐ Ⓑ Ⓒ	58	Ⓐ Ⓑ Ⓒ	68	Ⓐ Ⓑ Ⓒ Ⓓ	78	Ⓐ Ⓑ Ⓒ Ⓓ	88	Ⓐ Ⓑ Ⓒ Ⓓ	98	Ⓐ Ⓑ Ⓒ Ⓓ
9	Ⓐ Ⓑ Ⓒ Ⓓ	19	Ⓐ Ⓑ Ⓒ Ⓓ	29	Ⓐ Ⓑ Ⓒ Ⓓ	39	Ⓐ Ⓑ Ⓒ Ⓓ	49	Ⓐ Ⓑ Ⓒ	59	Ⓐ Ⓑ Ⓒ	69	Ⓐ Ⓑ Ⓒ Ⓓ	79	Ⓐ Ⓑ Ⓒ Ⓓ	89	Ⓐ Ⓑ Ⓒ Ⓓ	99	Ⓐ Ⓑ Ⓒ Ⓓ
10	Ⓐ Ⓑ Ⓒ Ⓓ	20	Ⓐ Ⓑ Ⓒ Ⓓ	30	Ⓐ Ⓑ Ⓒ Ⓓ	40	Ⓐ Ⓑ Ⓒ Ⓓ	50	Ⓐ Ⓑ Ⓒ	60	Ⓐ Ⓑ Ⓒ	70	Ⓐ Ⓑ Ⓒ Ⓓ	80	Ⓐ Ⓑ Ⓒ Ⓓ	90	Ⓐ Ⓑ Ⓒ Ⓓ	100	Ⓐ Ⓑ Ⓒ Ⓓ

READING (Part Ⅴ～Ⅶ)

NO.	A B C D	NO.	A B C D	NO.	A B C D	NO.	A B C D	NO.	A B C D	NO.	A B C D	NO.	A B C D	NO.	A B C D	NO.	A B C D	NO.	A B C D
101	Ⓐ Ⓑ Ⓒ Ⓓ	111	Ⓐ Ⓑ Ⓒ Ⓓ	121	Ⓐ Ⓑ Ⓒ Ⓓ	131	Ⓐ Ⓑ Ⓒ Ⓓ	141	Ⓐ Ⓑ Ⓒ Ⓓ	151	Ⓐ Ⓑ Ⓒ Ⓓ	161	Ⓐ Ⓑ Ⓒ Ⓓ	171	Ⓐ Ⓑ Ⓒ Ⓓ	181	Ⓐ Ⓑ Ⓒ Ⓓ	191	Ⓐ Ⓑ Ⓒ Ⓓ
102	Ⓐ Ⓑ Ⓒ Ⓓ	112	Ⓐ Ⓑ Ⓒ Ⓓ	122	Ⓐ Ⓑ Ⓒ Ⓓ	132	Ⓐ Ⓑ Ⓒ Ⓓ	142	Ⓐ Ⓑ Ⓒ Ⓓ	152	Ⓐ Ⓑ Ⓒ Ⓓ	162	Ⓐ Ⓑ Ⓒ Ⓓ	172	Ⓐ Ⓑ Ⓒ Ⓓ	182	Ⓐ Ⓑ Ⓒ Ⓓ	192	Ⓐ Ⓑ Ⓒ Ⓓ
103	Ⓐ Ⓑ Ⓒ Ⓓ	113	Ⓐ Ⓑ Ⓒ Ⓓ	123	Ⓐ Ⓑ Ⓒ Ⓓ	133	Ⓐ Ⓑ Ⓒ Ⓓ	143	Ⓐ Ⓑ Ⓒ Ⓓ	153	Ⓐ Ⓑ Ⓒ Ⓓ	163	Ⓐ Ⓑ Ⓒ Ⓓ	173	Ⓐ Ⓑ Ⓒ Ⓓ	183	Ⓐ Ⓑ Ⓒ Ⓓ	193	Ⓐ Ⓑ Ⓒ Ⓓ
104	Ⓐ Ⓑ Ⓒ Ⓓ	114	Ⓐ Ⓑ Ⓒ Ⓓ	124	Ⓐ Ⓑ Ⓒ Ⓓ	134	Ⓐ Ⓑ Ⓒ Ⓓ	144	Ⓐ Ⓑ Ⓒ Ⓓ	154	Ⓐ Ⓑ Ⓒ Ⓓ	164	Ⓐ Ⓑ Ⓒ Ⓓ	174	Ⓐ Ⓑ Ⓒ Ⓓ	184	Ⓐ Ⓑ Ⓒ Ⓓ	194	Ⓐ Ⓑ Ⓒ Ⓓ
105	Ⓐ Ⓑ Ⓒ Ⓓ	115	Ⓐ Ⓑ Ⓒ Ⓓ	125	Ⓐ Ⓑ Ⓒ Ⓓ	135	Ⓐ Ⓑ Ⓒ Ⓓ	145	Ⓐ Ⓑ Ⓒ Ⓓ	155	Ⓐ Ⓑ Ⓒ Ⓓ	165	Ⓐ Ⓑ Ⓒ Ⓓ	175	Ⓐ Ⓑ Ⓒ Ⓓ	185	Ⓐ Ⓑ Ⓒ Ⓓ	195	Ⓐ Ⓑ Ⓒ Ⓓ
106	Ⓐ Ⓑ Ⓒ Ⓓ	116	Ⓐ Ⓑ Ⓒ Ⓓ	126	Ⓐ Ⓑ Ⓒ Ⓓ	136	Ⓐ Ⓑ Ⓒ Ⓓ	146	Ⓐ Ⓑ Ⓒ Ⓓ	156	Ⓐ Ⓑ Ⓒ Ⓓ	166	Ⓐ Ⓑ Ⓒ Ⓓ	176	Ⓐ Ⓑ Ⓒ Ⓓ	186	Ⓐ Ⓑ Ⓒ Ⓓ	196	Ⓐ Ⓑ Ⓒ Ⓓ
107	Ⓐ Ⓑ Ⓒ Ⓓ	117	Ⓐ Ⓑ Ⓒ Ⓓ	127	Ⓐ Ⓑ Ⓒ Ⓓ	137	Ⓐ Ⓑ Ⓒ Ⓓ	147	Ⓐ Ⓑ Ⓒ Ⓓ	157	Ⓐ Ⓑ Ⓒ Ⓓ	167	Ⓐ Ⓑ Ⓒ Ⓓ	177	Ⓐ Ⓑ Ⓒ Ⓓ	187	Ⓐ Ⓑ Ⓒ Ⓓ	197	Ⓐ Ⓑ Ⓒ Ⓓ
108	Ⓐ Ⓑ Ⓒ Ⓓ	118	Ⓐ Ⓑ Ⓒ Ⓓ	128	Ⓐ Ⓑ Ⓒ Ⓓ	138	Ⓐ Ⓑ Ⓒ Ⓓ	148	Ⓐ Ⓑ Ⓒ Ⓓ	158	Ⓐ Ⓑ Ⓒ Ⓓ	168	Ⓐ Ⓑ Ⓒ Ⓓ	178	Ⓐ Ⓑ Ⓒ Ⓓ	188	Ⓐ Ⓑ Ⓒ Ⓓ	198	Ⓐ Ⓑ Ⓒ Ⓓ
109	Ⓐ Ⓑ Ⓒ Ⓓ	119	Ⓐ Ⓑ Ⓒ Ⓓ	129	Ⓐ Ⓑ Ⓒ Ⓓ	139	Ⓐ Ⓑ Ⓒ Ⓓ	149	Ⓐ Ⓑ Ⓒ Ⓓ	159	Ⓐ Ⓑ Ⓒ Ⓓ	169	Ⓐ Ⓑ Ⓒ Ⓓ	179	Ⓐ Ⓑ Ⓒ Ⓓ	189	Ⓐ Ⓑ Ⓒ Ⓓ	199	Ⓐ Ⓑ Ⓒ Ⓓ
110	Ⓐ Ⓑ Ⓒ Ⓓ	120	Ⓐ Ⓑ Ⓒ Ⓓ	130	Ⓐ Ⓑ Ⓒ Ⓓ	140	Ⓐ Ⓑ Ⓒ Ⓓ	150	Ⓐ Ⓑ Ⓒ Ⓓ	160	Ⓐ Ⓑ Ⓒ Ⓓ	170	Ⓐ Ⓑ Ⓒ Ⓓ	180	Ⓐ Ⓑ Ⓒ Ⓓ	190	Ⓐ Ⓑ Ⓒ Ⓓ	200	Ⓐ Ⓑ Ⓒ Ⓓ

LISTENING COMPREHENSION

In this section of the test, you will have the chance to show how well you understand spoken English. There are four parts to this section, with special directions for each part.

PART I

Directions: For each question, you will see a picture in your test book and you will hear four short statements. The statements will be spoken just one time. They will not be printed in your test book, so you must listen carefully to understand what the speaker says.

When you hear the four statements, look at the picture in your test book and choose the statement that best describes what you see in the picture. Then, on your answer sheet, find the number of the question and mark your answer. Look at the sample below.

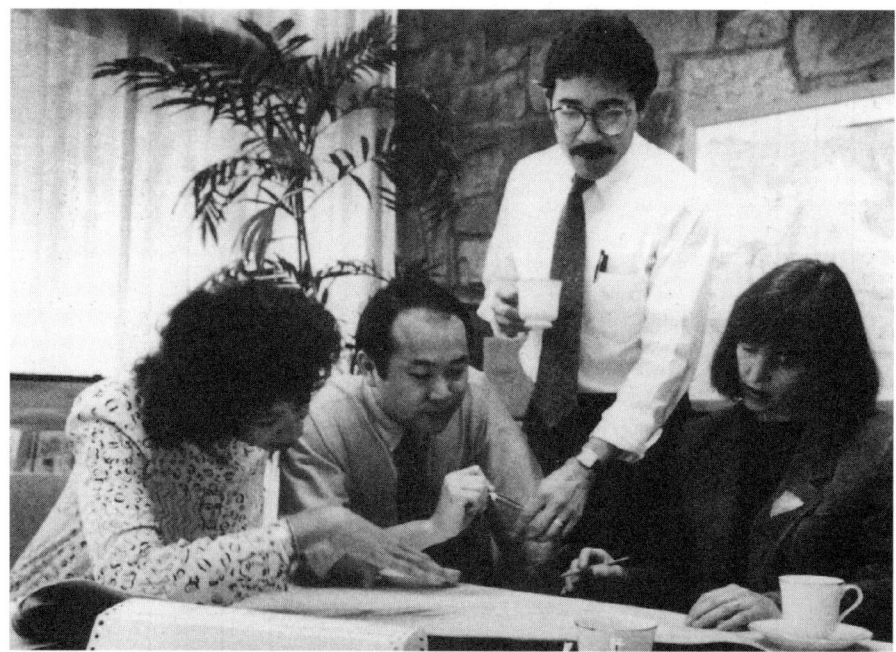

Sample Answer

Ⓐ ● Ⓒ Ⓓ

Now listen to the four statements.

Statement (B), "They're having a meeting," best describes what you see in the picture. Therefore, you should choose answer (B).

1.

2.

GO ON TO THE NEXT PAGE →

3.

4.

5.

6.

GO ON TO THE NEXT PAGE

7.

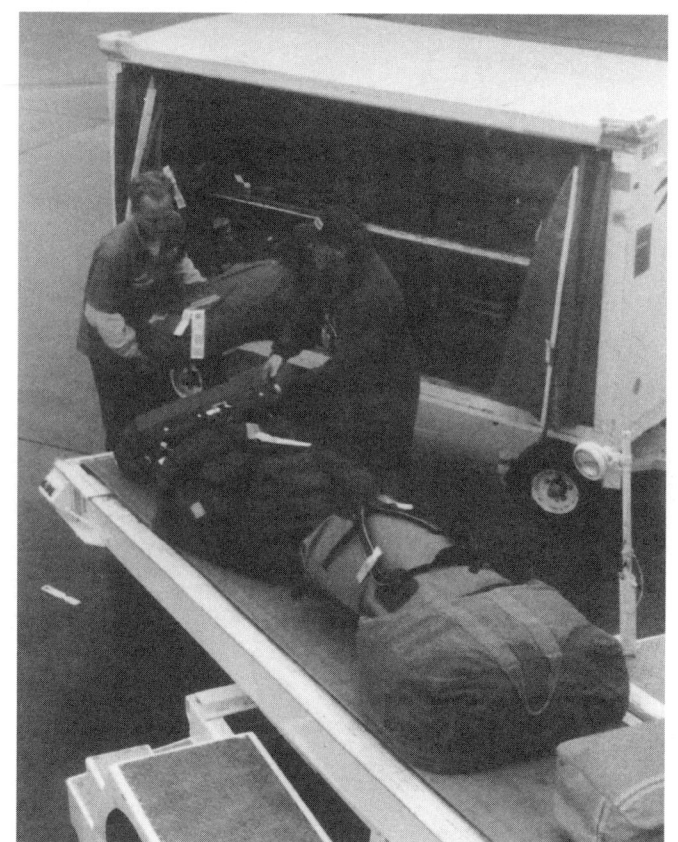

8.

9.

10.

GO ON TO THE NEXT PAGE ➡

11.

12.

13.

14.

GO ON TO THE NEXT PAGE

15.

16.

17.

18.

GO ON TO THE NEXT PAGE

19.

20.

PART II

Directions: In this part of the test, you will hear a question spoken in English, followed by three responses, also spoken in English. The question and the responses will be spoken just one time. They will not be printed in your test book, so you must listen carefully to understand what the speakers say. You are to choose the best response to each question.

Now listen to a sample question.

Sample Answer
● Ⓑ Ⓒ

You will hear:

You will also hear:

The best response to the question "How are you?" is choice (A), "I am fine, thank you." Therefore, you should choose answer (A).

21. Mark your answer on your answer sheet.

22. Mark your answer on your answer sheet.

23. Mark your answer on your answer sheet.

24. Mark your answer on your answer sheet.

25. Mark your answer on your answer sheet.

26. Mark your answer on your answer sheet.

27. Mark your answer on your answer sheet.

28. Mark your answer on your answer sheet.

29. Mark your answer on your answer sheet.

30. Mark your answer on your answer sheet.

31. Mark your answer on your answer sheet.

32. Mark your answer on your answer sheet.

33. Mark your answer on your answer sheet.

34. Mark your answer on your answer sheet.

35. Mark your answer on your answer sheet.

36. Mark your answer on your answer sheet.

37. Mark your answer on your answer sheet.

38. Mark your answer on your answer sheet.

39. Mark your answer on your answer sheet.

40. Mark your answer on your answer sheet.

41. Mark your answer on your answer sheet.

42. Mark your answer on your answer sheet.

43. Mark your answer on your answer sheet.

44. Mark your answer on your answer sheet.

45. Mark your answer on your answer sheet.

46. Mark your answer on your answer sheet.

47. Mark your answer on your answer sheet.

48. Mark your answer on your answer sheet.

49. Mark your answer on your answer sheet.

50. Mark your answer on your answer sheet.

GO ON TO THE NEXT PAGE

PART III

Directions: In this part of the test, you will hear thirty short conversations between two people. The conversations will not be printed in your test book. You will hear the conversations only once, so you must listen carefully to understand what the speakers say.

In your test book, you will read a question about each conversation. The question will be followed by four answers. You are to choose the best answer to each question and mark it on your answer sheet.

51. Who called and left a message?

(A) Mr. Murphy.
(B) The operator.
(C) Mr. Murphy's secretary.
(D) The committee chairperson.

52. Where does this conversation take place?

(A) In a coffee shop.
(B) In an office.
(C) In a post office.
(D) In a supermarket.

53. Why is Mrs. Sompong leaving?

(A) To join another company.
(B) To start her own business.
(C) To enter a race.
(D) To have a break from working.

54. When does Claudia want to go to the play?

(A) Monday.
(B) Wednesday.
(C) Thursday.
(D) Saturday.

55. What is the woman's job?

(A) Telephone operator.
(B) Computer technician.
(C) Sales representative.
(D) Personnel supervisor.

56. When will the men see the movie?

(A) At 1:00.
(B) At 2:00.
(C) At 4:00.
(D) At 7:00.

57. What are the people doing with the furniture?

(A) Rearranging it.
(B) Designing it.
(C) Buying it.
(D) Assembling it.

58. How will they travel to the conference?

(A) By plane.
(B) By car.
(C) By train.
(D) By bus.

59. Why is the woman NOT able to buy *Business News*?

(A) The magazines have all been sold already.
(B) The truck was delayed because of the weather.
(C) The store is closed on Mondays.
(D) The delivery schedule has been changed.

60. Who is going to the convention?

(A) Juan.
(B) Ricardo.
(C) Ms. Ortega.
(D) Carla.

61. What are they likely to eat for lunch?

(A) Soup.
(B) Salad.
(C) Sandwiches.
(D) Hamburgers.

62. Where is the man's luggage?

(A) In New York.
(B) At the hotel.
(C) In San Francisco.
(D) On the bus.

63. How much vacation time is Susanna allowed this year?

(A) One week.
(B) Two weeks.
(C) Three weeks.
(D) Four weeks.

64. Where are the speakers?

(A) In the cafeteria kitchen.
(B) In the first-aid room.
(C) In the mail room.
(D) In the staff lounge.

65. Who are they talking about?

(A) Yuri's daughter.
(B) Yuri's son.
(C) Yuri.
(D) Yuri's wife.

66. When will Tom need to use Alan's office?

(A) Thursday morning.
(B) Friday morning.
(C) Friday afternoon.
(D) Monday afternoon.

67. What is Patricia looking for?

(A) A file cabinet.
(B) A report.
(C) A memo.
(D) A check.

68. Where does this conversation take place?

(A) At the library.
(B) At a restaurant.
(C) At the office.
(D) At a hotel.

69. Why is the man unable to speak to Ms. Krishnan?

(A) She is on a sales trip overseas.
(B) She no longer works for the company.
(C) She has moved to another department.
(D) She is too busy.

70. Where will the two men go next week?

(A) To a hospital.
(B) To a greenhouse.
(C) To a building site.
(D) To a factory.

71. Why is Ms. Mura pleased?

(A) She won a contest.
(B) She bought a new company.
(C) She was just hired.
(D) She finished her résumé.

72. What is the woman going to do?

(A) Sell the camera.
(B) Pay by check.
(C) Fill out a form.
(D) Write her name on the card.

73. Who will be sent to room 512?

(A) A plumber.
(B) An accountant.
(C) An electrician.
(D) A driver.

74. What is Ms. Lee waiting for?

(A) A fax.
(B) Her clients.
(C) A document.
(D) A phone call.

GO ON TO THE NEXT PAGE

75. Why is Heidi leaving?

(A) To go home.
(B) To handle an urgent matter.
(C) To make a telephone call.
(D) To attend an office party.

76. What does the woman want to do?

(A) Get a credit card.
(B) Buy a sweater.
(C) Return a present.
(D) Pay a fine.

77. When will the presentation be made?

(A) Monday.
(B) Wednesday.
(C) Over the weekend.
(D) In seven weeks.

78. Why was the driver stopped?

(A) He was driving too fast.
(B) He turned the wrong way.
(C) His car was not working properly.
(D) He did not have a license.

79. When will the order be ready?

(A) In a few minutes.
(B) At 9:00 tonight.
(C) Tomorrow.
(D) The day after tomorrow.

80. Why did Olivia leave?

(A) There was not enough work to do.
(B) The division office asked her to.
(C) She decided to retire.
(D) Her contract was not approved.

PART IV

Directions: In this part of the test, you will hear several short talks. Each will be spoken just one time. They will not be printed in your test book, so you must listen carefully to understand and remember what is said.

In your test book, you will read two or more questions about each short talk. The questions will be followed by four answers. You are to choose the best answer to each question and mark it on your answer sheet.

81. How long will the tour be?

(A) 15 minutes.
(B) 30 minutes.
(C) 1 hour.
(D) 3 hours.

82 . What will the 3:00 talk be about?

(A) Photography.
(B) Sculpture.
(C) Modern art.
(D) Art collecting.

83. Who is speaking?

(A) A hotel clerk.
(B) A chef.
(C) A waiter.
(D) A farmer.

84. When is the speaker talking?

(A) Early morning.
(B) Late morning.
(C) Mid-afternoon.
(D) Evening.

85. Where would this announcement most likely be heard?

(A) On a ship.
(B) At a taxi stand.
(C) On a train.
(D) At an airport.

86. What must passengers have?

(A) A seat assignment.
(B) A credit card.
(C) A local map.
(D) A dinner reservation.

87. Who is the talk directed to?

(A) Customer service representatives.
(B) Potential franchise owners.
(C) Shopping-center designers.
(D) Bank officers.

88. What kind of business is Milton's?

(A) A food retailer.
(B) An employment service.
(C) A recreational facility.
(D) A travel agency.

89. What is Mr. Sandoval's position with the firm?

(A) Sales manager.
(B) Head of research and development.
(C) Personnel manager.
(D) Director of franchising.

90. What is Ms. Suzuki's profession?

(A) Photographer.
(B) Magazine editor.
(C) Advertising director.
(D) Newspaper publisher.

91. Where was Ms. Suzuki's most recent assignment?

(A) Australia.
(B) Japan.
(C) Brazil.
(D) The United States.

92. What is the purpose of the event?

(A) To celebrate a new merger.
(B) To honor workers.
(C) To plan next year's strategies.
(D) To announce profits.

GO ON TO THE NEXT PAGE ➡

93. How can you get tickets to the banquet?

(A) Go to the hotel.
(B) Call the president.
(C) Contact the board of directors.
(D) Telephone the personnel office.

94. What is the theme of the series?

(A) Geology.
(B) World history.
(C) Travel.
(D) Filmmaking.

95. How many films will be shown this week?

(A) Two.
(B) Five.
(C) Seven.
(D) Nine.

96. How long is tonight's film?

(A) A half hour.
(B) One hour.
(C) An hour and a half.
(D) Two hours.

97. What will happen after tonight's film?

(A) The theater will be closed for renovations.
(B) A short documentary film will be shown.
(C) A prize will be awarded.
(D) The filmmakers will be interviewed.

98. Who is speaking?

(A) A political candidate.
(B) A weather forecaster.
(C) A radio-show host.
(D) A newspaper reporter.

99. What is Ms. Valmont's job?

(A) Computer programmer.
(B) Government official.
(C) Journalist.
(D) Publisher.

100. What will be heard next?

(A) Last week's election results.
(B) A political commentary.
(C) A candidate's speech.
(D) Local news stories.

This is the end of the Listening Comprehension portion of the test. Turn to Part V in your test book

YOU WILL HAVE ONE HOUR AND FIFTEEN MINUTES TO COMPLETE PART V, VI AND VII OF THIS TEST.

READING

In this section of the test, you will have a chance to show how well you understand written English. There are three parts to this section, with special directions for each part.

PART V

Directions: **Questions 101-140** are incomplete sentences. Four words or phrases, marked (A), (B), (C), (D), are given beneath each sentence. You are to choose the **one** word or phrase that best completes the sentence. Then, on your answer sheet, find the number of the question and mark your answer.

You will read:

Because the equipment is very delicate,
it must be handled with -------.

(A) caring
(B) careful
(C) care
(D) carefully

Sample Answer
Ⓐ Ⓑ ● Ⓓ

The sentence should read "Because the equipment is very delicate, it must be handled with care." Therefore, you should choose answer (C).

Now, begin work on the questions.

---

101. Answering telephone calls is the ------- of an operator.

(A) responsible
(B) responsibly
(C) responsive
(D) responsibility

102. A free watch will be provided with every purchase of $20.00 or more for a ------- period of time.

(A) limit
(B) limits
(C) limited
(D) limiting

103. The president of the corporation has ------- arrived in Copenhagen and will meet with the Minister of Trade on Monday morning.

(A) still
(B) yet
(C) already
(D) soon

104. Because we value your business, we have ------- for card members like you to receive one thousand dollars of complimentary life insurance.

(A) arrange
(B) arranged
(C) arranges
(D) arranging

GO ON TO THE NEXT PAGE

105. Employees are ------- that due to the new government regulations, there is to be no smoking in the factory.

(A) reminded
(B) respected
(C) remembered
(D) reacted

106. Ms. Galera gave a long ------- in honor of the retiring vice-president.

(A) speak
(B) speaker
(C) speaking
(D) speech

107. Any person who is ------- in volunteering his or her time for the campaign should send this office a letter of intent.

(A) interest
(B) interested
(C) interesting
(D) interestingly

108. Mr. Gonzales was very concerned ------- the upcoming board of directors meeting.

(A) to
(B) about
(C) at
(D) upon

109. The customers were told that no ------- could be made on weekend nights because the restaurant was too busy.

(A) delays
(B) cuisines
(C) reservations
(D) violations

110. The sales representative's presentation was difficult to understand ------- he spoke very quickly.

(A) because
(B) although
(C) so that
(D) than

111. It has been predicted that an ------- weak dollar will stimulate tourism in the United States.

(A) increased
(B) increasingly
(C) increases
(D) increase

112. The firm is not liable for damage resulting from circumstances ------- its control.

(A) beyond
(B) above
(C) inside
(D) around

113. Because of ------- weather conditions, California has an advantage in the production of fruits and vegetables.

(A) favorite
(B) favor
(C) favorable
(D) favorably

114. On international shipments, all duties and taxes are paid by the -------.

(A) recipient
(B) receiving
(C) receipt
(D) receptive

115. Although the textbook gives a definitive answer, wise managers will look for ------- own creative solutions.

(A) them
(B) their
(C) theirs
(D) they

116. Initial ------- regarding the merger of the companies took place yesterday at the Plaza Conference Center.

(A) negotiations
(B) dedications
(C) propositions
(D) announcements

117. Please ------- photocopies of all relevant documents to this office ten days prior to your performance review date.

(A) emerge
(B) substantiate
(C) adapt
(D) submit

118. The auditor's results for the five-year period under study were ------- the accountant's.

(A) same
(B) same as
(C) the same
(D) the same as

119. ------- has the marketing environment been more complex and subject to change.

(A) Totally
(B) Negatively
(C) Decidedly
(D) Rarely

120. All full-time staff are eligible to participate in the revised health plan, which becomes effective the first ------- the month.

(A) of
(B) to
(C) from
(D) for

121. Contracts must be read ------- before they are signed.

(A) thoroughness
(B) more thorough
(C) thorough
(D) thoroughly

122. Passengers should allow for ------- travel time to the airport in rush hour traffic.

(A) addition
(B) additive
(C) additionally
(D) additional

123. This fiscal year, the engineering team has worked well together on all phases of project -------.

(A) development
(B) developed
(C) develops
(D) developer

124. Mr. Dupont had no ------- how long it would take to drive downtown.

(A) knowledge
(B) thought
(C) idea
(D) willingness

125. Small-company stocks usually benefit ------- the so-called January effect that causes the price of these stocks to rise between November and January.

(A) unless
(B) from
(C) to
(D) since

126. It has been suggested that employees ------- to work in their current positions until the quarterly review is finished.

(A) continuity
(B) continue
(C) continuing
(D) continuous

127. It is admirable that Ms. Jin wishes to handle all transactions by -------, but it might be better if several people shared the responsibility.

(A) she
(B) herself
(C) her
(D) hers

128. This new highway construction project will help the company -------.

(A) diversify
(B) clarify
(C) intensify
(D) modify

GO ON TO THE NEXT PAGE

129. Ms. Patel has handed in an ------- business plan to the director.

(A) anxious
(B) evident
(C) eager
(D) outstanding

130. Recent changes in heating oil costs have affected ------- production of furniture.

(A) local
(B) locality
(C) locally
(D) location

131. That is the position for ------- Mr. Kaslov has applied, but a final decision has not yet been made.

(A) which
(B) whom
(C) that
(D) what

132 . Any unsatisfactory item must be returned within 30 days and ------- by the original receipt from this store.

(A) altered
(B) adjusted
(C) accepted
(D) accompanied

133. A list of telephone ------- that will be out of service while the new communications system is installed is available from the main office.

(A) extensions
(B) extending
(C) extended
(D) extends

134. Please ------- your flight number at least 24 hours in advance.

(A) confirm
(B) concur
(C) conduct
(D) concord

135. The first year's sales of the new calculator were so ------- that the firm decided to withdraw it from the market.

(A) discouragement
(B) discourage
(C) discouraging
(D) discouraged

136. From an investor's viewpoint, getting ------- advice is the key to making sound investment decisions.

(A) unjudged
(B) unbiased
(C) inanimate
(D) impatient

137. Staff members are reminded that professional ------- is a daily requirement of the company.

(A) attire
(B) ambivalence
(C) assembly
(D) approach

138. Ms. Lee did ------- good work on that project that she was quickly offered a promotion.

(A) too
(B) such
(C) so
(D) much

139. We have approached the proposal with a good deal of ------- since some of the ideas put forward are very unconventional.

(A) cautioned
(B) caution
(C) cautious
(D) cautiously

140. ------- higher ticket prices this year, attendance at area theaters remains above average.

(A) Even though
(B) Nevertheless
(C) In spite of
(D) Consequently

PART VI

Directions: In **Questions 141-160**, each sentence has four words or phrases underlined. The four underlined parts of the sentence are marked (A), (B), (C),(D). You are to identify the **one** underlined word or phrase that should be corrected or rewritten. Then, on your answer sheet, find the number of the question and mark your answer.

Example:

All employee are required to wear their
    A   B

identification badges while at work.
      C   D

The underlined word "employee" is not correct in this sentence. This sentence should read, "All employees are required to wear their identification badges while at work." Therefore, you should choose answer (A).

Now begin work on the questions.

---

141. The Pinebrook Inn has a courtesy bus
                     A

which runs every thirty minutes both
   B   C

to from the downtown area.
  D

142 . We appreciate it your interest in our
         A   B

company and look forward to hearing from
             C   D

you soon.

143. In the event for any changes need
             A

to be made in the document, please
  B   C

call our office immediately.
           D

144. Each banking transaction were handled
      A   B

quickly and efficiently by well-trained
          C   D

tellers.

145. We recommend that you follow the

formatted shown in this sample when
  A   B

preparing announcements to be displayed
    C   D

on the bulletin board.

146. Bennett International has decided to
                  A

expand its borrowing to make up with a
      B   C

decline in investment returns.
      D

147. Ms. Rivera is going to write to manager to
               A   B

complain about the poor service she
       C

received during her stay at the hotel.
            D

148. One proposal suggests relocating the
              A   B

central offices at the suburbs to obtain
         C

needed space.
      D

GO ON TO THE NEXT PAGE ▶

149. Consumers are usually willing to buy <u>more</u>
                                              A
of an item <u>as</u> its price falls <u>because of</u> they
            B   C
want <u>to save</u> money.
      D

150. Substantial penalties <u>will be charging</u>
                            A
whenever <u>a</u> customer withdraws <u>funds</u> from
          B   C
this account <u>prior to</u> the maturity date.
              D

151. We have <u>taken</u> special <u>caring</u> to see that
              A   B
the merchandise <u>has been</u> packed
                  C
<u>according</u> to your instructions.
  D

152. For a list of books <u>available</u> through the
      A   B
library system, <u>consultation</u> the computer
                  C
terminal <u>near</u> the reference desk.
          D

153. Mr. Webber <u>was taken surprise</u> when he
                  A
<u>was told</u> the building he <u>was working</u> on
  B   C
had a severe <u>structural flaw</u>.
              D

154. <u>At</u> our company meeting the marketing
      A
analyst <u>reported that</u> we have too <u>much</u>
          B   C
sales representatives in Europe <u>these</u>
                                  D
days.

155. All passengers <u>must present</u> their boarding
                      A
passes <u>to</u> the <u>designate</u> agent <u>at</u> the
          B   C   D
airport gate.

156. <u>Without</u> we receive a definite commitment
      A
<u>by</u> the end of the month, we will be forced
  B
to reconsider <u>our</u> original proposal.
  C   D

157. The governor's panel of experts
reported <u>that</u> supervisors should <u>continue</u>
          A   B
to review <u>safety standard</u> on <u>a regular</u>
            C   D
basis.

158. For <u>each</u> workshop, you <u>must register</u> and
          A   B
pay <u>prior</u> to the date on which the
      C
conference <u>begin</u>.
            D

159. Francesca Rosati is <u>perfect</u> candidate
                          A
for the position <u>because of her</u> experience
  B   C
in <u>administration</u>.
    D

160. Travel club application forms <u>can find</u>
      A   B
<u>in front of</u> the main desk in the <u>hotel lobby</u>.
  C   D

PART VII

Directions: Questions 161-200 are based on a selection of reading materials, such as notices, letters, forms, newspaper and magazine articles, and advertisements. You are to choose the **one** best answer (A), (B), (C), or (D), to each question. Then, on your answer sheet, find the number of the question and mark your answer. Answer all questions following each reading selection on the basis of what is **stated** or **implied** in that selection.

Reading the following example.

The Museum of Technology is a "hands-on" museum, designed for people to experience science at work. Visitors are encouraged to use, test, and handle the objects on display. Special demonstrations are scheduled for the first and second Wednesdays of each month at 13:30. Open Tuesday-Friday 12:00-16:30, Saturday 10:00-17:30, and Sunday 11:00-16:30.

When during the month can visitors see special demonstrations?

Sample Answer

(A) Every weekend
(B) The first two Wednesdays
(C) One afternoon a week
(D) Every other Wednesday

The reading selection says that the demonstrations are scheduled for the first and second Wednesdays of the month. Therefore, you should choose answer (B).

Now begin work on the questions.

GO ON TO THE NEXT PAGE

Questions 161-162 refer to the following advertisement.

ESTATE AUCTION

An auction for the estate of Martina Jovanovic has been set for Saturday, July 19, at 12:00 noon. (Preview starts at 10:00 a.m.)

Location: The Jovanovic residence at 433 Walnut Drive

Some of the items to be auctioned:
* 1997 Sports Car
* Home Queen Appliances
* Oriental Carpets
* Stamp Collection
* Hand-Carved Wooden Boxes, Dolls, and Utensils
* China Teacups from Colonial America
* Antique Furnishing

Parking three blocks south, in the Municipal Building lot, at 119 Walnut Drive

Questions? Please call Estate Planners Associates, 546-7000. The Jovanovics request that you do not phone their home.

161. What event is being advertised?

(A) A party for the Jovanovic family
(B) A fund-raising event at the Municipal Building
(C) A sale of the possessions of Martina Jovanovic
(D) A private viewing of museum pieces

162. Where will the event be held?

(A) At the Municipal Building
(B) At 433 Walnut Drive
(C) At the Estate Planners Associates' office
(D) In the city parking lot

Department of Public Health
Wellington, New Zealand

FOOD ESTABLISHMENTS CLOSED FOR HEALTH-CODE VIOLATIONS

Name of Business	Date Closed	Reasons Cited for Closing
Mandy's 910 12th St.	1/16	Inadequate ventilation Improper food storage
Valley Restaurant 815 23rd Ave.	1/16	Plumbing fixtures in poor repair No certified food supervisor
Market Grill 770 Golden Rd.	1/16	No certified food supervisor Improper food temperature
Peppo Mart (food sales section only) 104 Main St.	1/17	Operating without a health department permit Inadequate refrigeration
Lawville's 872 N. Jackson	1/18	No hot water Unclean food contact surfaces

163. Why are these establishments closed?

(A) They are in violation of the building code.
(B) They have been cited for unsanitary conditions.
(C) They are undergoing renovations.
(D) They are open for only part of the year.

164. Which business will remain partially open?

(A) Peppo Mart
(B) Valley Restaurant
(C) Mandy's
(D) Lawville's

165. What should the Valley Restaurant do?

(A) Check its sinks and pipes.
(B) Offer take-out service.
(C) Change its menu.
(D) Renew its permit.

GO ON TO THE NEXT PAGE

MEMORANDUM

TO: All Office Employees

FROM: Ruth Crawford   *RC*

RE: New Phone System

DATE: May 22

As you know, we badly need to modernize our communications system. I have enclosed with this memo some descriptions of phone systems sent by sales representatives. Please read the materials carefully and send your recommendations to me.

The system should be able to handle at least one hold line and eight extension lines. My opinion is that a built-in answering machine is necessary. Conference calls and speed-dialing features are now standard in many systems and could prove useful.

At the present time our office uses twelve phones, and although we do not have a fixed limit for the unit price, it should be mid-range. Recommendations should be in my office by the end of the week so an order can be placed through Supplies and Equipment by the first of the month.

Enclosures

166. What does the memo discuss?

(A) Holding a conference on telecommunications
(B) Repairing old telephone units
(C) Communicating by telephone less frequently
(D) Choosing a new telephone system

167. What should people do after reading the memo?

(A) Organize a conference to discuss the matter.
(B) Order new phones right away.
(C) Notify Ruth Crawford of a preference.
(D) Contact Supplies and Equipment as soon as possible.

168. What is a criterion for selecting equipment?

(A) Use of standard colors
(B) One hold line and at least eight extension lines
(C) Separate answering machine
(D) Low price per unit

Questions 169-171 refer to the following news article.

This week Merrymaker Cruise Lines has filed a $700 million lawsuit against Wambaugh Marine Industries, a shipyard that filed for bankruptcy last November before completing a three-ship contract for Merrymaker. The suit contends that Merrymaker suffered $400 million in additional construction costs and lost passenger bookings and also seeks $300 million in punitive damages. In 1987, Merrymaker signed the $600 million contract with Wambaugh for three 2,600-passenger ships, but the bankruptcy halted all work at the shipyard. The suit also contends that the yard misrepresented its financial condition in order to get the Merrymaker contract.

169. What had Wambaugh agreed to do?

(A) Provide 2,600 passengers
(B) Build three ships
(C) File suit against Merrymaker
(D) Revise the Merrymaker contract

170. What was the value of the Wambaugh-Merrymaker agreement?

(A) $300 million
(B) $400 million
(C) $600 million
(D) $700 million

171. Why did work stop at the shipyard?

(A) Costs of materials were too high.
(B) Passenger bookings had decreased.
(C) The shipyard filed for bankruptcy.
(D) The ships were completed.

GO ON TO THE NEXT PAGE

Questions 172-173 refer to the following notice.

If you need to cancel or change your reservation for this tour, we will refund your deposit, in full, up to thirty days prior to departure. If you need to cancel your reservation after thirty days, no refund is possible, but you may sell your place or send a friend in your place. All group reservations are subject to a 90-day cancellation policy.

172 . What percentage of the deposit will be refunded with a 30-day cancellation notice?

(A) 0
(B) 30
(C) 90
(D) 100

173. What is suggested as an alternative to cancellation?

(A) Joining a group tour
(B) Giving your place to a friend
(C) Traveling 30 days earlier
(D) Sending in a refund request

Questions 174-176 refer to the following notice.

XYZ
MACHINERY

We would like to welcome you to the XYZ Machinery Company's International Symposium. As you are aware, XYZ employees from over twenty countries are in attendance at this year's conference. If you would like to meet your counterparts from other countries on a more personal level, be sure to sign up at the registration desk for special dinners, lunches, or breakfast meetings that are described below. Whether you are in Personnel, Sales, Management, or Research, you'll be able to discuss topics of common interest with colleagues of diverse backgrounds. Find out what your Indian, Japanese, or Moroccan counterpart can suggest for your department's current problems. Help your French, Colombian, or Russian colleague with a problem that you've tackled before. Take advantage of this rare opportunity to collaborate with your international partners. All meetings will be held in Lounge B.

TIME	TOPIC
Monday Breakfast 7:00-9:00	Legal Implications of Establishing Branch Offices in Asia
Tuesday Lunch 12:00-14:00	Technologies in the Former Soviet Republics
Wednesday Dinner 19:00-21:00	International Personnel Issues
Thursday Breakfast 7:00-9:00	New Markets in Western Europe

174. Who is the conference aimed at?

(A) International politicians
(B) People learning foreign languages
(C) International chefs
(D) Employees of a machinery company

175. What is the purpose of the notice?

(A) To give a list of participants
(B) To indicate room changes
(C) To announce special events
(D) To cancel several sessions

176. Which session would most likely deal with human resources?

(A) Monday breakfast
(B) Tuesday lunch
(C) Wednesday dinner
(D) Thursday breakfast

GO ON TO THE NEXT PAGE

Questions 177-180 refer to the following instructions.

 Softwind's technical support staff provides free telephone assistance to registered Softwind users. In order to receive this free assistance, you must first register your product with Softwind. To do this, fill in the enclosed registration card, including the name of the retail outlet where you purchased this product. Softwind will then send you a personal identification number (PIN), which must be supplied to support staff whenever you request assistance. Registering your product will also enable us to send you timely information on updates and future releases. Before calling technical support, please try to find the answer to your question in the handbook that accompanies this product. In particular, we recommend that you check the section on frequently asked questions that begins on page 286.

177. Who were these instructions written for?

(A) Technical support staff
(B) Softwind engineers
(C) Retail sales personnel
(D) Softwind customers

178. What information is necessary in order to register this product?

(A) The name of the store that sold the product
(B) The user's personal identification number
(C) The dates of future releases
(D) The user's forwarding address

179. How can you receive a PIN?

(A) By requesting one from support staff
(B) By telephoning technical support
(C) By mailing in the registration card
(D) By signing up for one at a retail outlet

180. What should you do first if you have a problem with the product?

(A) Read the manual.
(B) Change your PIN.
(C) Telephone technical support.
(D) Request updated instructions.

Smooth Skin
3949 Marina Way West
Alta Vista, CA 92458

Mr. George Mackie   May 11
IFS Freight Forwarding
8471 S. Eastern Avenue
Chicago, IL 60647

Dear Mr. Mackie:

We have just received a complaint about a mishandled delivery from one of our trusted customers, Mr. C. Benson of Butterfly Beauty Care in Dubuque, Iowa.

Apparently, a member of your staff delivered two cartons of goods to the Butterfly Beauty Care facility despite the fact that the items they contained had been damaged in transit. Enclosed, you will find a copy of the transmittal form signed by Mr. Benson, on which he clearly indicated that he noticed the damage while your driver was still on the premises.

Mr. Benson reports that the driver refused to take the goods back, contrary to your company's stated policy. Furthermore, the driver indicated that our packing was responsible for the breakage. We can assure you that these boxes were packed with the usual care, and left our warehouse in perfect condition. We can only conclude that they were damaged during shipment.

We expect you to pick up the boxes immediately at absolutely no cost to Mr. Benson or Smooth Skin. We are far from satisfied with the actions of your employee, and in view of the fact that this is the third complaint we have received in six months, any further incidents of this nature will force us to reconsider the renewal of our contract with your firm.

Sincerely,

Peggy S. Rolf

Peggy S. Rolf
Shipping Manager

Enclosure

181. What was sent to Mr. Mackie with this letter?

(A) A check
(B) Two cartons
(C) A new contract
(D) A shipping document

182. According to the letter, what did the delivery driver say?

(A) Smooth Skin was responsible for the damage.
(B) Butterfly Beauty should file a complaint.
(C) The shipment was damaged in transit.
(D) IFS should refund the customer's money.

183. Ms. Rolf refers to the IFS policy about

(A) shipping charges
(B) returns
(C) weight limits
(D) travel expenses

184. How does Ms. Rolf want the firm to respond to her letter?

(A) By contacting her directly
(B) By renewing the contract
(C) By retrieving the goods
(D) By paying for the damage

GO ON TO THE NEXT PAGE

Questions 185-186 refer to the following notice.

FUEL ADJUSTMENT NOTICE

With the approval of the Price Control Commission, Velcorp Power announces that the fuel adjustment will be decreased to 1.8747 cents per kilowatt hour sold, effective with meter readings taken on or after November 1, and until further notice.

VELCORP

185. Who issued this notice?

(A) A law office
(B) A gasoline station
(C) The Price Control Commission
(D) An electric company

186. What will happen on November 1?

(A) The commission will have its monthly meeting.
(B) Fuel will be sold by cubic meter.
(C) Prices will change.
(D) Meters will be read more often.

Questions 187-188 refer to the following news article.

LONDON--One of the Mitchell Motor Company's main British plants remained closed today by an ~~unofficial strike,~~ even though the company's assembly-line workers have accepted a pay increase. About 550 maintenance technicians are on strike at the Hightower factory in northern England. In response, Mitchell has laid off 8,000 assembly-line workers there.

Mitchell's 32,000 assembly-line workers voted to accept a 6.2 percent pay increase this week. But the technicians argued that they were losing ground against unskilled workers and threatened to spread their strike to other plants. The strike has forced Framm to halt production of vans at its facility in southern England.

187. What have the assembly-line workers agreed to do?

(A) Go on strike
(B) Support the technicians' demands
(C) Accept a pay increase
(D) Move to another plant

188. What has been the result of the technicians' strike?

(A) Assembly-line workers have been laid off.
(B) 8,000 technicians have been fired.
(C) Van models have been redesigned.
(D) Their salaries have increased.

GO ON TO THE NEXT PAGE

HOW TO INVEST MORE
AT
SMITH MUTUAL FUNDS

By Mail
To add to your account, send a check or money order payable to Smith Funds along with the additional investment form that is attached to this statement. Please see minimum investment requirements for each fund in the appropriate prospectus.

By Electronic Transfer
After an account has been established, you may purchase additional shares by electronic transfer. Please call Smith Funds for instructions.

By Exchange
You can open a new account by exchanging from one Smith Funds account to an identically registered account. Please verify the investment guidelines for each Fund in the appropriate prospectus. The Fund may modify, suspend, or terminate the exchange privilege at its discretion.

189. What should clients do to invest by electronic transfer?

(A) Mail a written request.
(B) Telephone for information.
(C) Send in another form.
(D) Terminate their exchange privilege.

190. What can the Fund change at any time?

(A) The investment guidelines
(B) The account registration number
(C) The minimum investment
(D) The exchange privilege

4-13-14 Shinohara Kitamachi
Chuo-ku, Osaka 541, Japan
March 22

Mr. S. Kayasit, President
Golden Crown Resorts
31/66 Raya Road
Patong Beach
Phuket 83150
Thailand

Dear Mr. Kayasit:

Thank you very much for offering me the position of Properties Agent for your office in Phuket. I appreciate your discussing the details of the position with me and giving me time to consider your offer. I also enjoyed meeting Mr. Van Vliet, the current Properties Agent in Phuket.

You have a fine organization and there are many aspects of the position which are very appealing to me. However, I believe it is in our mutual best interest that I decline your kind offer. I have decided to accept a position as the Sales Director for a smaller company located in Kyoto. This has been a difficult decision for me, but I believe it is the appropriate one for my career and family at this time.

I want to thank you for the consideration and courtesy given to me. It was a pleasure meeting you and Mr. Puapondh, the Head of Operations.

Sincerely,

Ryusuke Hayashida

Ryusuke Hayashida

191. Why was this letter written?

(A) To accept a new position
(B) To turn down a job offer
(C) To discuss employment opportunities
(D) To request further information from the personnel office

192 . Who offered the opportunity for employment?

(A) The Company President
(B) The Head of Operations
(C) The Properties Agent
(D) The Sales Director

193. Who does NOT work for Golden Crown Resorts?

(A) Mr. Van Vliet
(B) Mr. Kayasit
(C) Mr. Hayashida
(D) Mr. Puapondh

GO ON TO THE NEXT PAGE

All computer disks must be scanned immediately upon entry to this building. Standard Chemical Company policy prohibits the possession of any personal disks on site. Disks authorized for business must be declared, accompanied by a pass, and scanned for viruses. When entering the facility, failure to declare disks will result in confiscation. The term "disk" refers to any computer-data medium.

194. Where would this notice most likely be seen?

(A) In a health clinic
(B) At a computer terminal
(C) At the entrance of Standard Chemical
(D) In the company cafeteria

195. What will happen if a disk is not declared?

(A) It will be erased.
(B) It will be scratched.
(C) It will be duplicated.
(D) It will be taken away.

Questions 196-197 refer to the following newspaper article.

New Terminal For Digili

DIGILI–Chaldea's Ministry of Planning and Investment has proposed building a new terminal at Digili International Airport. The *Economic Times* said the project would cost between US $180 million and $195 million, more than half of which would come from overseas. The plan calls for building a terminal that can process at least eight million passengers a year.

The ministry's proposal also calls for enlargement of the existing terminal to handle five million passengers a year. Late last year, the Aviation Science Institute unveiled an ambitious plan to renovate the country's four existing airports and build as many as six new airports.

196. Where is most of the funding for the project coming from?

(A) The *Economic Times*
(B) The Chaldean Ministry of Planning and Investment
(C) International investors
(D) The Digili Airport Authority

197. What is NOT included in the proposal?

(A) Investing at least US $180 million
(B) Increasing the size of an existing building
(C) Constructing more than five new airports
(D) Demolishing the old terminal at Digili

GO ON TO THE NEXT PAGE

Suarez Drilling Corporation

1217 Isabella Avenue, Buenos Aires, Argentina

Ms. Ursula Kahanian
Dienst and Klein Auditors
1001 Wellington Avenue
Toronto, Ontario
Canada

Dear Ms. Kahanian:

We will be pleased to welcome you to our headquarters for the year-end auditing procedures.

Paula Jenkins tells us that you will arrive in Buenos Aires on flight BA 209 on Monday, January 30, at 10:10 a.m. I have instructed my assistant, Carmen Sierra, to drive you directly to our main office and make sure that all the arrangements for your stay are satisfactory. We will put a computer terminal at your disposal in a private office. Should you have any special requirements, I would appreciate it if you would phone or fax us to let us know before your arrival.

We have booked a room at the Santa Catalina Hotel in the center of town, which serves breakfast and dinner. Alternatively, we can recommend many fine restaurants in the center of town. We have arranged for you to have prepaid lunches at our staff cafeteria. Ms. Sierra will take care of the transport arrangements for your return to the airport on Friday the third.

I look forward to meeting you next month.

Sincerely,

Rafael Ortiz
Financial Director

198. Why is Ms. Kahanian going to Buenos Aires?

(A) To visit a drilling site
(B) To upgrade a computer system
(C) To conduct an audit
(D) To review various restaurants

199. Why might it be necessary for Ms. Kahanian to contact Mr. Ortiz prior to her arrival?

(A) To arrange to use a computer
(B) To tell him her flight number
(C) To reserve hotel accommodations
(D) To find out if she will have access to a copy machine

200. Where will Ms. Kahanian probably have her midday meals?

(A) At the Suarez Drilling headquarters
(B) At the Santa Catalina Hotel
(C) In one of the town's restaurants
(D) At a local coffee shop

Stop! This is the end of the test. If you finish before one hour and fifteen minutes have passed, you may go back to Parts V, VI, and VII and check your work.

APPENDIX

付録 A

Contents

- ■ TOEIC ミニ・テストの正解
- ■ TOEIC ミニ・テストの解説
- ■ TOEIC ミニ・テストの音声スクリプト

TOEIC ミニ・テストの正解

正解				

1. (D)	29. (A)	81. (C)	107. (D)	161. (A)
2. (C)	30. (B)	82. (C)	108. (C)	162. (B)
3. (C)		83. (A)	109. (A)	163. (B)
4. (B)	51. (C)	84. (C)	110. (D)	164. (D)
5. (C)	52. (C)	85. (C)	111. (C)	165. (D)
6. (B)	53. (D)	86. (C)	112. (C)	166. (C)
7. (A)	54. (C)	87. (B)	113. (B)	167. (A)
	55. (D)	88. (B)	114. (D)	168. (C)
21. (B)	56. (A)			169. (A)
22. (C)	57. (D)	101. (D)	141. (C)	170. (B)
23. (C)	58. (B)	102. (B)	142. (A)	171. (D)
24. (A)	59. (D)	103. (B)	143. (D)	172. (C)
25. (A)	60. (A)	104. (A)	144. (D)	173. (B)
26. (B)		105. (D)	145. (C)	174. (A)
27. (A)		106. (B)	146. (A)	
28. (C)			147. (B)	

TOEIC ミニ・テストの解説

Part I：写真描写問題

1. **(D)** 女性がpay phone（公衆電話）のような硬貨やクレジットカードで支払える電話の受話器に向かって話している。(A)hallは大きい開放的な部屋のこと。写真では女性は小さな囲われた場所に座っている。(B)女性はマイクではなく、電話を使っている。(C)電話の下にキーボードがあるが、女性はタイプしてはいない。

2. **(C)** 女性がディスプレイ・ボードの近くに立ってグラフを指差し、部屋にいる人たちに説明している。(A)写真の中で空いている椅子はひとつだけ。(B)女性は説明あるいはpresentation（プレゼンテーション）をしているのであり、プレゼントを渡しているのではない。(D)人々はテーブルではなく、ディスプレイ・ボードを見ている。

3. **(C)** 男性が新聞のような紙を持っている。(A)新聞紙は写っているが、壁紙ではない。(B)男性は書いているのではなく、読んでいる。(D)前面に椅子があるが、男性は立っている。

4. **(B)** 3名の人たちがバスに乗りこむところである。(A)バスの運転手は運転席に座っており、バスから降りようとはしていない。(C)写真に写っている乗客はバスに乗り込もうとしている3人だけであり、窓には乗客は見えない。(D)人々がバスに乗り込むところで、バスは止まっている。

5. **(C)** 両側に木が生えている狭いpath（歩道）が写っている。(A)家は写っていない。(B)hikersは人を指すが、人は写っていない。(D)木には葉がついているが、地面に舞い落ちている落ち葉はない。

6. **(B)** 男性が鏡を見ている。reflectionは鏡に写る姿のことである。(A)2本のタオルはきちんとタオルかけにかかっている。床に落ちてはいない。(C)鏡に2つのものが写っているが、鏡は壊れたり、ひびが入ったりはしていない。(D)男性は衣服を着ており、衣服を脱ごうとはしていない。彼がこれから入浴するとは考えられない。

7. **(A)** crowd（大勢の人々）がミュージシャンのまわりに集まっている。**(B)** ミュージシャンは一種類ではなく様々な種類の楽器を演奏している。**(C)** 車は1台も写っていない。**(D)** バイオリンを弾いている男性はコートを着ているが、帽子はかぶっていない。

Part II：応答問題

21. **(B)** 質問では場所を尋ねているので(B)が適切な返答である。(A)男性がパリにいる理由を答えてはいるが、滞在している場所を答えていない。(C)も場所を答えていない。

22. **(C)** 建物がいつ完成するかという時期を答えているのは(C)のみ。(A)建物の材料が何であるかを尋ねてはいない。(B)建物の建設費用を尋ねてはいない。

23. **(C)** 方針の変更理由について尋ねている。変更したのは方針に対し多くの不満が寄せられたからである。(A)場所を答えており、理由は述べていない。(B)a board of directors（取締役会）は人々のグループである。この返答は「彼」個人について述べている。

24. **(A)** Would you mind...は誰かに依頼するときに使われる表現である。"Not at all." は話し手がかばんを開けることを意に介さず、同意したことを意味する。(B)と(C)は場所を答えており、適切な返答ではない。

25. **(A)** priced fairlyは価格が高すぎないということを示している。これがその製品が良く売れるはずだという理由である。(B)と(C)では、質問が新製品を話題にしているにもかかわらず、製品を表わすitではなく、Iを主語として女性が自分のことを答えている。

26. **(B)** Ms.Garcíaの職業についての質問である。(B)のみが職業について言及している。(A)質問文にあるworkではなくwalkが返答に使われている。(C)質問では、kindは「種類（この場合は職種）」という意味の名詞であるのに対し、返答では「親切な」という意味の形容詞としてkindが使われている。

27. **(A)** 質問では女性がファイルを机の上に置くべきか、それともファイリング・キャビネットの中にしまうべきかを尋ねたのに対して、"I'll take it."（自分が受け取る）という返事をしたのである。(B)どこにファイルをしまえばよいかを尋ねているのであり、今どこにあるかを尋ねているのではない。(C) in the afternoonは時間を表わすが、質問は時間について尋ねていない。

28. (C) 女性が男性に対し、会社のオフィスが建物の何階分を占有しているかを知っているかどうかを尋ねている。男性は正確には何階分持っているかを知らないということを示している。(A)女性がいる場所について尋ねてはいない。(B)特定の部屋が使用中かどうかという質問ではない。

29. (A) 質問ではMrs. Martelliが誰をその仕事の担当に選んだかを尋ねたのに対し、実習生が選ばれたと答えている。(B)Mrs. Martelliについて述べているが、彼女が誰を選んだかは述べていない。(C) Mrs. Martelliが選んだ人ではなく、希望する職位を答えている。

30. (B) レンタカーの代理店がどこにあるかという質問に対して、男性がレンタカーを借りられそうな場所を答えている。(A)と(C)はレンタカーの代理店の場所について答えていない。

Part III：会話問題

51. (C) 女性はMr. Olmosが14日間すなわち2週間いなくなると言っている。(A) Mr. Olmosは4日間不在にするのではない。(B) Mr. Olmosは1週間（7日間）不在にするのではない。(D)40日間は1ヵ月以上になるが、40日間ではなく、14日間不在にするのである。

52. (C) overseasはこの文章では「海外への」という意味である。女性は外国に電話をかけたいのである。(A)男性はdialing direct（ダイレクトコール）について述べており、女性にオフィスまでのdirections（行き方）を教えているのではない。(B)女性は特別な電話を使う必要がないので喜んでいる。(D)オフィスの電話の変更については何も述べられていない。

53. (D) 男性は旅行費用について尋ねており、価格を低く抑えたいと思っている。女性が一番安いのはバスを使うことだと言ったので、男性はそれに従い土曜日のバスの予約をしている。女性は(A)電車、(B)車、(C)飛行機の旅行についても述べているが、男性はバスで行くことを決めている。

54. (C) 2人の男性はballgame（野球の試合）、チーム、シーズンといったスポーツに関する言葉を出している。スポーツイベントについて話しているのである。(A)休暇、(B)会議、(D)パーティーについては言及していない。

55. (D) 女性はMr. Mizunoが彼女の代わりにメモをファックスしたと言っている。(A)話し手の一人であるMs. Tanakaは忙しすぎるのでファックスを送れなかったと言っている。(B)男性はsales meeting（営業会議）について話しているが、sales representative（販売代理人）については言及していない。(C)メモは経理担当者宛にファックスされたのである。

56. (A) 顧客は2日後に荷物が届く速達を利用することを決めている。(B)普通便であれば、4〜6営業日かかる。(C)2人は8日とは言っていない。(D)速達の追加料金を10ドルと言っているが、10日間とは言っていない。

57. **(D)** 女性は出発前に食事をしたいので飛行機の出発時間について尋ねている。食事をする時間があるとわかって安心している。(A)女性は飛行機がまだ離陸していないことは知っている。彼女が知りたいのは出発までどのくらい時間があるかということである。(B)男性はチケットの販売店について述べているが、チケットに関する情報については述べていない。(C)搭乗まで1時間ある。飛行機が予定より早く出発するのではない。

58. **(B)** 2人の会話に show, lead, plays, set design という言葉が出ており、これらは劇場の上演に関する言葉である。(A)講堂、(C)スタジアム、(D) 待合室はどれも座席のたくさんある場所であるが、演劇を見るための場所としてはふさわしくない。

59. **(D)** 男性は新聞に広告が載っていた仕事へ応募すると言っている。彼は薬剤師の職を探している。(A)男性は今日の新聞のコピーをとるか、新聞を買うと言っている。コピー機が欲しいわけではない。(B)男性自身が薬剤師である。薬剤師を探しているのではない。(C)女性は benefit package（付加給付）について言及しているが、男性は package（包み）を探しているのではない。

60. **(A)** 女性は医者の予約があると言っている。つまり、彼女は病院に行く予定なのである。(B)女性ではなく男性がタクシーに乗るのである。(C)女性はダウンタウンには行かないと言っている。(D)女性ではなく男性が駅に行くのである。

Part IV：説明文問題

81. **(C)** 交通情報はラジオで放送されることがよくある。話し手はラジオのアナウンサーだと考えられる。(A)警察官、(B)天気予報士、(D)バスの運転手が交通情報をラジオで発表することはない。

82. **(C)** レポートでは道路舗装と橋の架け替えについて述べている。この2つは道路工事の部類に入る。(A)交通の遅れについて述べているが、交通事故については述べられていない。また、(B)霧、(C)洪水についても述べていない。

83. **(A)** 宣伝はアパートについて modern（現代的）だと言っている。(B)アパートの寝室は1つだと述べられている。(C)アパートは街の近くではあるが、街の中心部ではない。(D)アパートは spacious（広い、大きい）と表現されている。

84. **(C)** 賃貸料にはフィットネスクラブの会員権も含まれている。(A)アパートはカントリークラブにあると述べられているが、その会員料については述べられていない。(B)ガーデニングができるといっているが、その費用が賃貸料に含まれているとは言っていない。(D)賃貸希望者向けビデオは無料である。

85. (C) 話し手はまず会社の年度表彰式に来た聴衆を歓迎し、次に従業員に対し感謝の意を示し、賞を授与する。(A)Jill Smithは会社の南西支部に勤務しているが、写真については述べられていない。(B)話し手はテレビの視聴者に向かって話してはいない。(D)新たな販売促進活動については述べられていない。

86. (C) Joan BerryはJill Smithを招き、聴衆に向かって一言述べさせる。すなわち、Ms. Smithが次に話すのである。(A)Joan Berryは社長に代わって聴衆を歓迎している。つまり、社長はパーティには出席していないということになる。(B)Joan Berryは今話している人である。(D)社長室の人が話すということは述べられていない。

87. (B) 工事は当初計画よりも早く開始される必要がある。これは、従来の規約に代わる新たな建築規約が来年初めに施行されることになっており、会社は従来の建築規約に従ってビルを建てたいからである。(A)政府は新たな建築規約を施行することになっており、その遅延は要求していない。(C)設計者の仕事が減ったとすれば、計画変更の結果であり、原因ではない。(D)顧客が新たな建築場所を要求したとは言っていない。

88. (B) ラフ図面、敷地見取り図と完成見取り図はすべて設計計画に含まれる。計画は2週間後には準備できていなければならない。(A)話し手は今日締切のものがあるとは言っていない。(C)来年3月は当初の工事開始予定月である。(D)今年の11月は新たな工事開始月である。

Part V：文法・語彙問題

101. (D) 誰宛てに封筒が送られたかを示すためには、toの後に代名詞の目的格themが必要である。(A)theyは主格代名詞であり、前置詞の目的語にはなれない。(B)theirは名詞の前に置かれ名詞を修飾する代名詞の所有格である。(C)theirsは所有代名詞であり、the publishersを指すことにはならない。

102. (B) 原形の動詞defineの前に助動詞が必要である。should defineで、取締役会が決定する義務があるという意味になる。(A)と(D)の助動詞hadまたはhaveの後には動詞の過去分詞形が置かれる。(C)used toは助動詞であるが、usedだけでは不適切である。

103. (B) both reached and signedという句を完成させるためには接続詞bothが必要である。both ...and ...という句は二つの行動（合意することと署名すること）が行なわれなければならないという事実を強調している。(A)yetは接続詞として使われることもあるが、この場合は位置がふさわしくないし、文意も通らない。(C)eitherという接続詞はしばしばorとともに使われ、通常は後にand が来ることはない。(D)as well asはin addition to（加えて）という意味。文中のandと置き換えることはできるが、空欄に入れることはできない。

104. (A) 前置詞forの後には出来事の継続時間や期間を表わす語句が続く。(B)onは曜日や日付の前に置かれる。(C)from ... to...はある出来事の始まりから終わりまでの継続時間を示す。この文では、具体的な時点については述べられていない。(D)前置詞sinceの後には時間を表わす語句が続き、過去のある時点からの継続を表わす。ここでも具体的な時点は述べられていない。

105. (D) (A)のsternlyはwith severityまたはwith harshness（厳しく、過酷に）という意味。(C)のstringentlyはwith strictness（厳しく）という意味である。(A)，(C)ともに否定的な意味を持ち、この文には不適切である。(B)strikinglyはnoticeably（目立って）という意味で、この文脈には不適切。したがって、強く勧められているという意味になる(D)のstronglyがもっともふさわしい。

106. **(B)** 文意から考えて「照合する」という意味を持つ動詞が必要である。アシスタントは到着するレポーターの名前を照合確認しなければならない。(A)remark on...で notice and comment on...（...に気がつき、コメントする）という意味である。これは会合におけるアシスタントのする仕事ではない。(C)notify は inform または tell（知らせる、伝える）という意味。notify の目的語は物ではなく、人。例：They notified the reporters of the schedule change. (D)ensure は guarantee（保証する）という意味である。

107. **(D)** 文意から考えて「機会」を意味する名詞が必要である。have an opportunity to do something（何かする機会を持つ）という表現はよく使われる。(A)popularity, (B)regularity, (C)celebrity は名詞だが、excellent という形容詞に修飾される名詞ではない。

108. **(C)** 文意から考えて「目に見える」あるいは「はっきりとわかる」という意味の形容詞が必要である。(A)は形容詞ではなく動詞である。(B)は動名詞である。(D)は形容詞ではなく副詞である。

109. **(A)** 文意から考えて「給与」を表わす名詞が必要である。compensation（給与）の増加は勤労、すなわち productivity（生産性）に対する報酬である。(B)commodity（商品）は売買されるものであり、生産性に対する報酬ではない。(C)compilation（寄せ集め）はものの集合である。(D)complacency は「満足」または「自己満足」という意味で、労働者に報酬として与えられるものではない。

110. **(D)** 文意から考えて「固定の」あるいは「変わらない」という意味を表わす形容詞が必要である。remain stable は一定期間変わらないでいるという意味である。(A)authoritative は「正式の」という意味の形容詞である。(B)summarized は「短くまとめられた」という意味の分詞である。(C)examined は状態を表わさない。

111. **(C)** Mr. Kobayashi がどのように話したかを説明する副詞が必要である。(A)と(B)は形容詞である。(D)の excitement は名詞である。

112. **(C)** parameters は「限界、制限」という意味である。仕事が与えられた時間と予算内で行われていることを示す前置詞 within が必要である。(A)among は「～の中で、間で」という意味で、通常、3つ以上のものに使われる。(B)about は「あたりに、あちこちに」という意味で、おおまかに言えば within と反対の意味である。(D)onto は動いていく方向、または何かと接触することを示す。

113. **(B)** 2つの名詞 success と process の関係を表わす前置詞が必要。この場合は所有を表わす前置詞が入る。この文は製造工程の成功について述べているのである。(A), (C), (D)は所有を示すためには使うことのできない前置詞である。

114. (D) reading と waiting が同時に行われていることを表わす接続詞が必要。(A)during は時間を表わす前置詞で、ふつう名詞を伴う。(B)接続詞 after は、ある物事の後の行為を表わす場合に用いられ、同時に起こった物事を表わすことはない。(C)with は 2 つの行為を結びつける接続詞ではない。

Part VI：誤文訂正問題

141. (C) 動詞句 plan on の後には動名詞が続かなければならない。この文では動詞の introduce が続いているため、on ではなく to 不定詞を使うべきである。

142. (A) thousands of という句は「無数の、多数の」というニュアンスで、正確な数値がわからない時に使われる。ここでは使われた金額が明らかなので、具体的な金額を示す形容詞 ten thousand が正しい形である。英語では形容詞は複数形の名詞を修飾しても複数形に変化することはない。

143. (D) この文では、work は形容詞として使われており、located のような分詞ではなく、名詞を修飾すべきである。the normal work location と名詞句にすればよい。

144. (D) on は特定の曜日や日付を含む時間表現に使われる。the end of the year は特定の時点を示していないので、前置詞 on ではなく at が置かれるべきである。

145. (C) 関係代名詞 that の主格にあたる benefits は複数形の名詞なので、これに対応する動詞は provides ではなく、provide である。

146. (A) last week のように過去の特定の時点が示される場合には過去形が使われる。この文は、Last week President announced... となるべきである。

147. (B) 最上級の形にする必要があるので、定冠詞 the を加え、one of the most competitive とするのが正しい。

Part VII：読解問題

161. (A) この通知は、会議が今後 10 年間の目標あるいは計画についての話し合いで始まることを伝えている。a decade は 10 年間のことである。(B)ビデオ会議には 20 の事業所が参加するが、20 年間の目標については述べられていない。(C)現在の課題は二つ目の議題であり、最初の議題ではない。(D)従業員の質疑応答は会議の最後に行われる。

162. (B) 南米とアジアの従業員は、outside of regular business hours（通常の就業時間の前後）に会議に参加しなければならない。彼らは時間外労働に対しては additional pay（追加手当）を受け取る。(A)会議で発言する従業員もいるが、発言に対する追加手当については述べられていない。(C)すべての事業所は衛星で結ばれているので、従業員が移動する必要はない。(D)この通知は将来の目標について言及しているが、すでに達成された目標については述べていない。

163. **(B)** この研究では、企業に対して、電子データをスクランブル（波長を変える）させる方法であるencryption（暗号化）を実施することを勧めている。(A) curbは「抑制する」という意味である。研究では企業に対し通信と情報の共有を制限することは勧めていない。(C)委員会は企業ではなく、政府が輸出規制を緩和することを提案している。(D)政府の研究への投資については何も述べられていない。

164. **(D)** 暗号化技術は銀行取引をより安全に行えるようにし、電気通信のプライバシーを保護する。(A)政府の研究諮問委員会はすでに企業に対して科学技術のアドバイスを提供している。(B)より速いデータ処理能力については書かれていない。(C)暗号化の目的は企業情報の秘密を守り、安全な状態に置くことであり、共有することではない。

165. **(D)** この広告は大学の医療センターが出したもので、major health-care facilityと説明されていることから、広告主は病院であると推定できる。(A)秘書の養成学校については述べていない。(B)ドバイにある医療センターの情報担当責任者は募集されているのであり、広告主ではない。(C)募集している職にはコンピュータ技術も必要とされるが、広告主は病院であり、コンピュータ会社ではない。

166. **(C)** 応募者は最低4年の管理職としての経験を持っていなければならない。(A)プログラミングの経験は必要ないと述べてある。(B)募集広告によれば、7年間の関連業務経験があれば十分である。(D)応募者は修士以上の学位が必須だが、医師の資格とは特定していない。

167. **(A)** 履歴書には応募者の学歴と職歴が記載される。応募者に(B)応募料金、(C)照会状、(D)既往症歴の提出は求めていない。

168. **(C)** 応募者には履歴書を記載されている大学医療センターの住所宛に送付するよう求めている。(A)医療センターに直接応募書類を持ち込むことは求めていない。(B)と(D)については広告の最後で「電話、ファックス及び電子メールでの応募は受け付けない」と書かれている。

169. **(A)** 手紙の冒頭部分から、Mach Motors Companyはこの手紙をSpectraを購入した顧客に送っていると判断できる。(B)と(C)は顧客に生じた問題を解決するMach Motors Companyの従業員を指しているので、手紙の宛先ではない。(D)この手紙では顧客に対し、SpectraをMachの代理店あるいは販売店に持っていくことを依頼しているのであって、店舗に対して宛てられたものではない。

170. **(B)** この手紙はSpectraの所有者に車の部品の一つを改善すること（improvement）を伝えるものである。(A)この手紙はSpectraの所有者に新しいシートベルトの部品を取り付けるように勧めているが、シートベルトの使用については特に勧めていない。(C)駐車するときにシートベルトの問題が起こるが、小さなスペースに駐車するためのアドバイスについては何も述べられていない。(D)Spectraはこの手紙に出てくる唯一の車種であり、新車種ではない。

171. **(D)** Mach Motors CompanyはSpectraの所有者に新しいシートベルトのリトラクターを無料で提供している。手紙では(A)サイドブレーキ、(B)シートカバーについては述べていない。(C)問題があるのは後部座席のシートベルトであり、前の座席ではない。

172. **(C)** From:Georges Bemanajaraとあるので、彼がこのメッセージの差出人で、15日までアムステルダムにいると述べている。(A)Stacie Drese と(B)Amy Little はGeorges Bemanajara が会いたいと思っている人たちである。(D)Robert O'Neillはメッセージの受取人であり、差出人ではない。

173. **(B)** until 15th は15日がその場所に滞在する最後の日だということである。(A) 7 日はこのメッセージが書かれた日付である。(C)と(D)は彼のロンドン滞在の初日と最終日である。

174. **(A)** 空港の航空交通管制官がストライキに入ると、飛行機のフライトはキャンセルされ、Mr. Bemanajaraはセミナーに間に合うように帰宅できない可能性がある。(B)天気については何も述べられていない。(C)セミナーの他の会議については何も述べられていない。(D)噂とは非公式の情報で、真実とは異なる場合がある。キャンセルの噂があっても実際には起こらないかもしれないので、遅延の原因にはならない。

CD1 No.1

Part I

1. (A) She's working in the hall.
   (B) She's speaking into the microphone.
   (C) She's typing on the computer.
   (D) She's using a pay phone.

2. (A) All of the seats in the room are empty.
   (B) A man is giving a present to his colleagues.
   (C) A woman is explaining a point to the group.
   (D) They're demonstrating a new product on the table.

3. (A) He's getting ready to paper the wall.
   (B) He's writing a story on the board.
   (C) He's reading an article in the paper.
   (D) He's sitting in front of the class.

4. (A) The driver is stepping down from the bus.
   (B) The passengers are boarding the bus.
   (C) Some passengers are waving from the window.
   (D) The bus is moving into another lane.

5. (A) The house is made of wood.
   (B) The hikers are entering the forest.
   (C) The path winds through the trees.
   (D) The leaves are blowing across the ground.

6. (A) The towels have fallen off the rack.
   (B) He's looking at his reflection.
   (C) The mirror's cracked in two places.
   (D) He's ready to take a bath.

7. (A) A crowd has gathered to listen to the musicians.
   (B) They're all playing the same instruments.
   (C) There are many cars parked next to the building.
   (D) The violinist is wearing a hat and coat.

CD1 No.2

Part II

21. (Man 1) Where are you staying in Paris?
    (Man 2) (A) To study French.
             (B) At the Grand Hotel.
             (C) No, we're just visiting.

22. (Woman) When does Mr. Gustavson predict the construction of the building will be finished?
    (Man)   (A) Out of steel and concrete.
             (B) Twenty million dollars.
             (C) In about a month.

23. (Man)   Why did the board of
               directors change its policy?
    (Woman)   (A) Yes, in the boardroom.
               (B) He changed jobs
                   several weeks ago.
               (C) There had been too
                   many complaints.

24. (Man 1)   Would you mind opening
               your bag so I can inspect it,
               sir?
    (Man 2)   (A) Not at all.
               (B) In my suitcase.
               (C) Next to my passport.

25. (Woman 1) This new product should
               sell well, shouldn't it?
    (Woman 2) (A) Yes, it is priced fairly.
               (B) Yes, I feel well.
               (C) Yes, I should.

26. (Man 1)   What kind of work does Ms.
               García do?
    (Man 2)   (A) Yes, I like to walk.
               (B) She's a computer
                   programmer.
               (C) That's very kind of
                   you.

27. (Woman 1) Shall I put this file on your
               desk or back in the filing
               cabinet?
    (Woman 2) (A) I'll take it.
               (B) No, it's behind the
                   desk.
               (C) In the afternoon.

28. (Woman)   Did you realize that this
               firm occupies all three
               floors of the building?
    (Man)   (A) No, she's on the fourth
                   floor.
               (B) Yes, the room is
                   occupied.
               (C) No, I thought it was
                   just the first two.

29. (Woman 1) Who did Mrs. Martelli pick
               to fill the position?
    (Woman 2) (A) A young intern from
                   the marketing
                   department was chosen.
               (B) Mrs. Martelli met with
                   us after all.
               (C) She wanted a position
                   with more benefits.

30. (Man)   Do you know where I can
               rent a car?
    (Woman)   (A) I've been looking all
                   over for my keys.
               (B) I would try the airport.
               (C) No, I'll take a taxi.

 **CD1 No.3**

Part III
51. (Woman)   Have you heard? Mr. Olmos
               is going to Africa.
    (Man)   Is that right? I guess he'll be
               gone for some time.
    (Woman)   Not too long really, just for
               fourteen days.

52. (Woman)   Which phone can I use to
               make an overseas call?
    (Man)   You can dial direct from any
               of the office phones.
    (Woman)   Great, then I don't need an
               operator or a special line.

53. (Man) How much will it cost for me to get from New York to Boston?

(Woman) It depends on whether you travel by car, bus, train, or plane. The best deal I could find for you would probably be on a bus.

(Man) That sounds fine to me. I'll want a ticket for Saturday morning.

54. (Man 1) We're planning on going to the ball game on Friday. Would you like to join us?

(Man 2) That sounds like fun. I know the team is doing well, but unfortunately I have plans this Friday.

(Man 1) OK. There will be plenty of other opportunities this season.

55. (Man) Good morning, Ms. Tanaka. Were you able to fax the notes from the sales meeting to our accountant?

(Woman) No, I've been too busy, but Mr. Mizuno did it for me.

(Man) Just as long as they were sent out.

56. (Woman) How long will it take for me to receive my order?

(Man) We usually ship via Global Services, which takes from four to six business days; they also have a two-day express service for an extra ten dollars.

(Woman) OK. I'll go with the express service.

57. (Woman) What time does the plane leave? I'm getting pretty hungry.

(Man) According to the ticket agent, we have to board at two o'clock.

(Woman) Good, that means we still have an hour. Why don't we head up to the restaurant?

58. (Woman) I didn't expect to see so many people here this early. The show doesn't start for another hour, and half the seats are already full.

(Man) Well, the lead is very popular these days. He's been in a number of successful plays.

(Woman) Not only that, but the set design is supposed to be quite unique.

59. (Man) Have there been any job advertisements for pharmacists lately?

(Woman) Yes, I just saw one in the newspaper that included a good salary and benefit package.

(Man) Great! I'll get a copy of today's paper and send in my application right away.

60. (Man) Could you take me to the station after my meeting?

(Woman) Sorry, I'm not going downtown. I have a doctor's appointment near here.

(Man) That's OK, I'll get a taxi.

Part IV

Questions 81 and 82 refer to the following report.

And for all of you getting ready for your drive home, I'm happy to report that there are no major traffic delays in the metropolitan area. There are, however, a few minor problems. On Route 9 near River Road, expect delays due to paving. Also, because of the rebuilding of the Lincoln Bridge, only one lane will be open. Stay tuned for an update in twenty minutes.

Questions 83 and 84 refer to the following radio advertisement.

It's your life. Live each moment to the fullest! Imagine living in a spacious, modern apartment in a country-club setting where activities and facilities can keep you constantly busy. Close to the city, yet rural enough to grow a garden and have a pet. We offer luxurious one-bedroom apartments for $1,500 [fifteen hundred dollars] a month. Your rent includes membership in our private health and fitness club. Find out how beautiful life can be. Call or write for a free brochure or video, or make an appointment for a tour. Don't delay, call today. Only a limited number of one-bedroom apartments remain.

Questions 85 and 86 refer to the following talk.

Good evening. I'm Joan Berry and tonight I have the pleasure of welcoming you on behalf of our president to our annual awards banquet. This year's sales were up in all regions, but the southwest division had the most impressive figures. Would all of you join me in congratulating the person responsible for this growth, Jill Smith, on her fine accomplishments. Ms. Smith, would you please come up to the podium to accept this token of our appreciation and say a few words about your strategy?

Questions 87 and 88 refer to the following short talk.

Our next topic today is the schedule change for the new office building on Center Street. As of the first of next year, the city government will be enforcing new building codes. To operate within last year's codes, we need to begin work as soon as possible. Therefore, the construction start is being moved from March of next year to November of this year. As a result, we will need all preliminary drawings, site plans, and renderings ready for the client in two weeks. I realize this may present a challenge to many of you, so we will adjust your workload to accommodate this change.

APPENDIX **B**

付録 B

Contents

TOEIC練習テストの正解

1.	(C)	34.	(B)	67.	(B)	101.	(D)	135.	(C)	167.	(C)
2.	(A)	35.	(B)	68.	(D)	102.	(C)	136.	(B)	168.	(B)
3.	(B)	36.	(C)	69.	(C)	103.	(C)	137.	(A)	169.	(B)
4.	(B)	37.	(C)	70.	(D)	104.	(B)	138.	(B)	170.	(C)
5.	(B)	38.	(A)	71.	(C)	105.	(A)	139.	(B)	171.	(C)
6.	(A)	39.	(B)	72.	(B)	106.	(D)	140.	(C)	172.	(D)
7.	(C)	40.	(B)	73.	(C)	107.	(B)			173.	(B)
8.	(A)	41.	(A)	74.	(D)	108.	(B)	141.	(D)	174.	(D)
9.	(D)	42.	(B)	75.	(B)	109.	(C)	142.	(A)	175.	(C)
10.	(A)	43.	(C)	76.	(C)	110.	(A)	143.	(A)	176.	(C)
11.	(D)	44.	(B)	77.	(B)	111.	(B)	144.	(B)	177.	(D)
12.	(A)	45.	(B)	78.	(C)	112.	(A)	145.	(A)	178.	(A)
13.	(B)	46.	(C)	79.	(D)	113.	(C)	146.	(C)	179.	(C)
14.	(D)	47.	(A)	80.	(C)	114.	(A)	147.	(B)	180.	(A)
15.	(D)	48.	(B)			115.	(B)	148.	(C)	181.	(D)
16.	(A)	49.	(B)	81.	(B)	116.	(A)	149.	(C)	182.	(A)
17.	(B)	50.	(A)	82.	(B)	117.	(D)	150.	(A)	183.	(B)
18.	(C)			83.	(C)	118.	(D)	151.	(B)	184.	(C)
19.	(D)	51.	(C)	84.	(D)	119.	(D)	152.	(C)	185.	(D)
20.	(C)	52.	(B)	85.	(C)	120.	(A)	153.	(A)	186.	(C)
		53.	(A)	86.	(A)	121.	(D)	154.	(C)	187.	(C)
21.	(C)	54.	(B)	87.	(B)	122.	(D)	155.	(C)	188.	(A)
22.	(B)	55.	(A)	88.	(A)	123.	(A)	156.	(A)	189.	(B)
23.	(B)	56.	(D)	89.	(D)	124.	(C)	157.	(C)	190.	(D)
24.	(C)	57.	(A)	90.	(A)	125.	(B)	158.	(D)	191.	(B)
25.	(B)	58.	(C)	91.	(A)	126.	(B)	159.	(A)	192.	(A)
26.	(A)	59.	(D)	92.	(B)	127.	(B)	160.	(B)	193.	(C)
27.	(B)	60.	(A)	93.	(D)	128.	(A)			194.	(C)
28.	(B)	61.	(B)	94.	(C)	129.	(D)	161.	(C)	195.	(D)
29.	(A)	62.	(A)	95.	(D)	130.	(A)	162.	(B)	196.	(C)
30.	(C)	63.	(C)	96.	(C)	131.	(A)	163.	(B)	197.	(D)
31.	(B)	64.	(A)	97.	(D)	132.	(D)	164.	(A)	198.	(C)
32.	(A)	65.	(A)	98.	(C)	133.	(A)	165.	(A)	199.	(D)
33.	(C)	66.	(A)	99.	(C)	134.	(A)	166.	(D)	200.	(A)
				100.	(D)						

TOEIC練習テストのスコア算出方法

第6章の練習テストを終了すると、スコアを算出することができます。

ステップ1
前ページにある正解を参照し、正解した問題をチェックしてください。各セクションの正解数がそのセクションの素点になります。Section I Listening の正解数を数え、下の適切な空欄に記入します。Section II Reading についても同様にします。

	素点	換算点レンジ
Section I Listening	95	470-495
Section II Reading	87	400-435
トータル・スコア・レンジ		870-930

素点はそのセクションのTOEICスコアではありません。TOEICテストの各フォームでは素点を換算点に変換するための統計的手法を採用しています。この手続きにより、異なるテスト・フォームでも、そのスコアが表わす意味は同一となります。したがって、あるテスト・フォームにおいて、トータル・スコアが550ということは、他のテスト・フォームにおける550と同等の英語能力を示すことになります。

ステップ2
上の空欄に各セクションの素点を記入しましたら、次ページのスコア換算表を参照してください。この表はTOEICテストの各フォームと同等であり、第6章の練習テスト用に開発されたものです。この表は素点を換算点レンジに変換するためのものです。たとえば、Listening の素点が61から65のいずれかであれば、換算点のレンジは300から345となります。このことはかならずしも、素点61が換算点300に相当し、素点65が換算点345に相当することを意味しません。**練習テストの換算点レンジはおおよその英語能力を示すものであり、実際のTOEICテストのスコア算出に使われたことはありません。**

スコア換算表でSection I Listeningの素点レンジと書かれている欄を見て、あなたの素点にあてはまる換算点レンジを見つけます。ご自分のListeningの換算点レンジを素点の欄のとなりに記入します。Section II Readingについても同様にして換算点レンジを記入して下さい。

ステップ3

次にListeningとReadingの換算点レンジの合計を計算します。これにより第6章にあるあなたのTOEIC練習テストのトータル・スコア・レンジが算出されます。次ページにあるスコア算出例をご参照ください。

> **注意**：異なった時期に異なった状況で受験した場合、異なる結果が出るということを知っておいてください。通常のテスト会場でTOEICテストを受験した場合、そのスコアはTOEIC練習テストのスコア・レンジ内に収まる公算が大きいと考えられます。しかし、スコア・レンジを上回ったり、下回ったりする可能性もあります。

スコア換算表

Section I Listening		Section II Reading	
素点レンジ	換算点レンジ	素点レンジ	換算点レンジ
96-100	480-495	96-100	450-495
91-95	470-495	91-95	420-465
86-90	440-490	86-90	400-435
81-85	410-460	81-85	370-410
76-80	390-430	76-80	340-380
71-75	360-400	71-75	310-355
66-70	330-370	66-70	280-325
61-65	300-345	61-65	260-300
56-60	270-315	56-60	230-270
51-55	240-285	51-55	200-245
46-50	210-255	46-50	170-215
41-45	180-225	41-45	140-185
36-40	150-195	36-40	120-160
31-35	120-165	31-35	90-130
26-30	90-135	26-30	60-105
21-25	60-105	21-25	30-75
16-20	40-75	16-20	10-50
11-15	10-45	11-15	5-20
6-10	5-20	6-10	5
1-5	5	1-5	5
0	5	0	5

スコア算出例

Section I Listening の素点が45で、Section II Reading の素点が64だった場合、以下の空欄に数字を書き入れます。

	素点	換算点レンジ
Section I Listening	45	
Section II Reading	64	
トータル・スコア・レンジ		

次に、スコア換算表から換算点レンジを見つけ、その数字を記入し、合計値を出します。

	素点	換算点レンジ
Section I Listening	45	180-225
Section II Reading	64	260-300
トータル・スコア・レンジ		440-525

TOEIC練習テストのトータル・スコアは440から525の間ということになります。

TOEIC練習テストの解説

Section I Listening

Part Ⅰ：写真描写問題

1. (C) 女性のうち一人がタイプを打っている写真である。つまり、彼女はキーボードを使っているのである。(A)女性はまだ働いているので、業務はまだ終わっていない。(B)ペンや鉛筆を使って手で書いている女性はいない。(D)スクリーンはコンピュータのものであり、テレビではない。

2. (A) 人々は２、３のテーブルのみに着席している。(B)レストラン沿いの川または湖のような場所が見えるが、床に水はまかれてない。(C)テーブルは丸い形をしている。(D)客がいるということはレストランはまだ営業中である。

3. (B) 男性が電話で話しながら写真を見ている。つまり２つのことを同時に行なっているのである。(A)写真はすでに現像されている。(C)彼は風景写真を手にしているようだが、窓の外を眺めてはいない。(D)彼はまだ電話機を耳に当て、話しをしている最中である。

4. (B) 駐車場には天井がついている。(A)車の中には運転手はいないし、ライトもついていない。(C)写真にはcars（車）は写っているが、cards（カード）は写っていない。(D)車はpark（公園）ではなくparking area（駐車場）にある。

5. (B) 男性と女性がソファに隣り合って座っている。(A)ソファの上にバッグがあるが、誰もそれに触れてはいない。(C)２人はソファに座っており、ソファを移動させてはいない。(D)２人は互いに見つめ合っているが、ディスプレイを見てはいない。

6. (A) 市場は大勢の人でにぎわっている。(B)男性は野菜を持ち上げているが、庭にいるのではない。(C)野菜は売られているので、すでに収穫はすんでいる。yet to be harvestedは「まだ収穫が残っている」という意味である。(D)女性は量りの近くにはいるが、上に乗ってはいない。scaleは野菜を量るために使われている。

7. (C) 男性たちは荷物を別の場所へ運んでいる。(A)彼らはバッグを前にある台に置いているが、頭上ではなく、ひざくらいの高さの位置である。(B)スーツケースは運ばれる前にすでに荷造りされている。(D)写真には荷物が検査されている様子は写っていない。

8. (A) 男性はmerchandise（売られている商品）を見ている。あるいは確かめている(examine)。(B)ケースは商品で一杯である。男性は腕時計を見ているので、(C)商品のケースを並べ替えたり、(D)映画を見ているのではない。

9. **(D)** 男性と女性が向かいあって(facing each other)立っている。(A)階段は女性の後ろにあり、人は階段を登っているのではなく、立ち止まっている。(B)2人は向き合っているので、the same direction（同じ方向）を見ることはできない。(C)手すりはあるが、2人ともそれに触れてはいない。

10. **(A)** 電車はたくさんの人で混雑している。(B)写真にはrain（雨）ではなくtrain（電車）が写っている。男性は立っているが、電車の扉を閉めようとしているのではない。(C)電車はまだ駅に停車しており、出発していない。(D)男性はブリーフケースを抱えて、まだ電車に乗っている。ブリーフケースをどこかに置き忘れてはいない。

11. **(D)** 一人の女性が別の女性の髪の毛を切っている。(A)女性の労働時間が短くなったことについては何も述べられていない。(B)女性は記事を切り抜いている(clipping out the article)のではない。(C)写真に写っているのはair（空気）ではなくhair（髪の毛）である。

12. **(A)** 何人かの人がエスカレーターで上の階へ上がっている。(B)人々はエスカレーターを歩いて登ってはいない。つまり、エスカレーターは正常に動いていることになる。(C)エスカレーターがあるので、建物は少なくとも二階建てである。(D)たくさんの人がいるので、この建物は一般に公開されていると考えられる。

13. **(B)** ウェイターは男性と女性がメニューを見ているときに、何かを書いているので、注文を取っている(taking their order)と考えられる。(A)彼らはまだ食べていないので、食事代を支払う段階ではない。(C)女性は食べ物を注文しているのであって、男性たちに立ち去るよう求めているのではない。(D)テーブルの上に皿は見当たらない。つまり、片づけるべき皿はないのである。

14. **(D)** 女性は腕を延ばして一番上の棚に手を届かせようとしている。(A)もう1人は女性に手を貸していない。(B)店は商品で一杯なので、在庫は十分である。(C)男性は棚の前でひざまずいており、レジの前で支払おうとしているのではない。

15. **(D)** 男性が女性に紙を渡そうとしている。(A)ファイルはあるが、男性はそれを片づけてはいない。(B)女性は男性の向かい側にいるが、座っているのではなく、立っている。(C)紙はあるが、新聞ではない。

16. **(A)** 3人が一緒に楽器を演奏している。彼らはtrio（トリオ）である。(B)この演奏はおそらくミュージカルではない。しかも、まだ上演中である。(C)楽器は使用中で、ケースの中にしまわれてはいない。(D)オーケストラであれば、もっと人数が多いはずである。写真の3人は部屋に入ろうとしているのではなく、すでに演奏を始めている。

17. **(B)** 数人が自転車に乗っている。(A)川のようなものが写っているが、誰もその中に入ってはいない。(C)木にはたくさんの葉がついている。(D)水は近くの岸まであふれてはいない。

18. **(C)** 3人の女性が屋外で働いているようである。(A)紙と花はあるようだが、花柄の壁紙はない。(B)彼女たちは歩いているのではなく座っている。ツアーをしている(taking a tour)のではない。(D)彼女たちの前に紙が広げられているが、誰も食べ物を食べてはいない。

19. **(D)** 女性が部屋にいる人たちに、うちとけた雰囲気でスピーチ、あるいはpresentation（プレゼンテーション）をしている。(A)女性は座っているのではなく立っている。(B)女性の話を聞いている人々は立っているのではなく座っている。(C)部屋にある椅子はすべて使われており、空いている椅子はない。

20. **(C)** 大きな箱がトラックの近くの地面に積まれている(stacked)。(A)トラックは道路脇に駐車されている。写真には信号は写っていない。(B)男性はすでにトラックの中にいる。(D)数人の男性と箱が写っているが、箱を運んでいる(carrying boxes)男性はいない。

Part Ⅱ：応答問題

21. **(C)** 質問文のキーワードはwhenであり、日付を答えたものが正解となる。(A)whereに対する答えである。(B)how longに対する答えである。

22. **(B)** 飛行機の到着時間を尋ねた質問である。女性は到着時間を知らないし、知ろうともしなかったのである。(A)では質問に出てくるarriveという単語が使われているが、(A)も(C)も問題の到着時間についての答えにはなっていない。

23. **(B)** 誰がメモを届けられるか(who can deliver a memo)を尋ねている。(B)"I can do it."（自分がやる）と答えており、適切な答えである。(A)住んでいる場所を答えている。(C)どこから来たかについて述べている。

24. **(C)** 「パーティに行かないのか」と尋ねられて、行けない理由（体調不良）を答えている。(A)どこでパーティが行われるかについての答えであり、男性がパーティに行きたいかどうかについてではない。(B)receptionは正式なパーティのことであり、receiptは支払いの明細書である。

25. **(B)** 旅行会社の名前を尋ねた質問である。(B)のみが名前を答えている。(A)話し手は人の名前ではなく会社の名前を尋ねている。(C)何かを推奨してもらうための質問ではない。

26. **(A)** キーワードはwhereなので、場所を表わす答えであるべきである。(B)when（時間）に対する答えである。(C)why（理由）に対する答えである。(C)でview（景色）について述べられているが、Oceanviewは会社の名前であり、窓からの眺めではない。

27. **(B)** 工場を訪問したかどうかを相手に尋ねている。過去形で答えている(B)が正しい。(A)主語と時制が誤りである。(C)plantを「工場」ではなく「植物」と解している。

28. **(B)** 質問文のキーワードはwhoであり、応答は人の名前を含んでいるべきである。(A)where（場所）に対する答えである。この場合はin the main officeがポイント。main officeに何かがある場合は、It's...でもかまわないが、人の場合はHe..., She...など人称代名詞を使って表わす。(C)新しい受付係はすでに雇われ

ていると判断できる。

29. **(A)** どこで会議が開催されるかを尋ねているので、場所を答えるべきである。(B)here と hear は同じ発音なので注意。質問は hear とは無関係である。(C)質問者は会議が開催されることをすでに知っており、場所を知りたいのである。この答えは質問の前半を確認しているにすぎない。

30. **(C)** 質問文のキーワードは why と early である。(C)のみが会議が早く始まった理由を述べている。(A)時間を挙げているが、これは when の質問に答えるものである。(B)何についての会議が行なわれたかを説明しており、なぜ早く始まったかは説明されていない。

31. **(B)** 質問文のキーワードは total と figures であり、答えには数字と金額が含まれると考えられる。(A)何が生産されているかを答えているが、その生産量は述べられていない。(C)は工場の部門名をあげているが、生産量についてはふれていない。

32. **(A)** how far とあるので、距離について尋ねている。(A)公園まで行くのにかかる時間を答えているので、適切である。(B)この表現は反対意見を述べる丁寧な表現である。(C)質問は parking（駐車）に関してではなく、park（公園）に関してである

33. **(C)** 議題が準備されているかどうかを尋ねる質問である。(C)議題は見直される必要があると述べられており、まだ準備はされていないのである。(A)男性は議題が準備されているか(prepared)を尋ねており、修理されたか(repaired)を尋ねているのではない。(B)議題は他との類似点を比較される(compared)ものではなく、準備される(prepared)ものである

る。

34. **(B)** インフォーマルな言い方で映画に誘っているところである。(B)形式ばらずに誘いを受け入れており、適切である。(A)映画館への行き方を尋ねているのではない。(C)仕事があとどのくらいかかるかを尋ねているのではない。

35. **(B)** 質問が過去形なので、答えも過去形でなければならない。(B)大量の在庫があったと答えており、適切である。(A)と(C)はどちらも現在形で答えている。(A)stock exchange（証券取引所）と在庫という意味の stock とを混同している。

36. **(C)** 援助を求める依頼に対し、(C)は丁寧な答え方で快諾しており、適切である。(A)質問は files（ファイル）の場所についてであり、fire exit（非常口）についてではない。(B)merger は emergency（非常事態）と発音が似ているが、「二つの会社の合併」という意味である。

37. **(C)** 質問文のキーワードは budget（予算）である。機器を買うための資金がどこから出たかを尋ねる質問である。regular（通常の）の予算からではなく、special funding（特別の財源）を使ったのである。(A)sound equipment（音声機器）について尋ねており、sounds（音声）についてではない。(B)departmental と rental は音が似ているが、機器ではなく、room rental（部屋の賃借）にかかるお金について述べている。

38. (A) (A)のみがどこに男性が滞在するかという質問の答えになっている。男性の会社が滞在場所を取り計らってくれるのである。(B)男性がパリに行く理由を述べている。(C)男性がパリに滞在する期間を述べている。

39. (B) 男性からの夕食への招待に対し、(B)は丁寧に断っている。(A)過去形の答えになっているが、夕食はまだ始まっていない。(C)招待に対する答えになっていない。

40. (B) ここでのdealは特別な値引きのことである。(B)は値引き率を示しており、適切である。(A)質問文のcompanyは会社のことであり、旅行の同行者のことではない。(C)ここでのdealはカードゲームでカードを配るという意味の動詞である。

41. (A) モリ氏が自由になる時間を尋ねているので、その時間を答えている(A)が適切である。(B)と(C)は場所を答えている。

42. (B) この質問のポイントはもっと文具(便箋と封筒)を手に入れるにはどうしたらよいかということである。(B)入手方法を述べており、適切である。(A)文具についてではなく、郵送された郵便物について述べている。(C)letterheadは会社の正式な便箋であり、department head(部門長)のことではない。

43. (C) Ms. Duboisが会議に出席したかどうかという質問に対し、(C)は彼女が欠席したと述べており、適切である。(A)会議の頻度について述べている。(B)presentを「出席」という意味ではなく贈り物という意味でとらえている。

44. (B) 男性は女性が誰の下で仕事をしているかを確認している。(B)彼の誤りを丁寧に訂正しており、適切である。(A)質問文の単語はassistance(補助)ではなく、assistantである。補助が必要かどうかを尋ねている質問ではない。(C)ではnewとknewの二つの発音の同じ単語で混乱させられる。男性は女性が何か知っているかを尋ねているのではなく、彼女が新しいアシスタントかどうかを尋ねている。

45. (B) 質問文のキーワードはwhenである。いつ報告書をもらえるかという質問に対し、(B)は報告書が仕上がる時間を挙げているので適切である。(A)質問は実際の売上についてではなく、売上報告書について尋ねている。(C)報告書がどのくらい前のものかを答えており、どのようにして手に入れるかについては述べていない。

46. (C) 質問は従業員の過ちの理由を尋ねているので、それを説明している(C)が適切である。(B)はnoで始まっている。これはyes-noで答える質問の場合にしか使われない答え方であり、情報を求める質問の答えにはならない。(A)Mr. Danforthがどこにいるかを答えてはいるが、彼の行動については説明していない。

47. (A) 商品がセール中で値下げされているかという質問であると答えている。質問文のmarked downは「値下げされた」という意味の動詞。(B)はmarketを「市場」という意味の名詞として答えている。market being closed downで「市場が閉鎖された」ということ。(C)質問はコートの価格についてであり、色についてではない。

48. **(B)** why の質問に対し、(B)では Ms. Ortiz がなぜインボイスを見たいのかという理由を述べており、適切である。(A)質問は invoices（商品の明細書）に関してであり、voice（声）に関してではない。(C)Ms. Ortiz はまだ明細書を見ていないので、答えは過去形にはならない。また、invoices は複数形なのに対して単数形の it で受けているので、不適切である。

49. **(B)** 質問はどこにキャビネットを置くかについてであるので、場所を答えると考えられる。(B)「現在置いてある場所がいい」という意見であり、答えとして適切である。(A)right（右）というのはこの質問では方向を示しており、correct（正しい）という意味ではない。(C)質問文中に copy machine という語句が使われているが、内容はファイル・キャビネットの位置についてである。コピー機で取ったコピーについてではない。

50. **(A)** same と last time があるのである行動が繰り返されていることがわかる。(A)その時以来(since then)状況が変わったことを説明しており、適切である。(B)質問は business proposal（業務提案）についてであり、marriage proposal（結婚の申込）についてではない。(C)rejected は「受け入れられない」という意味である。injection は「注射」という意味。

Part Ⅲ：会話問題

51. **(C)** 二番目の女性が Mr. Murphy の秘書が電話をかけてきたかを尋ねているのに対し、最初の女性は yes と答えている。つまり、電話でメッセージを残したのは Mr. Murphy の秘書である。(A)Mr. Murphy 自身は電話をかけてはいない。(B)電話の operator（オペレーター）や

(D)委員会の chairperson（議長）については述べていない。

52. **(B)** 2人は employee lounge（従業員用のラウンジ）と mailroom（郵便室）のことを述べているので、彼らはおそらく office（オフィス）の建物の中にいると考えられる。男性はコーヒーが飲める場所を探しているところなので、まだ(A)コーヒーショップ、あるいは(D)スーパーマーケットにはいない。(C)mailroom は post office（郵便局）とは違う。

53. **(A)** 話し手は Ms. Sompong の仕事の状況について話している。ライバル会社が彼女を採用するために仕事を提示したのである。(B)2人は事業を始めることについては述べていない。(D)話し手は休暇をとって仕事を休むことについては述べていない。(C)ライバル会社どうしで競合しているかもしれないが、この会話ではその話題には触れていない。

54. **(B)** Claudia は最初の話し手であり、水曜日のチケットが欲しいと言っている。演劇の上演は(A)月曜日から(C)木曜日までだが、(B)水曜日が正解である。(D)土曜日は上演されない。

55. **(A)** 女性は電話を受け、電話をかけた人が話したい相手に電話をつないでいるので、telephone operator（電話オペレーター）である。(B)会社は Standard Computer Services という名前だが、女性は computer technician（コンピューター技師）ではない。(C)女性は電話を営業部にまわそうかと打診しているが、自分は営業にかかわる仕事をしていない。(D)Mr. Fong が人事部で働いているのである。

56. **(D)** 2人の男性は二つの上映のうちの遅い方、すなわち7時に始まる映画に行くことに決めている。(A)1時の上映については述べられていない。(B)映画は2時にではなく、2回上映される。(C)早い方の上映が4時である。

57. **(A)** 2人はどこに机を置くかを話している。彼らは家具の配置変えをしているのだと考えられる。家具はすでに部屋の中にあるので、(B)設計したり、(C)買ったり、(D)組み立てたりするはずはない。

58. **(C)** 2人は途中で仕事ができるので、電車を使うことに決めたのである。(A)会議が行なわれる場所は飛行機で行くには近すぎる。(B)車を運転していくことも考えたが、やはり電車で行くことを選んだ。(D)男性は電車のチケットを購入すると言っているので、ここでのstationはバス停を指すものではない。

59. **(D)** 配達のトラックが新しいルートを使っているので、ニュース誌はまだ配達されていない。男性はすぐにトラックは来るだろうと言っている。(A)ニュース誌はまだ到着していないので、販売されたり売り切れたりしているのではない。(B)トラックはいつもより遅いが、天候による遅れではない。(C)月曜日は配達日であり、店休日ではない。

60. **(A)** いくつかの名前が挙がっている。女性(Ms. Ortega)はRicardoの代わりに会議に行くことを依頼するJuanという名の男性に電話をかけている。(B)Ricardoは会議に行くことができなくなった人物である。(C)Ms. OrtegaはJuanに会社を代表して行くように頼んでいるので、彼女自身は行かない。(D)Carlaは出張の手配を担当している人物である。

61. **(B)** saladはここで述べられている唯一のメニューである。女性がサラダ・バーのクーポンを持っていることから、お金を節約するために2人は(A)スープ、(C)サンドイッチ、(D)ハンバーガーではなく、サラダを注文すると考えられる。health food restaurant（健康食品レストラン）ではふつうハンバーガーは出さない。

62. **(A)** 航空会社は男性の荷物を誤ってニューヨークに運んでしまったのである。男性は(C)サンフランシスコの(B)ホテルに滞在している。(D)男性はバスでショッピングモールへ行くことができるが、バスに彼の荷物があるわけではない。

63. **(C)** Susannaは2年間勤めたので3週間の休暇をもらう権利がある。(A)Susannaはすべての休暇を一度にとってもよいかと尋ねている。onceと言っているが、oneとは言っていない。(B)一度にとれそうな休暇は2週間である。(D)4週間とはどこにも述べられていない。

64. **(A)** 2人の男性はkitchen staff（厨房のスタッフ）、とうもろこしの缶詰、メニューなど、食材に関連する語句を使用していることから、cafeteria kitchen（カフェテリアの台所）での会話だと考えられる。また、shelf, counterといった具体的な場所を指した語も使われている。(B)救急室、(C)メールルーム、(D)スタッフ・ラウンジとは考えられない。

65. **(A)** Yuriは娘のAnnaが旅行中に病気になったと言っている。(B)AnnaはYuriの末娘である。(C)Yuriは話し手である。彼については話題にしていない。(D)Yuriが言ったourはYuri自身と彼の妻を指すものと考えられるが、妻のことが話題になっているのではない。

66. **(A)** いくつかの時間があげられている。木曜日の朝はTomのオフィスにペンキが塗られる日なので、彼はAlanのオフィスを使いたがっている。(B)金曜日の朝は、その時までAlanが不在にしているのである。(C)金曜日の午後については述べられていない。(D) 月曜日の午後はTomのプロジェクトの締切日である。

67. **(B)** Patriciaはマーケティング・レポートについて尋ねている。(A)Patriciaは相手の女性にファイルキャビネットの中を探すよう頼んでいるのである。(C)メモは机の上にある。紛失したのではない。(D)Patriciaはcheckを「探す」という意味の動詞で使っており、「小切手」という意味の名詞としては使っていない。

68. **(D)** その夜男性が滞在できる部屋を探すことについての会話なので、男性とホテルの予約係との会話だと考えられる。(A)bookedはここでは「予約された」という意味の形容詞であり、図書館などにあるbook（本）という意味の名詞ではない。(A)図書館、(B)レストラン、(C)オフィスは宿泊施設ではない。

69. **(C)** Ms. Krishnanは海外営業部に異動になったのである。(A)Ms. Krishnanは現在海外営業部で働いているが、海外に営業の出張に出ているとは言っていない。2つの句の語順の違いに注意。(B)Ms. Krishnanはこの部門ではもう働いていないが、まだ同じ会社で働いている。(D)女性はMs. Krishnanが忙しすぎるとは言っていない。

70. **(D)** plantはこの会話ではfactory（工場）のことである。2人の男性が工場訪問を計画している。(A)operation はここでは操業方法を指し、病院の患者に行われる手術のことではない。(B)greenhouse（温室）は plants（植物）が育つ所である。(C)工場はすでに建てられているので、建設現場は存在しない。

71. **(C)** Mr. Shimaが女性を会社に採用したところである。(A)Ms. Muraは入社が決まったのであって、コンテストに優勝したのではない。(B)Ms. MuraはMr. Shimaの会社で働く予定だが、会社を買ったわけではない。(D)Mr. ShimaはMs. Muraの履歴書を見てそれが非常に良いと言っているので、彼女はすでに履歴書の作成は終えているはずである。

72. **(B)** 女性はカメラの支払いをするために小切手を書くのである。(A)彼女はカメラを売っているのではなく買っている。(C)用紙に記入しても、支払うことにはならない。(D)彼女は小切手を書くにあたって、クレジットカードを見せるかもしれないが、カードにはすでに彼女の名前が書いてあるはずである。

73. **(C)** 女性はドライヤーが使えず、部屋の電気もつかないと言っている。これは電気の故障なので、electrician（電気技師）が修理に向かうと考えられる。(A)plumber（配管工）は建物の配管を修理する人である。(B)accountant（会計士）は財務諸表を作成する人である。(D)女性は急いでいるが、どこかへ行くために運転手を手配しているのではない。

74. **(D)** Ms. Díaz は Ms. Lee に彼女が待っている国際電話には対応するのかと尋ねている。(A)Ms. Lee はその日のうちにファックスを送る予定である。(B) Ms. Lee は顧客を待っているのではなく、しばらくの間、誰にも邪魔をされたくないのである。(C) Ms. Lee は顧客用の書類を作成しているところである。

75. **(B)** Heidi はオフィスから呼び出しを受けた。すぐに出かけなければならないということは、重要な、あるいは急ぎの用件だと考えられる。(A)彼女は家ではなく、オフィスに戻るのである。(C)彼女は電話を受けたばかりである。後で電話をかけると言っているが、電話をかけるために出かけるのではない。(D)彼女はすでにパーティに来ている。

76. **(C)** 女性は贈り物としてもらったセーターを返したいのである。(A)男性はクレジット・カードについては述べていない。男性は女性に credit を与えると言っている。これは、セーターと同額の買い物をできる権利を与えるという意味である。(B)女性が欲しいのはセーターではなくスーツである。(D)彼女はクレジットをもらえればよい(fine)と言っている。彼女は fine（罰金）を払うためにそこにいるのではない。

77. **(B)** いくつかの時間が挙げられているが、来週の水曜日がプレゼンテーションの日として挙げられている。(A)来週の月曜日は最終的な変更を加える日である。(C)「広告部門のスタッフは週末も働かなければならない」と言っている。プレゼンテーションを行なうのではない。(D)「スタッフはこれまでの7週間働きづめだった」と言っている。7週間後にプレゼンテーションが行なわれるのではない。

78. **(C)** 車のウィンカーが故障していたため、警察官が呼び止めたのである。(A)男性はスピード違反かと尋ねているが、警察官はそうではないと答えている。(B)turn signal（ウィンカー）に問題はあるが、男性は間違った方向に曲がっているのではない。(D 男性は警察官の求めに応じて免許証を提示している。

79. **(D)** いくつかの時間が挙げられているが、男性が注文の品を受け取れるのは明後日である。(A)男性は急いでいるが、注文の品は数分後にはできない。(B)店が開店するのは朝の9時である。今晩の9時とは言っていない。(C)店は明日棚卸しのために閉店するので、男性は注文の品を受け取ることはできない。

80. **(C)** 2人は Olivia が辞めた後、彼女のポジションがどうなるかについて話している。彼女は自己都合で退職したと考えられる。(A)最近大きな契約が結ばれたので、2人は仕事が増えると予測している。(B)彼女がやめるように頼まれたかどうかについては述べられていない。実際、その部門では彼女のポジションは空けたままにしてある。(D)ここで述べられている契約書は Olivia とのものではない。会社全体のものである。

Part Ⅳ：説明文問題

81. **(B)** ツアーは about half an hour（約30分）かかる。(A)アナウンスでは15分とは言っていない。(C)ツアーは an hour（1時間）ではない。(D)彫刻についての話は3時に始まる。three hours（3時間）とは言っていない。

82. **(B)** ツアーガイドは彫刻の好きな人を sculpture garden（彫刻の庭）で行われる３時の講演に招待している。講演は彫刻についてであると考えられる。(A)美術館には写真も展示されることもあるが、写真については述べられていない。(C)現代美術のツアーは３時からではなく、これから始まるのである。(D)美術館は美術品を収集するが、美術品の収集については述べられていない。

83. **(C)** Ivan は注文をとり、料理を出すと言っており、いくつかのメニューを挙げている。彼はレストランのウェイターであると考えられる。(A)ホテルにはレストランがある場合がほとんどだが、フロント係が自ら給仕することはない。(B)シェフはレストランで料理を作るが、給仕はしない。(D)農夫は食べ物を育てるが、食事を作って出すことはしない。

84. **(D)** Ivan は今夜は(tonight)自分が料理を出す担当だと言っているので、夕刻に違いない。(A)早朝、(C)朝の遅い時間、あるいは(D)午後半ばはいずれも不適切である。

85. **(C)** limited express（特別特急）と rear car（最終号車）という言葉が使われているので、電車でのアナウンスと考えられる。ここでの car は客車のことである。(A)船には客車はない。(B)タクシーには指定席、あるいは食べ物のサービスはないし、このように長い旅行はできない。また、タクシー乗り場では通常アナウンスは流れない。(D)このアナウンスのほとんどが飛行機で聞かれるものと似ているが、機内であれば、座席によってサービスが限定されることはない。

86. **(A)** すべての座席が指定席だと言っている。つまり、席はあらかじめ決められているのである。(B)クレジット・カードについては何も述べられていない。(C)地図についても述べられていない。(D)乗客は座席の予約が必要だが、食べ物のサービスには予約は不要である。

87. **(B)** franchise は特定の会社の製品を販売する権利である。Dave Sandoval は聴衆に、フランチャイズのオーナーになり、フランチャイズ店舗を開店する方法を話している。(A)聴衆はまだ Milton's Pies で働いていない。(C) Milton's のパイの店はショッピングセンターにあると述べられているが、講演はパイのフランチャイズ事業についてである。(D)聴衆は新しいフランチャイズを開店するために銀行から資金を借りられるが、この講演は銀行の役員に向けられたものではない。

88. **(A)** Milton's はパイを扱っているので、food retailer（食べ物の小売業者）ということになる。(B)講演では雇用についても話されているが、Milton's が職業斡旋会社だとは述べられていない。講演では食べること、買物、異なる地域について話されているが、Milton's が(C)娯楽施設、あるいは(D)旅行代理店だとは述べられていない。

89. **(D)** Dave Sandoval は自分のことを director of franchising（フランチャイズ事業の責任者）だと述べている。彼は自分の会社を大きくして店の売上げや事業の拡大を図りたがっているが、自分の身分を (A) sales manager（販売部長）、(B) head of research and development（研究開発所長）、(C) personnel manager（人事部長）であると言っていない。

90. (A) Ms. Suzuki は photojournalist（写真ジャーナリスト）だと紹介されている。(B)彼女は雑誌制作のスタッフとして加わるが、編集を行ったり、記事の構成を行ったりする訳ではない。News Journal や magazine という言葉は出てくるが、Ms. Suzuki が(C) advertising director または(D)newspaper publisher だとは述べていない。

91. (A) 女性はこの3年間をオーストラリアで過ごしたのである。(B)女性は日本生まれだが、最近日本では働いていない。(C) 女性がブラジルで仕事をするのは6カ月後である。(D)米国については述べられていない。

92. (B) 盛大な夕食会や晩餐会で、経営者は従業員を表彰することがある。この場合、従業員に栄誉を与えるとは賞を授与するという意味になる。(A)会社の合併、あるいは2組織の統一といったことについては述べられていない。(C) year という言葉は出てくるが、受賞者に関連する言葉であって、戦略に関連する言葉ではない。(D)会社の利益については述べられていない。

93. (D) チケットを入手するには、すぐ personnel office へ電話するようにと述べられている。(A)晩餐会が行われるホテルへ行く前に、チケットを入手しなければならない。(B)the president も(D)the board of directors（取締役会）も晩餐会に出席することになっているが、チケットは発行しない。

94. (C) テーマは travel である。キーワードとなる travel, journey, voyage という言葉が使われている。(A)geology とは地理学のことである。映画のタイトルは The Earth Is Round だが、地理学についての映画ではない。(B)映画の内容は世界史ではなく、世界中を旅する物語となっている。(D)映画製作者が質疑応答に対応するが、映画製作についての映画ではない。

95. (D) 上映期間中、9本の映画が上映されるのである。(A)a couple は「2つの」という意味だが、ここでの couple は映画に出てくる二人の登場人物のことを指している。(B)five years とは映画の登場人物二人が旅した期間である。(C)seven days とは映画が上映される期間のこと。

96. (C) 映画の上映時間は90分、つまり、an hour and a half（1時間30分）となる。(A)a half hour, (B)one hour, (D)two hours についてはいずれも述べられていない。

97. (D) 映画製作者が質問を受けるのである。つまり、インタビューを受けるということである。(B)上映される映画はドキュメンタリーだが、その後に何かが上映されるのではない。(A)修繕のために上映場が閉鎖されること、あるいは (C)賞の授与については述べられていない。

98. (C) 話し手の Vanessa Evans が彼女の番組のゲストとして Ms. Valmont を招いたのである。(A)Ms. Valmont が選挙の立候補者について語ることになっている。(B)天気予報はこの後放送されるが、話し手が気象予報士というわけではない。(D)Ms. Valmont がリポーターあるいはジャーナリストである。

99. (C) Ms. Valmont は新聞記者か記事の執筆者である。(A)コンピュータについては何も述べられていない。(B)Ms. Valmont は政府を組織している政党について執筆しているが、彼女自身がその政府の一員というわけではない。(D)彼女は本の執筆者であり、本の発行者ではない。

100. (D) インタビューの前に地域のニュースが放送される。(A)インタビューは先週の選挙結果に焦点が当てられる。(B)論評はニュースの後放送される。(C)立候補者についてのトークが行われるが、立候補者が番組で演説を行なうのではない。

Part Ⅴ：文法・語彙問題

101. (D) ここでは「義務」という意味の名詞が必要となる。(A)responsible は形容詞。(B)responsibly は副詞。(C)responsive は形容詞。

102. (C) limited は period of time という名詞句を修飾する形容詞として使用されている。for a limited period of time は for a short time only という意味。(A)limit は名詞なので、名詞句 period of time を修飾することはない。(B)limits は名詞の複数形か、動詞の三人称単数形である。どちらも period of time を修飾することはない。(D)動名詞 limiting は形容詞として使われることがあるが、この場合は文意と合わない。

103. (C) この文では、直前に完了した出来事を表わす現在完了形が必要である。already という副詞は現時点よりも以前に起こった出来事に対して使われる。(A)副詞としての still は、過去に起こった出来事が現在も続いている状況を表わす。(B)yet は現時点までに起こった出来事に対して使われるが、多くの場合、否定文か疑問文で用いられる。(D)soon は近い未来の出来事を表わす場合に用いられ、過去を表わすことはない。

104. (B) 現在完了形〈have ＋動詞の過去分詞形〉の形をとって have arranged とする。(A)arrange は原形なので現在完了形とはならない。(C)arranges は現在形なので完了形とはならない。(D)have been arranging のように現在完了進行形とすることはできるが、動名詞としての arranging を適用することはできない。

105. (A) 動詞の過去分詞形をもって受動態とする。従業員に規則を守ってもらうように注意をうながしているのである。(B)respected は後に for を伴うので、Employees are respected for working hard. のような使われ方をする。同様に名詞を伴い、The employees respected the rule. とすることもある。(C)remembered では文意に合わない。(D)reacted は自動詞なので受動態にすることはできない。

106. (D) a long に続く名詞が必要である。(A)speak は動詞なので不適切。(B)speaker は人を表わす名詞だが、long は人を修飾することはない。(C)動名詞は名詞として扱われるが、不定冠詞の a を伴うことはない。

107. **(B)**「興味がある」という意味になる形容詞が必要となる。(A)interest は動詞。(C)interesting は形容詞だが、前置詞 in が後に続くことはない。(D)interestingly は副詞。

108. **(B)** be concerned と the upcoming meeting を結べるのは about である。concerned は (A)to や (C)at を伴うことはない。(D)concerned は upon を伴うこともあるが、ふつうは I was concerned upon hearing the news.のように動名詞が続く場合のみである。

109. **(C)** レストランなどでなされることを表わす名詞が入ると考えられる。(A)delays とともに用いられる動詞は cause などで、make では不適切。(B)cuisine は料理の種類で、serve や prepare といった動詞とともに使われる。(D)violations も make とともに用いられることはない。

110. **(A)** 接続詞の because を用いて、プレゼンテーションが理解しにくかった理由を表わすことができる。(B)although は理由を表わすのではなく、2つの節の対比を表わす場合に用いられる。(C)so that は行為の目的を表わす。(D)than は more difficult than のように比較を表わす場合に用いられる。

111. **(B)** 形容詞 weak を修飾する副詞が必要。(A)increased は動詞。(C)increases は名詞の複数形か3人称単数形の動詞である。(D)increase は名詞。副詞ではない。

112. **(A)** 前置詞 beyond は、circumstances beyond its control のように、慣用的な表現として使われる。「企業は自らの力が及ばない状況で発生した損失に対しては責任をとることはない」という意味になる。(B)above, (C)inside, (D)around はこのような慣用的表現に用いられることはない。

113. **(C)** 天気が良いという状況を表わす形容詞があてはまる。(A)favorite は形容詞だが、人の好みなどを話す場合に使われる。(B)名詞の favor, 動詞の favor のいずれも weather condition の前に置かれることはない。(D)副詞は名詞を修飾しない。

114. **(A)** 受動態の文なので by の後には動作を行なう人を表わす名詞が必要。この場合は「受取人」という意味の名詞が必要である。(B)は動名詞である。(C)receipt は支払いの証拠となる紙である。(D)は形容詞である。

115. **(B)** 所有格 their を用いることによって、creative solutions が managers' own ideas であることが示される。(C)theirs は所有代名詞で、the textbook is theirs.のように単独で名詞を指す。(A)them と (D)they は代名詞で、所有を表わす場合には使われない。

116. **(A)** 2つの企業が合併すること(merger)に関連した名詞が適切と考えられる。また、合併には合意に達するための交渉や論議が行われることからも推測できる。(B)dedications（貢献）はmergerとは関係ない。(C)propositions（提案）はtake placeの主語にはならない。（D）Announcements are madeという言い方はするが、announcementsはtake placeの主語にはならない。

117. **(D)** 空欄には、従業員が自分たちの書類の写しをどう取り扱うかを表わす動詞が入る。submitは「提出する、送り付ける」という意味。（A）この文でphotocopiesは目的語となるため、自動詞であるemergeでは不適切。(B)substantiate（実証する）は前置詞句to this officeを後に続けることはできない。(C)to adapt somethingは「(何かを)変える」という意味。この文では、提出する前に必要書類に何らかの変更を加えるということは述べられていない。

118. **(D)** ここでは、2つの結果が比較されている。the same asは2つの物事が等しいことを表わす場合に使われる。(A), (B), (C)は正解のthe same asの一部を含んでいるにすぎない。

119. **(D)** 頻度が少ないという意味の副詞が必要となる。文頭に置かれて強調されているため、倒置（主語と動詞の位置の逆転）が起こっている。(A)Totally, (B)Decidedly, (C)Negativelyはいずれも副詞だが、頻度を表わすことはない。

120. **(A)** この文でのthe firstは、the first dayを表わし、the first day of the monthという意味である。したがって、dayとmonthを結びつける前置詞はofとなる。(B)toは時間を表現する場合によく用いられるが、その場合はfrom the first to the fifthのように、「〜まで」という意味になる。(C)fromはfrom the end of the monthのように物事の開始時を表わす。(D)forは期間を表わす場合に用いられる。

121. **(D)** 契約書がどのように校正されなければならないかを表わす副詞が必要となる。thoroughlyは「注意深く」という意味。(A)thoroughnessは前置詞withを前に伴えば適切な形となる。(B)more thorough, (C) thoroughはいずれも形容詞なので誤り。

122. **(D)** 空欄には「余分な」という意味の形容詞が入る。(A)additionは名詞なので、travel timeを修飾することはない。(B)additive（付加された）は形容詞だが、文意と合わない。(C)additionallyは副詞なので、名詞を修飾することはない。

123. **(A)** 複合名詞を構成する名詞が入る。project development は「プロジェクトの進展」という意味。(B)developed, (C)develops は動詞。(D)developer は何かを開発する主体を表わす名詞。

124. **(C)** had no idea で、did not know と同様「わからなかった」という意味になる。(A)名詞 knowledge は後に of を伴う。(B)「わからなかった」と言う場合、had no thought という表現は使わない。(D) willingness では文意と合わない。

125. **(B)** この文で benefit は動詞となり、後に〈from + 名詞〉を伴う。(A)接続詞 unless は条件節を導く際に用いられる。この場合は条件節ではないので誤り。(C)to が動詞 benefit の後に続くことはない。(D)前置詞 since は理由または物事の始まりを表わす場合に用いられるが、この場合はそのどちらでもない。

126. **(B)** suggested の後には that 節が続いていることから判断する。(A)continuity は名詞。主語の employees の後には動詞が必要。(C)continuing では意味が通じない。(D)continuous は形容詞。

127. **(B)** Ms. Jin に対応した再帰代名詞が入る。by herself で「(他の力を借りずに)彼女自身で」という意味。(A)she, (C)her, (D)hers は代名詞だが、再帰代名詞ではない。

128. **(A)** 会社がこれから何を行なうかを表わす自動詞が入る。diversify は「(事業内容を)多角化する」という意味になる。(B)clarify, (C)intensify, (D)modify はいずれもふつうは他動詞として用いられ、目的語を必要とする。自動詞になると文意と合わない。

129. **(D)** business plan(事業計画)が「優れている」、あるいは「傑出した」という意味の形容詞が入る。(A)anxious, (C)eager は人を形容することはあるが、business plan を修飾するには不適切。(B)ふつう、形容詞の evident が business plan を修飾することはない。

130. **(A)** production を修飾する形容詞が入る。(B) locality は名詞、(C)locally は副詞、(D) location は名詞なので production(名詞)を修飾することはない。

131. **(A)** 関係代名詞 which は前置詞 for を伴うことができる。この場合の先行詞は the position。(B)whom は先行詞が人である場合の関係代名詞。(C)that は the position を受けることはできるが、for を伴うことはできない。(D)関係代名詞としての what はこの場合は不適切。

132. **(D)** 空欄には前置詞 by を伴うことができる動詞が入る。accompanied by で「～を伴って、～と一緒に」という意味になる。(A)altered(変更する)、(B)adjusted(適合させる)、(C)accepted は文意と合わない。

133. (A) telephone とともに複合名詞として意味の通じる名詞が入る。telephone extensions とは、電話回線の本線から個々に引かれた内線のことである。(B)extending, (C)extended, (D)extends は、いずれも動詞なのでこの場合は不適切。

134. (A)「チェックする、確認する」という意味の動詞が必要。(B)concur は「（物事に）同意する」という意味。(C)conduct は「導く、案内する」という意味で、フライトナンバーとは関係ない。(D)concord は「合意」という意味の名詞。

135. (C)「売上げが悪かった」という内容になる形容詞が入る。(A)discouragement は名詞で、so の後には続かない。(B)discourage は動詞。(D)discouraged は動詞 discourage の過去分詞形。

136. (B) unbiased は「偏見のない、公平な」という意味の形容詞。(A)unjudged は「判断されない」という意味で、文意と合わない。(C)inanimate は「生命のない」という意味で、ふつう advice を修飾することはない。(D)impatient は「耐えられない、短気な」という意味で、人に対して使われる形容詞。

137. (A)attire は「衣類」という意味の不可算名詞。制服の着用が義務付けられる会社はよくある。(B)ambivalence は「不確定さ」という意味で文意と合わない。(C)professional assembly でも意味が通じるが、その場合は可算名詞なので professional の前に不定冠詞の a が必要となる。(D)approach も同様に不定冠詞の a が必要。

138. (B) ここでの such は good を強調している。その後に続く that 節で good work の結果を述べている。(B) 〈too ＋形容詞＋ for ...「...にとって〜すぎる」〉あるいは〈too ＋形容詞＋ to...「あまりに〜なので...できない」〉といった使い方はできるが、後に that 節を伴うことはできない。(C)so 〜 that 構文ととらえがちだが、その場合は her work was so good that ... のようになる。(D)much ... that のような使い方はできない。

139. (B) a good deal of 〜は「たくさんの〜」という意味で、後には名詞が続く。(A)cautioned は動詞の過去分詞形。(C)cautious は形容詞なので、後には名詞が続かなければならない。(D)cautiously は副詞。

140. (C) in spite of ...は「...にもかかわらず」という意味で対比を表わす前置詞句。この場合は higher ticket prices this year という名詞句を後半の節と対比させている。(A)Even though, (B)Nevertheless, (D)Consequently は後に節を伴い、句を伴うことはない。

Part VI：誤文訂正問題

141. (D) ダウンタウン地区へ向かうバス路線と、ダウンタウン地区から戻ってくるバス路線のどちらもあるという内容。英文の場合、downtown を2度使う必要はなく、The bus runs both to and from the downtown area. のように表記すればよい。

142. (A) 他動詞 appreciate は目的語を1つしかとらない。したがって、この場合 appreciate の目的語は your interest となり、it は不要。

143. (A) 〈in the event of ＋名詞句／＋ that 節〉で「（もしも）～の場合」という意味。したがって、for ではなく that が入ればよい。

144. (B) each は単数形なので、動詞の形はそれに対応しなければならない。したがって was handled となるのが正しい。

145. (A) 文中の動詞 follow の目的語となる名詞が必要なので、「配置、様式」という意味の format とする。formatted は動詞 format の過去形あるいは過去分詞形である。

146. (C)「～を補う」という意味の熟語は、make up for であり、make up with ではない。

147. (B) manager は Ms. Rivera が滞在したホテルの支配人である。すなわち、特定の個人について述べているので、名詞 manager の前に定冠詞 the が必要である。

148. (C)「オフィスを郊外へ移転する」という意味にするためには、前置詞 at ではなく、to を使う。

149. (C) I did not go out because of rain. のように、because of の後には節ではなく句が続く。この場合は節が続くので、because だけでよい。

150. (A) 前半の文は受動態となるので、charging ではなく、過去分詞形の charged でなければならない。

151. (B) take care は「気をつける、面倒をみる」という意味の熟語。caring とはならない。

152. (C) the computer terminal を目的語とする動詞が必要。したがって consultation ではなく動詞の consult が正しい。

153. (A)「～に驚く（驚かされる）」と言うときに名詞 surprise を使って表現する場合は、be taken by surprise のように by が必要となる。by を省略することはできない。

154. (C) 「非常に多くの」という場合、後に可算名詞が続く場合はmanyを使う。muchであれば後に続くのは不可算名詞でなければならない。例：I have too much work.

155. (C) 名詞agentを修飾する形容詞あるいは形容詞の役割を果たす過去分詞が必要となるので、designatedでなければならない。「空港の搭乗口では担当の職員に搭乗券を提示しなければならない」という意味。

156. (A) withoutの後には名詞あるいは名詞の役割を果たす動名詞が続く。接続詞unlessであれば、後に節を続けることができるので、文として成り立つ。

157. (C) 複合名詞safety standardは可算名詞である。見直されるsafety standard（安全基準）は1つとは限らないので、複数形のsafety standardsが正しい。

158. (D) beginを動詞とする主語conferenceは単数形である。したがって動詞も主語に合わせて3人称単数形現在のbeginsとなるのが正しい。

159. (A) candidateは可算名詞で、ここでは単数形として扱われている。したがって、冠詞のaまたはtheが必要となる。

160. (B) 動詞が受動態でなければならない。can findの受動態はcan be foundである。

Part Ⅶ：読解問題

161. (C) An auction for the estate of Martina Jovanovicという広告のタイトルがある。auctionとは物品を競売にかけることで、estateは故人の資産や財産のことである。(A)auctionはパーティーではない。(B)広告には資金を集めるとは述べていない。(D)なかには芸術的なものもあるが、美術館の収蔵品の一部だとは述べていない。

162. (B) オークションが開催される場所は広告の中にLocationとして記されている。433 Walnut Driveがオークションの開催場所である。(A)車はMunicipal Buildingの駐車場に停めることができるが、イベントがそこで開催されるわけではない。(C)イベントはEstate Planners Associatesが運営するが、彼らの事務所でイベントが開催されるのではない。(D)市営駐車場については述べられていない。

163. (B) これらの施設は衛生法が守られていなかったため閉鎖するのである。つまり、不衛生な環境にあったということ。(A)守られていなかったのは建築法ではなく衛生法である。(C)改修するとは述べていない。(D)1年のうちの一時期だけ営業するとは述べられていない。

164. **(A)** Peppo Mart では食品部門のみが閉鎖の対象となっているが、他の部門は営業している。(B), (C), (D)の施設に関しては、営業している部門があるという記述はない。

165. **(A)** Valley Restaurant では配水管設備の不整備が指摘されている。したがって Valley Restaurant は流し台や水道管の修理を行わなければならない。(B)食品のテイクアウト、(C)メニュー、(D)認可の更新については述べられていない。

166. **(D)** メモの主題は新しい電話回線についてである。従業員はいくつかあるサンプルの中から新しい回線を選ぶようにと言われている。(A)複数回線を使用した会議についてふれてはいるが、電気通信についての会議のメモではない。(B)会社は新しい電話回線システムを導入するのであって、修理を行なうのではない。(C)従業員の電話の使用頻度が高いとは述べられていない。

167. **(C)** 従業員は電話回線についての説明書を読んで、このメモの書き手である Ruth Crawford に自分の気に入ったものを知らせるようにと言われている。(A)従業員が会議を開く必要があるとは述べていない。(B)このメモを受け取った従業員が電話回線の申し込みをするのではない。(D)Supplies and Equipment 社に連絡を取るのは Ruth Crawford である。

168. **(B)** 従業員が考慮しなければならない条件の1つとして、1回線につき8つの内線機能がついていることが挙げられている。(A)従業員は色を考慮する必要はない。(C)Ruth Crawford は留守電機能が内蔵された電話回線が必要だと考えている。(D)メモには受話器の価格は中程度のものがよい述べられている。

169. **(B)** Wambaugh Marine Industries は造船所で、Merrymaker と3隻の客船を造る契約を交わしていたのである。(A)Wambaugh が供給することに合意したのは、乗客ではなく船体である。(C)Wambaugh が Merrymaker に対して訴訟を起こしたのではない。(D)契約の改訂については述べられていない。

170. (C) 契約額は6億ドルである。(A) 3億ドルはMerrymakerが損害を被ったと提訴した額である。(B) 4億ドルはMerrymakerが追加建造費用として、支払わなければならなかった額である。(D)7億ドルは賠償請求額である。

171. (C) Wambaughが倒産したため、造船所での作業ができなくなってしまったのである。(A)資材の価格高騰が作業を止めてしまったのではない。(B)作業が中止されたので、Merrymakerは乗客を失うことになったのである。(D)Wambaughは、船が完成する前に倒産してしまったのである。

172. (D) 出発日の30日前までに解約した場合、予約金は100%返金となる。(A)出発前30日を過ぎた場合、返金はゼロである。(B)30%ではなく、30日である。(C)a 90-day cancellation policyについては述べられているが、90%ではない。

173. (B) キャンセルする代わりに、友人にチケットを売ったり譲ったりすることができると述べられている。(A)団体旅行に参加することについては述べられていない。(C)キャンセルするかわりに早めに出発するとも言っていない。(D)返金の申請はキャンセルする場合にのみなされるのである。

174. (D) この通知はXYZ Machinery Companyの従業員たちに宛てて出されたものである。シンポジウムはこの会社の従業員を対象に開催される。(A)各国からXYZ Machinery Companyの従業員たちが集まるが、彼らは政治家ではない。(B)外国語を学ぶ人については述べられていない。(C)調理師のための会議ではない。

175. (C) 夕食、昼食、朝食のそれぞれに取り上げられる会議のテーマについて知らせた通知である。(A)参加者の国籍が挙げられている箇所はあるが、それが一覧表になっているのではない。(B)部屋の変更があったのではない。(D)キャンセルされた催しはない。

176. (C) human resources（人材）に関する問題を扱うのはpersonnel（人事）であることから考える。人事問題については水曜日の夕食時に会議が行われる。(A)月曜日の朝食は、法規問題についての会議である。(B)火曜日の昼食時には、テクノロジーについての会議が開催される。(D)木曜日の朝食は市場についてである。

177. (D) Softwind社の製品を購入した人に向けての指示書である。(A)指示書には、テクニカル・サポート・スタッフのサービスについて述べられている。(B)Softwind社の技術者たちについては述べられていない。(C)商品を販売するのは販売担当者である。これらの指示は販売担当者ではなく、既に製品を購入している人たちに向けて書かれたものである。

178. (A)顧客は製品を購入した店舗名を知らせなければならない。(B)購入者は、登録すれば認証番号を発行してもらえる。(C)購入者は登録した後、これから発売される商品の発売日を知ることができる。(D)購入者の宛先となる住所については述べられていない。

179. (C)Softwind社が登録カードを受け付ければ、購入者はPIN（認証番号）を発行してもらうことができる。(A)サポート・スタッフがPINを発行するのではない。(B)この通知は購入者が登録後、テクニカル・サポートを受けるための手順である。(D)小売店で登録するとは述べられていない。

180. (A)購入者は、テクニカル・サポートに電話する前にマニュアルを読むように、とある。(B)PINを変更するという記述はない。(C)購入者は、まずマニュアルを読み、それでもサポートが必要な場合に電話をかけるのである。(D)最新の指示については述べられていない。

181. (D)同封されているのは発送伝票のコピーである。これはIFS Freight Forwarding社がMr. Bensonに宛てて商品を発送した際に同梱した納品書である。(A)小切手については述べられていない。(B)手紙は商品2カートン分について述べているが、それらの商品とともにこの手紙が送られたのではない。(C)2社の契約に関する記述はあるが、この手紙に契約書が同封されていたのではない。

182. (A)運転手はSmooth Skin社に弁償の義務があると述べている。(B)運転手はButterfly Beauty社のMr. Bensonに苦情を申し立てるようには提案しなかった。(C)搬送中に損傷を被ったと言ったのは、この手紙を書いたPeggy Rolfである。(D)運転手は返金については何も言っていない。

183. (B)Ms. Rolfの手紙では、運転手が破損した商品に関しては引き取るというIFSの規定に反した行動をとったと述べている。つまり、運転手が返品の義務に従わなかったということである。(A)運送手数料については述べられていない。(C)重量制限については述べられていない。(D)travel expenses（旅費）という言葉は旅行にかかった費用であり、荷物の輸送などの際に使われることはない。

184. (C)Ms. Rolfは会社に商品を引き取るよう求めている。(A)IFSがMs. Rolfと連絡をとることを要求しているのではない。(B)Ms. Rolfは契約を打ち切る可能性を示唆している。契約更新をしないかもしれない。(D) Ms. RolfはIFSに弁償金を求めているのではない。

185. **(D)** これはVelcorp電力会社からの通達である。1時間当たりのキロワット料金が変更になることが述べられている。これは電力量の単位なので、電力会社が発行したものだと考えられる。(A)法律事務所に関する記述はない。(B)fuelという語は使われているが、ガソリンスタンドのことは述べていない。(C)Velcorp社は価格設定委員会の決定に従ってはいるが、委員会がこの通知を発行しているのではない。

186. **(C)** 通知によると、11月1日より価格が改訂になるとある。(A)会議については述べられていない。(B)単位である立方メートルについては述べられていない。(D)メーターのチェックがどのくらいの頻度で行われるかという記述はない。

187. **(C)** 工場の組立ラインの従業員は賃金の引き上げに同意したとあることから、従業員は賃金の引き上げを受け入れたことになる。(A)ストライキを行っているのはラインの従業員ではなく、メンテナンス技術者たちである。(B)ラインの従業員が技術者を支持しているとは述べられていない。(D)従業員が他の工場に移るという記述はない。

188. **(A)** Mitchell Motor Companyは技術者たちのストライキに対する報復として、ラインの従業員を解雇したとある。(B)解雇されたのは技術者ではなく、ラインの従業員である。(C)Vanのデザインの変更については述べられていない。(D)技術者たちの賃金が引き上げられたのではない。

189. **(B)** 電信取引についての問い合わせは電話で行なうことになっている。(A)書面による問い合わせについての記述はない。(C)これは郵便による投資に関してのみ該当する事項である。(D)電子取引にかかわる乗換え特権の解消についての記述はない。

190. **(D)** ファンドは必要に応じて随時、乗換え特権の変更を行なうことがあるという記述がある。(A)投資規約の確認については述べられているが、変更については述べられていない。(B)口座登録番号の変更に関しては述べられていない。(C)投資家は最小投資額を確認することはできるが、その変更に関する記述はない。

191. **(B)** Mr. Hayashidaは採用通知に対することわりを入れたのである。(A)Mr. Hayashidaは日本企業からの採用通知を受け入れたのである。この手紙はタイの会社に対して書かれたものである。(C)採用を申し込む前に、雇用主との話し合いの機会を持ちたいとの書面を送る場合はあるが、ここでは違う。(D)人事に関する問題ではあるが、Mr. Hayashidaはもっと詳しい情報を知りたいのではない。

192. (A)この手紙は彼を採用したいと考えている会社社長に対して書かれたものである。(B)Mr. Puapondhという事業部長の名前は出てくるが、彼が採用を決定するのではない。(C)Mr. Hayashidaが応募した職務が不動産業務の担当だったのである。(D)Mr. Hayashidaは別の企業に販売部長として就職すると述べている。

193. (C) Mr. Hayashidaは Golden Crown Resorts で働くのではない。(A)Mr. Van Vliet は Phuket の不動産会社 Golden Crown Resorts の社員である。(B)Mr. Kayasit は Golden Crown Resorts の社長である。(D)Mr. Puapondh は Golden Crown Resorts の事業部長である。

194. (C) 通知はこの建物、すなわち Standard Chemical Company に入館する際に必要なコンピュータディスクに関する指示である。(A)コンピュータウィルスのチェックを行なうのであって、健康クリニックに関することを述べているのではない。(B)この通知は人の目に付きやすいように建物の入り口に掲示されることはあっても、建物内のコンピュータ端末に掲示されることはない。(D)コンピュータのディスクに関する通知がカフェテリアに掲示されるとは考えられない。

195. (D) 申告されていないディスク、あるいは認知されなかったディスクは没収されることになっている。ディスクの(A)消去、(B)破棄、(C)複製に関しては述べられていない。

196. (C) 記事によると資金の大半が海外資本であるという記述がある。(A)The Economic Times は資本の出所がどこかを報告しているだけである。(B)The Chaldea's Ministry of Planning and Investment はこの事業計画の立案者である。(D)Digili Airport 当局に関する記述はない。

197. (D) ターミナルの敷地面積を拡大することが述べてあるのであって、建物を取り壊すのではない。(A)記事によると、1億8000万米ドルから1億9500万米ドルの資金が投入されるだろうということである。(B)ターミナルの敷地面積を拡大することは事業計画の一部に含まれている。(C)新空港建設は前年、ある研究機関によって打ち出された計画の1つである。

198. (C) 手紙によれば、Ms. Kahanian はブエノスアイレスにある Suarez Drilling Corporation 本社に年度末会計監査を行なうために訪れるのである。(A) Ms. Kahanian は掘削会社を訪問するが、掘削現場を視察するために来るのではない。(B)Mr. Ortiz は Ms. Kahanian が本社に滞在中、コンピュータ端末を提供するとは述べているが、コンピュータ・システムをアップグレードするとは述べていない。(D)Mr. Ortiz は Ms. Kahanian に良いレストランを教えられると述べているが、Ms. Kahanian が実際にレストランの品定めをするわけではない。

199. (D) Mr. Ortiz は Ms. Kahanian に対して、到着する前に電話かファックスで特別な要望があったら知らせて欲しいと書いている。コピー機はそうした要望のなかに入るものの一例と考えられる。(A) Ms. Kahanian がコンピュータ端末1台を自由に使えるようにすると手紙に書いている。(B)Mr. Ortiz はすでに Ms. Kahanian のフライト・ナンバーを知っている。(C) Ms. Kahanian が宿泊するホテルはすでに予約済みである。

200. (A) Ms. Kahanian が本社の社員食堂で無料で昼食がとれるように手配したのである。(B) Ms. Kahanian は朝食と夕食を Santa California ホテルで食べられるが、昼食については述べられていない。(C)街のレストランでの食事はホテルで朝食と夕食をとらない場合の代替案である。(D)コーヒー・ショップに関しては何も書かれていない。

Part I

1. (A) The transaction has been completed.
   (B) They're filling out the forms by hand.
   (C) The woman is using the keyboard.
   (D) They're watching a program on television.

2. (A) Few of the tables are occupied.
   (B) There's water on the floor of the restaurant.
   (C) The shape of the tables is square.
   (D) The restaurant has gone out of business.

3. (A) He's developing the photographs.
   (B) He's doing two things at once.
   (C) He's looking out the window at the scenery.
   (D) He's hanging up the telephone.

4. (A) The drivers have turned on their car lights.
   (B) The parking area is covered.
   (C) The cards are sorted by number.
   (D) The park is closed to traffic.

5. (A) They're picking up their bags.
   (B) They're sitting next to each other.
   (C) They're moving the sofa into the corner.
   (D) They're looking at a display in a museum.

6. (A) The market is open for business.
   (B) The man is working in his vegetable garden.
   (C) The crops have yet to be harvested.
   (D) The woman is weighing herself.

7. (A) They're placing the bags into the overhead compartment.
   (B) They're packing their suitcases.
   (C) They're moving the luggage.
   (D) They're going through customs inspection.

8. (A) The man is examining the merchandise.
   (B) There are not many products for sale.
   (C) The display cases are being rearranged.
   (D) The man is watching a movie.

9. (A) They're climbing the stairs together.
   (B) They're looking in the same direction.
   (C) They're holding onto the railing.
   (D) They're facing each other.

10. (A) There are a lot of people on the train.
    (B) The man is closing the door because of the rain.
    (C) The train has already departed from the station.
    (D) The man left his briefcase on the train.

11. (A) Her work hours have been cut.
    (B) She's finished clipping out the article.
    (C) There's not much air in this room.
    (D) She's giving the person a haircut.

12. (A) Some people are going up to the next level.
    (B) The escalator is out of order.
    (C) The building is only one story high.
    (D) The property is closed to the public.

13. (A) The customers are ready to pay their bill.
    (B) The waiter is taking their food order.
    (C) The woman is ordering the men to go away.
    (D) The waiter is taking away their dishes.

14. (A) The sales assistants are helping the customers.
    (B) The store inventory is low.
    (C) A man is paying for his purchases.
    (D) A woman is reaching for an item.

15. (A) He's putting her files away.
    (B) She's sitting across the desk from him.
    (C) They're reading the newspaper together.
    (D) He's handing her some papers.

16. (A) The musicians are playing as a trio.
    (B) The musical has just ended.
    (C) The instruments are in their cases.
    (D) The orchestra is entering the auditorium.

17. (A) Swimmers are getting out of the water.
    (B) People are cycling along the path.
    (C) The trees have lost all their leaves.
    (D) The river has flooded the surrounding area.

18. (A) They're putting up some flowered wallpaper.
    (B) They're taking a tour of the garden.
    (C) They're doing some work outside.
    (D They're eating their lunch in the park.

19. (A) The speaker is seated in front of the class.
    (B) The men and women are standing along the wall.
    (C) There are many empty seats in the room.
    (D) She's making a presentation to the group.

20. (A) The truck is waiting at the traffic light.
    (B) The man is climbing into the truck.
    (C) Boxes are stacked outside the truck.
    (D) Men are carrying boxes across the street.

CD2 No.2

Part II
21. (Man) When was Mr. Chen born?
    (Woman) (A) In Hong Kong.
            (B) Since last June.
            (C) In 1958.

22. (Woman 1) Did you ask them what time their flight would arrive?
    (Woman 2) (A) Yes, they were happy to arrive.
              (B) No, I didn't think of it.
              (C) No, it was too dark to tell.

23. (Man 1) Who can deliver this memo to Mr. Watanabe for me?
(Man 2)
(A) Yes, Mr. Watanabe lives in Japan.
(B) I can do it when I've finished typing this letter.
(C) No, the delivery person is from Osaka.

24. (Woman) Don't you want to go to the reception for Miss Gunther?
(Man)
(A) No, in the hotel ballroom.
(B) I have the receipt.
(C) Sorry, but I'm not feeling well.

25. (Man 1) What's the name of the travel agency this company uses?
(Man 2)
(A) Yes, that's his name.
(B) I think it's called All Points Travel.
(C) I recommend you use a carry-on bag.

26. (Woman 1) Where did Maria leave the Oceanview contract?
(Woman 2)
(A) She put it in Ms. García's mailbox.
(B) Just a minute ago, so you can still catch her.
(C) Because the mountain-view rooms were all booked.

27. (Man) Have you visited the main plant yet?
(Woman)
(A) Yes, they are.
(B) Yes, I went there last week with the director.
(C) Yes, the gardener is looking after them.

28. (Woman) Who is the new receptionist?
(Man)
(A) It's in the main office.
(B) Her name is Olga Kaminsky.
(C) Yes, we need a new receptionist.

29. (Woman 1) Will the conference be held here or at headquarters?
(Woman 2)
(A) It's scheduled for this building.
(B) No, you will not be able to hear.
(C) Yes, they will have the conference.

30. (Man 1) Why did the meeting begin so early?
(Man 2)
(A) Yes, at eight-thirty.
(B) About the upcoming acquisition.
(C) Everyone was in a hurry.

31. (Woman) What are your total production figures for this factory?
(Man)
(A) We produce pharmaceuticals.
(B) Over 1000 units a week.
(C) In the shipping department.

32. (Man) How far would you say Conrad Park is from here?

(Woman) (A) It's about a ten-minute walk.

(B) No, I wouldn't go so far as to say that.

(C) Yes, parking there is very expensive.

33. (Man) Is the agenda prepared?

(Woman) (A) No, it's still broken.

(B) Yes, they compared very well.

(C) Not yet, the vice president needs to review it.

34. (Woman 1) How about a movie when we finish up here?

(Woman 2) (A) Just down the street at the Cinema Center.

(B) That's a good idea.

(C) About a half hour more, I think.

35. (Man 1) The product was in stock last week, wasn't it?

(Man 2) (A) The stock exchange closes at five.

(B) Yes, there was a large inventory on hand then.

(C) No, they aren't.

36. (Woman) Can you locate the files on the merger, or should I ask Mr. Chang to do it?

(Man) (A) The fire exit is located at the end of the hall.

(B) Yes, I called security to handle the emergency.

(C) I'll have them ready for you in a minute.

37. (Man 1) Didn't the sound equipment come out of your regular departmental budget?

(Man 2) (A) We didn't hear any sounds.

(B) Yes, the room is rented.

(C) No, we got special funding.

38. (Woman) Where do you plan to stay while you're in Paris?

(Man) (A) Our company has an arrangement with the Hotel Odeon.

(B) I have a conference there next week.

(C) I'll be in France for four days.

39. (Man) I was wondering if you'd like to join us for dinner this evening?

(Woman) (A) Yes, it was a wonderful dinner.

(B) Sorry, I have other plans.

(C) I hope you weren't too lost.

40. (Woman) Does our company get any special deals on car rentals?

(Man) (A) Yes, I'd like some company on the trip.

(B) Twenty-five percent off the regular daily rate.

(C) No, it's your turn to deal.

41. (Woman 1) Exactly when will Mr. Mori be free?
(Woman 2) (A) In approximately two hours.
(B) At the International Airport.
(C) Near gate number 16.

42. (Man 1) How can I get more letterhead and envelopes?
(Man 2) (A) Yes, the mail is picked up three times a day.
(B) Contact Ms. McKay in the stockroom.
(C) No, he isn't the head of the department.

43. (Woman) Ms. Dubois was present at this morning's staff meeting, wasn't she?
(Man) (A) Once a week, on a Monday.
(B) No, it wasn't a gift.
(C) No, she wasn't there.

44. (Man) You're the new assistant to Mr. Lin, aren't you?
(Woman) (A) No, I don't need assistance.
(B) No, I work for Ms. Wong.
(C) Yes, I knew about that.

45. (Woman 1) When can you get me a copy of the most recent sales report?
(Woman 2) (A) Yes, they're selling well.
(B) Right after lunch.
(C) About four years old.

46. (Man 1) Why didn't Mr. Danforth bring the situation to the attention of his supervisor?
(Man 2) (A) Yes, at his workstation.
(B) No, he often doesn't pay attention.
(C) He thought he could handle it himself.

47. (Woman 1) Is this coat already marked down?
(Woman 2) (A) Yes, that's the sale price on the tag.
(B) The market is closed this evening.
(C) Yes, I have a red coat.

48. (Woman) Why does Ms. Ortiz want to see the invoices?
(Man) (A) Yes, they have loud voices.
(B) There's a problem with the shipment.
(C) No, she didn't see it.

49. (Man) Should they move the file cabinet to the right or over by the copy machine?
(Woman) (A) Yes, your thinking is correct.
(B) I think it looks good where it is.
(C) No, these copies didn't come out clearly.

50. (Man 1) Isn't that the same proposal we rejected last time?
(Man 2) (A) Yes, but things have changed since then.
(B) No, the wedding was called off.
(C) No, it was a different injection.

Part III

51. (Woman 1) I left a telephone message on your desk.
(Woman 2) Oh, did Mr. Murphy's secretary call again?
(Woman 1) Yes. She said the committee meeting is set for Tuesday.

52. (Man) Is there anywhere I can get coffee or tea around here?
(Woman) Yes, I think there is. Go have a look in the employee lounge.
(Man) That's next to the mailroom, right? Want me to bring you anything?

53. (Man) Did you hear about Mrs. Sompong's resignation?
(Woman) Yes. Our competitors made her an offer she couldn't resist.
(Man) I wonder if they'll appoint her as their new marketing manager?

54. (Woman 1) I need to call the theater to order tickets for Wednesday.
(Woman 2) Why don't you see the play over the weekend, Claudia?
(Woman 1) It runs only Monday through Thursday.

55. (Woman) Good morning, this is Standard Computer Services. Would you like to speak with someone in sales, service, or research?
(Man) Actually, I need to speak with Mr. Fong in personnel.
(Woman) Please hold while I transfer your call.

56. (Man 1) When does the movie start?
(Man 2) There are two showings—one at four and one at seven.
(Man 1) Let's go to the later show.

57. (Woman) Do you think the desk will fit under the window?
(Man) It might, but what about putting it next to the bookshelves? By the way, why are you changing things again?
(Woman) I just couldn't work comfortably in the old arrangement.

58. (Man) What do you think is the best way for us to get to the conference?
(Woman) Well, it's too close to bother flying. We could drive there, but I think if we took the train we could get some work done on the way.
(Man) Yes, that's the best plan. I'll pick up tickets at the station on my way home from work.

59. (Woman) Do you have this week's *Business News* yet?
(Man) No, the truck that used to deliver it on Monday has a different route. It should be here soon.
(Woman) I'll come back later this afternoon, I guess.

60. (Woman) Juan, Ricardo will not be able to attend the meeting next week in Panama, so I'd like you to represent the firm. Would you be able to do it?

(Man) Yes, Ms. Ortega, I'd really like to go to that meeting. What about travel arrangements?

(Woman) That's all been taken care of. See Carla. You'll leave Sunday evening — and thanks.

61. (Man) I've heard nothing but praise for that new health food restaurant.

(Woman) Same here. And I've got a coupon for the salad bar—buy one, get one free.

(Man) I'm always looking to save some money. Let's check it out for lunch.

62. (Man) The airline sent my luggage to New York by mistake and it doesn't look like they'll be able to deliver it to me in time for this evening's dinner. Where can I go to buy a few things?

(Woman) There's a shopping mall not far from here. You can get there by bus or cab from the hotel.

(Man) Oh, that's right. I was there the last time I was in San Francisco.

63. (Woman 1) Because you've worked here now for two years, Susanna, you are entitled to three weeks' vacation.

(Woman 2) Will I be allowed to take it all at once?

(Woman 1) Most supervisors allow two weeks at a time.

64. (Man 1) Let's get these boxes unloaded before the kitchen staff gets here.

(Man 2) Okay. Should I put these cans of corn on the shelf?

(Man 1) You can just leave them out on the counter. They're a part of today's menu.

65. (Woman) Hello, Yuri. I didn't think you would be back from your trip so soon.

(Man) Well, we didn't expect to be back now, but Anna, our youngest girl, got sick while we were away.

(Woman) I'm sorry to hear that. I hope she's feeling better now.

66. (Man 1) Alan, are you going to be in your office Thursday morning? If you're not, could I work there because my office is being painted then?

(Man 2) You're in luck, Tom. I'll be out until Friday morning.

(Man 1) That's great. I've got to get this project done by Monday afternoon.

67. (Woman 1) Did you leave that marketing report on my desk? I can't find it anywhere.

(Woman 2) No, Patricia, the only thing I've put on your desk recently is a memo.

(Woman 1) Could you please check in your file cabinet for it? I need it soon.

68. (Woman) I'm sorry, sir. We're completely booked tonight. There are no rooms available until tomorrow evening.

(Man) I see. Is there some place close by where I might be able to stay?

(Woman) Let me call around and see if I can find a room for you.

69. (Man) Excuse me, could I speak to Ms. Krishnan, please?

(Woman) Ms. Krishnan? I'm sorry, but she's no longer in this division. She was transferred last week to overseas sales.

(Man) Perhaps you could give me her new number?

70. (Man 1) Would you like to visit our plant while you're in town next week?

(Man 2) That would be great. I've always wanted to see your operation firsthand.

(Man 1) OK. Let me know when you're available and I'll show you around.

71. (Man) Your résumé looks very impressive, Ms. Mura, and I would like to offer you a job with our company.

(Woman) Thank you, Mr. Shima. I'm really looking forward to working with you.

(Man) Good. You can sign the papers at the personnel office.

72. (Man) And how would you like to pay for the camera?

(Woman) Could I write you a check?

(Man) Certainly. I'll need some form of identification or a major credit card.

73. (Woman) Hello. I'm in room 512 [five-twelve]. I just plugged in my hair dryer and all the lights went out.

(Man) I'm sorry. I'll send someone to take care of it right away.

(Woman) Thanks. I have to go out at six o'clock, so I'm really in a hurry!

74. (Woman 1) Ms. Díaz, please make sure I'm not interrupted for the next hour. I'll be working on a document that I have to fax to a client today.

(Woman 2) Will you take the international call that you're expecting, Ms. Lee?

(Woman 1) Yes. That's the one exception I will make.

75. (Woman) I'm sorry to have to leave in the middle of things here, but that was the office calling. They need my help right away.

(Man) Oh no, Heidi. You'll miss the rest of the party. Could you come back afterward?

(Woman) Maybe. I'll phone before I leave to see if anyone's still here.

76. (Woman) I'd like to return this sweater, but I don't have the sales slip. It was a gift.

(Man) In that case, we can only issue you a credit, not a refund.

(Woman) That would be fine. I'll use it toward this suit.

77. (Man) The advertising department has been working really hard these last seven weeks.

(Woman) I know, they've even been in the office on weekends. Do you think they'll be ready to make the presentation next Wednesday?

(Man) That's the plan. They're making their final revisions on Monday.

78. (Man 1) Excuse me, sir. Could I see your driver's license and your insurance papers, please?

(Man 2) Certainly, officer.... Here you are. I wasn't speeding, was I?

(Man 1) No sir, you weren't. The reason I pulled you over is because your left turn signal seems to be out of order.

79. (Man) Will my order be ready tomorrow? I must send it to a customer as soon as possible.

(Woman) I'm afraid our store will be closed tomorrow for inventory. I'm sure we'll have it the following day.

(Man) I see. I'll come and get it then. You open at nine, right?

80. (Woman) I thought the company wasn't going to hire anyone to take Olivia's place when she retired.

(Man) The division office decided to keep her position open in case the workload increased in her department.

(Woman) Oh, that's right. That big contract was signed just before she left.

Part IV
Questions 81 and 82 refer to the following announcement.

Good afternoon. I'm glad you could join me today for a tour of the museum's splendid modern art collection. The tour should last about half an hour, during which time we will try to focus on some of the museum's best-known pieces. For those of you who enjoy sculpture, I'll be giving another talk at three o'clock in the sculpture garden.

Questions 83 and 84 refer to the following speech.

Hello, my name is Ivan. I'll be serving you tonight. Let me tell you about some of our specials. We have grilled steak with sautéed vegetables. We also have a nice fresh salmon dish that comes with rice. Our soup of the day is clam chowder. I'll be back in a minute to take your order.

Questions 85 and 86 refer to the following short talk.

This is the limited express bound for Munich. We will be making a brief stop in Frankfurt before reaching our final destination. We expect our traveling time today to be three hours and twenty minutes. All seats are reserved. Please check your ticket and make sure that you are sitting in the correct seat. Telephones and food service are available in the rear car. Thank you for your attention. We will be departing in a few minutes.

Questions 87 through 89 refer to the following announcement.

Good evening. I'm Dave Sandoval, director of franchising for Milton's Pies. As you know, we're the fastest-growing franchisor in the southern region today. Last year we opened 300 shops, and now we hope to expand into the central region and put a Milton's Pie Shop in every mall and shopping center. No one should be too far from a great-tasting Milton pie. You're here tonight because you're interested in becoming a franchise owner, and we want to help you go into business! Most banks lend you the money you need to open a franchise because the Milton's name has customer appeal, and because our shops make money—for you, for us, and for the bank.

Questions 90 and 91 refer to the following excerpt from a speech.

It is my pleasure to introduce to you the world-renowned photojournalist Michiko Suzuki. A native of Japan, Ms. Suzuki has been working in Australia for the past three years as a staff photographer for *The Sydney News Journal*. I'm very pleased that Ms. Suzuki has agreed to join our magazine for six months before she takes her next long-term assignment in Brazil. She'll be working closely with our staff, sharing some of the secrets of her innovative techniques.

Questions 92 and 93 refer to the following announcement.

We are very pleased to announce that this year's annual employee awards banquet will be held in the grand ballroom of the elegant Adams Hotel. If you have not yet received your tickets, please call the personnel office immediately. We hope you'll join the president and board of directors in honoring this year's award winners.

Questions 94 through 97 refer to the following announcement.

Good evening, ladies and gentlemen, and welcome to the Regent Theater. Tonight's film, *The Earth is Round,* documents the experiences of a young couple as they travel around the world on a journey spanning more than five years. This film begins our week-long series in which we'll show nine different films, each depicting a unique voyage. *The Earth is Round* runs for 90 minutes, and we invite you to join us at the end of the movie for a question-and-answer session with the filmmakers. Thank you, and we hope you enjoy the show.

Questions 98 through 100 refer to the following talk.

This is Radio Talk Today. My name is Vanessa Evans and this afternoon we'll be talking with Sylvie Valmont about last week's election results. Ms. Valmont is a newspaper journalist and author of several books on politics and political parties. We'll be discussing her views on why some candidates fared well in the elections and why others didn't live up to expectations. She'll also tell us about the changing future of political parties in our country. But, before I bring on Ms. Valmont, here's the local and regional news and the weather forecast for the weekend.

TOEIC ミニ・テスト

（247ページ）

ANSWER SHEET

REGISTRATION NO.
受験番号

フリガナ
NAME 氏名

LISTENING (Part Ⅰ～Ⅳ)

NO.	ANSWER A B C D	NO.	ANSWER A B C	NO.	ANSWER A B C	NO.	ANSWER A B C D	NO.	ANSWER A B C D
1	A B C D	11	A B C D	21	A B C	31		41	
2	A B C D	12	A B C D	22	A B C	32		42	
3	A B C D	13	A B C D	23	A B C	33		43	
4	A B C D	14	A B C D	24	A B C	34		44	
5	A B C D	15	A B C D	25	A B C	35		45	
6	A B C D	16	A B C D	26	A B C	36		46	
7	A B C D	17	A B C D	27	A B C	37		47	
8	A B C D	18		28	A B C	38		48	
9	A B C D	19		29	A B C	39		49	
10	A B C D	20		30	A B C	40		50	

NO.	ANSWER A B C	NO.	ANSWER A B C D	NO.	ANSWER A B C D	NO.	ANSWER A B C D	NO.	ANSWER A B C D
51		61	A B C D	71		81	A B C D	91	
52		62	A B C D	72		82	A B C D	92	
53		63	A B C D	73		83	A B C D	93	
54		64	A B C D	74		84	A B C D	94	
55		65	A B C D	75		85	A B C D	95	
56		66	A B C D	76		86	A B C D	96	
57		67	A B C D	77		87	A B C D	97	
58		68	A B C D	78		88	A B C D	98	
59		69	A B C D	79		89	A B C D	99	
60		70	A B C D	80		90	A B C D	100	

READING (Part Ⅴ～Ⅶ)

NO.	ANSWER A B C D	NO.	ANSWER A B C D	NO.	ANSWER A B C D	NO.	ANSWER A B C D	NO.	ANSWER A B C D
101	A B C D	111	A B C D	121		131		141	
102	A B C D	112	A B C D	122		132		142	
103	A B C D	113	A B C D	123		133		143	
104	A B C D	114	A B C D	124		134		144	
105	A B C D	115	A B C D	125		135		145	
106	A B C D	116		126		136		146	
107	A B C D	117		127		137		147	
108	A B C D	118		128		138		148	
109	A B C D	119		129		139		149	
110	A B C D	120		130		140		150	

NO.	ANSWER A B C D	NO.	ANSWER A B C D	NO.	ANSWER A B C D	NO.	ANSWER A B C D	NO.	ANSWER A B C D
151	A B C D	161	A B C D	171	A B C D	181	A B C D	191	
152	A B C D	162	A B C D	172	A B C D	182	A B C D	192	
153	A B C D	163	A B C D	173	A B C D	183	A B C D	193	
154	A B C D	164	A B C D	174	A B C D	184	A B C D	194	
155	A B C D	165	A B C D	175	A B C D	185		195	
156	A B C D	166	A B C D	176	A B C D	186		196	
157	A B C D	167	A B C D	177	A B C D	187		197	
158		168	A B C D	178	A B C D	188		198	
159		169	A B C D	179	A B C D	189		199	
160		170	A B C D	180	A B C D	190		200	

TOEIC 練習テスト

(249ページ)

ANSWER SHEET

REGISTRATION NO.
受験番号

フリガナ

NAME
氏 名

LISTENING (Part Ⅰ～Ⅳ)

NO.	ANSWER A B C D	NO.	ANSWER A B C D	NO.	ANSWER A B C D	NO.	ANSWER A B C D	NO.	ANSWER A B C D	NO.	ANSWER A B C D	NO.	ANSWER A B C D	NO.	ANSWER A B C D	NO.	ANSWER A B C D	NO.	ANSWER A B C D
1	Ⓐ Ⓑ Ⓒ Ⓓ	11	Ⓐ Ⓑ Ⓒ Ⓓ	21	Ⓐ Ⓑ Ⓒ Ⓓ	31	Ⓐ Ⓑ Ⓒ Ⓓ	41	Ⓐ Ⓑ Ⓒ	51	Ⓐ Ⓑ Ⓒ Ⓓ	61	Ⓐ Ⓑ Ⓒ Ⓓ	71	Ⓐ Ⓑ Ⓒ Ⓓ	81	Ⓐ Ⓑ Ⓒ Ⓓ	91	Ⓐ Ⓑ Ⓒ Ⓓ
2	Ⓐ Ⓑ Ⓒ Ⓓ	12	Ⓐ Ⓑ Ⓒ Ⓓ	22	Ⓐ Ⓑ Ⓒ Ⓓ	32	Ⓐ Ⓑ Ⓒ Ⓓ	42	Ⓐ Ⓑ Ⓒ	52	Ⓐ Ⓑ Ⓒ Ⓓ	62	Ⓐ Ⓑ Ⓒ Ⓓ	72	Ⓐ Ⓑ Ⓒ Ⓓ	82	Ⓐ Ⓑ Ⓒ Ⓓ	92	Ⓐ Ⓑ Ⓒ Ⓓ
3	Ⓐ Ⓑ Ⓒ Ⓓ	13	Ⓐ Ⓑ Ⓒ Ⓓ	23	Ⓐ Ⓑ Ⓒ Ⓓ	33	Ⓐ Ⓑ Ⓒ Ⓓ	43	Ⓐ Ⓑ Ⓒ	53	Ⓐ Ⓑ Ⓒ Ⓓ	63	Ⓐ Ⓑ Ⓒ Ⓓ	73	Ⓐ Ⓑ Ⓒ Ⓓ	83	Ⓐ Ⓑ Ⓒ Ⓓ	93	Ⓐ Ⓑ Ⓒ Ⓓ
4	Ⓐ Ⓑ Ⓒ Ⓓ	14	Ⓐ Ⓑ Ⓒ Ⓓ	24	Ⓐ Ⓑ Ⓒ Ⓓ	34	Ⓐ Ⓑ Ⓒ Ⓓ	44	Ⓐ Ⓑ Ⓒ	54	Ⓐ Ⓑ Ⓒ Ⓓ	64	Ⓐ Ⓑ Ⓒ Ⓓ	74	Ⓐ Ⓑ Ⓒ Ⓓ	84	Ⓐ Ⓑ Ⓒ Ⓓ	94	Ⓐ Ⓑ Ⓒ Ⓓ
5	Ⓐ Ⓑ Ⓒ Ⓓ	15	Ⓐ Ⓑ Ⓒ Ⓓ	25	Ⓐ Ⓑ Ⓒ Ⓓ	35	Ⓐ Ⓑ Ⓒ Ⓓ	45	Ⓐ Ⓑ Ⓒ	55	Ⓐ Ⓑ Ⓒ Ⓓ	65	Ⓐ Ⓑ Ⓒ Ⓓ	75	Ⓐ Ⓑ Ⓒ Ⓓ	85	Ⓐ Ⓑ Ⓒ Ⓓ	95	Ⓐ Ⓑ Ⓒ Ⓓ
6	Ⓐ Ⓑ Ⓒ Ⓓ	16	Ⓐ Ⓑ Ⓒ Ⓓ	26	Ⓐ Ⓑ Ⓒ Ⓓ	36	Ⓐ Ⓑ Ⓒ Ⓓ	46	Ⓐ Ⓑ Ⓒ	56	Ⓐ Ⓑ Ⓒ Ⓓ	66	Ⓐ Ⓑ Ⓒ Ⓓ	76	Ⓐ Ⓑ Ⓒ Ⓓ	86	Ⓐ Ⓑ Ⓒ Ⓓ	96	Ⓐ Ⓑ Ⓒ Ⓓ
7	Ⓐ Ⓑ Ⓒ Ⓓ	17	Ⓐ Ⓑ Ⓒ Ⓓ	27	Ⓐ Ⓑ Ⓒ Ⓓ	37	Ⓐ Ⓑ Ⓒ Ⓓ	47	Ⓐ Ⓑ Ⓒ	57	Ⓐ Ⓑ Ⓒ Ⓓ	67	Ⓐ Ⓑ Ⓒ Ⓓ	77	Ⓐ Ⓑ Ⓒ Ⓓ	87	Ⓐ Ⓑ Ⓒ Ⓓ	97	Ⓐ Ⓑ Ⓒ Ⓓ
8	Ⓐ Ⓑ Ⓒ Ⓓ	18	Ⓐ Ⓑ Ⓒ Ⓓ	28	Ⓐ Ⓑ Ⓒ Ⓓ	38	Ⓐ Ⓑ Ⓒ Ⓓ	48	Ⓐ Ⓑ Ⓒ	58	Ⓐ Ⓑ Ⓒ Ⓓ	68	Ⓐ Ⓑ Ⓒ Ⓓ	78	Ⓐ Ⓑ Ⓒ Ⓓ	88	Ⓐ Ⓑ Ⓒ Ⓓ	98	Ⓐ Ⓑ Ⓒ Ⓓ
9	Ⓐ Ⓑ Ⓒ Ⓓ	19	Ⓐ Ⓑ Ⓒ Ⓓ	29	Ⓐ Ⓑ Ⓒ Ⓓ	39	Ⓐ Ⓑ Ⓒ Ⓓ	49	Ⓐ Ⓑ Ⓒ	59	Ⓐ Ⓑ Ⓒ Ⓓ	69	Ⓐ Ⓑ Ⓒ Ⓓ	79	Ⓐ Ⓑ Ⓒ Ⓓ	89	Ⓐ Ⓑ Ⓒ Ⓓ	99	Ⓐ Ⓑ Ⓒ Ⓓ
10	Ⓐ Ⓑ Ⓒ Ⓓ	20	Ⓐ Ⓑ Ⓒ Ⓓ	30	Ⓐ Ⓑ Ⓒ Ⓓ	40	Ⓐ Ⓑ Ⓒ Ⓓ	50	Ⓐ Ⓑ Ⓒ	60	Ⓐ Ⓑ Ⓒ Ⓓ	70	Ⓐ Ⓑ Ⓒ Ⓓ	80	Ⓐ Ⓑ Ⓒ Ⓓ	90	Ⓐ Ⓑ Ⓒ Ⓓ	100	Ⓐ Ⓑ Ⓒ Ⓓ

READING (Part Ⅴ～Ⅶ)

NO.	ANSWER A B C D	NO.	ANSWER A B C D	NO.	ANSWER A B C D	NO.	ANSWER A B C D	NO.	ANSWER A B C D	NO.	ANSWER A B C D	NO.	ANSWER A B C D	NO.	ANSWER A B C D	NO.	ANSWER A B C D	NO.	ANSWER A B C D
101	Ⓐ Ⓑ Ⓒ Ⓓ	111	Ⓐ Ⓑ Ⓒ Ⓓ	121	Ⓐ Ⓑ Ⓒ Ⓓ	131	Ⓐ Ⓑ Ⓒ Ⓓ	141	Ⓐ Ⓑ Ⓒ Ⓓ	151	Ⓐ Ⓑ Ⓒ Ⓓ	161	Ⓐ Ⓑ Ⓒ Ⓓ	171	Ⓐ Ⓑ Ⓒ Ⓓ	181	Ⓐ Ⓑ Ⓒ Ⓓ	191	Ⓐ Ⓑ Ⓒ Ⓓ
102	Ⓐ Ⓑ Ⓒ Ⓓ	112	Ⓐ Ⓑ Ⓒ Ⓓ	122	Ⓐ Ⓑ Ⓒ Ⓓ	132	Ⓐ Ⓑ Ⓒ Ⓓ	142	Ⓐ Ⓑ Ⓒ Ⓓ	152	Ⓐ Ⓑ Ⓒ Ⓓ	162	Ⓐ Ⓑ Ⓒ Ⓓ	172	Ⓐ Ⓑ Ⓒ Ⓓ	182	Ⓐ Ⓑ Ⓒ Ⓓ	192	Ⓐ Ⓑ Ⓒ Ⓓ
103	Ⓐ Ⓑ Ⓒ Ⓓ	113	Ⓐ Ⓑ Ⓒ Ⓓ	123	Ⓐ Ⓑ Ⓒ Ⓓ	133	Ⓐ Ⓑ Ⓒ Ⓓ	143	Ⓐ Ⓑ Ⓒ Ⓓ	153	Ⓐ Ⓑ Ⓒ Ⓓ	163	Ⓐ Ⓑ Ⓒ Ⓓ	173	Ⓐ Ⓑ Ⓒ Ⓓ	183	Ⓐ Ⓑ Ⓒ Ⓓ	193	Ⓐ Ⓑ Ⓒ Ⓓ
104	Ⓐ Ⓑ Ⓒ Ⓓ	114	Ⓐ Ⓑ Ⓒ Ⓓ	124	Ⓐ Ⓑ Ⓒ Ⓓ	134	Ⓐ Ⓑ Ⓒ Ⓓ	144	Ⓐ Ⓑ Ⓒ Ⓓ	154	Ⓐ Ⓑ Ⓒ Ⓓ	164	Ⓐ Ⓑ Ⓒ Ⓓ	174	Ⓐ Ⓑ Ⓒ Ⓓ	184	Ⓐ Ⓑ Ⓒ Ⓓ	194	Ⓐ Ⓑ Ⓒ Ⓓ
105	Ⓐ Ⓑ Ⓒ Ⓓ	115	Ⓐ Ⓑ Ⓒ Ⓓ	125	Ⓐ Ⓑ Ⓒ Ⓓ	135	Ⓐ Ⓑ Ⓒ Ⓓ	145	Ⓐ Ⓑ Ⓒ Ⓓ	155	Ⓐ Ⓑ Ⓒ Ⓓ	165	Ⓐ Ⓑ Ⓒ Ⓓ	175	Ⓐ Ⓑ Ⓒ Ⓓ	185	Ⓐ Ⓑ Ⓒ Ⓓ	195	Ⓐ Ⓑ Ⓒ Ⓓ
106	Ⓐ Ⓑ Ⓒ Ⓓ	116	Ⓐ Ⓑ Ⓒ Ⓓ	126	Ⓐ Ⓑ Ⓒ Ⓓ	136	Ⓐ Ⓑ Ⓒ Ⓓ	146	Ⓐ Ⓑ Ⓒ Ⓓ	156	Ⓐ Ⓑ Ⓒ Ⓓ	166	Ⓐ Ⓑ Ⓒ Ⓓ	176	Ⓐ Ⓑ Ⓒ Ⓓ	186	Ⓐ Ⓑ Ⓒ Ⓓ	196	Ⓐ Ⓑ Ⓒ Ⓓ
107	Ⓐ Ⓑ Ⓒ Ⓓ	117	Ⓐ Ⓑ Ⓒ Ⓓ	127	Ⓐ Ⓑ Ⓒ Ⓓ	137	Ⓐ Ⓑ Ⓒ Ⓓ	147	Ⓐ Ⓑ Ⓒ Ⓓ	157	Ⓐ Ⓑ Ⓒ Ⓓ	167	Ⓐ Ⓑ Ⓒ Ⓓ	177	Ⓐ Ⓑ Ⓒ Ⓓ	187	Ⓐ Ⓑ Ⓒ Ⓓ	197	Ⓐ Ⓑ Ⓒ Ⓓ
108	Ⓐ Ⓑ Ⓒ Ⓓ	118	Ⓐ Ⓑ Ⓒ Ⓓ	128	Ⓐ Ⓑ Ⓒ Ⓓ	138	Ⓐ Ⓑ Ⓒ Ⓓ	148	Ⓐ Ⓑ Ⓒ Ⓓ	158	Ⓐ Ⓑ Ⓒ Ⓓ	168	Ⓐ Ⓑ Ⓒ Ⓓ	178	Ⓐ Ⓑ Ⓒ Ⓓ	188	Ⓐ Ⓑ Ⓒ Ⓓ	198	Ⓐ Ⓑ Ⓒ Ⓓ
109	Ⓐ Ⓑ Ⓒ Ⓓ	119	Ⓐ Ⓑ Ⓒ Ⓓ	129	Ⓐ Ⓑ Ⓒ Ⓓ	139	Ⓐ Ⓑ Ⓒ Ⓓ	149	Ⓐ Ⓑ Ⓒ Ⓓ	159	Ⓐ Ⓑ Ⓒ Ⓓ	169	Ⓐ Ⓑ Ⓒ Ⓓ	179	Ⓐ Ⓑ Ⓒ Ⓓ	189	Ⓐ Ⓑ Ⓒ Ⓓ	199	Ⓐ Ⓑ Ⓒ Ⓓ
110	Ⓐ Ⓑ Ⓒ Ⓓ	120	Ⓐ Ⓑ Ⓒ Ⓓ	130	Ⓐ Ⓑ Ⓒ Ⓓ	140	Ⓐ Ⓑ Ⓒ Ⓓ	150	Ⓐ Ⓑ Ⓒ Ⓓ	160	Ⓐ Ⓑ Ⓒ Ⓓ	170	Ⓐ Ⓑ Ⓒ Ⓓ	180	Ⓐ Ⓑ Ⓒ Ⓓ	190	Ⓐ Ⓑ Ⓒ Ⓓ	200	Ⓐ Ⓑ Ⓒ Ⓓ

Memo

Memo

Memo

Memo

TOEIC®公式ガイド&問題集
日本語版(音声CD2枚付)

2000年3月1日	第1版第1刷発行
2003年6月15日	第2版第1刷発行
2004年1月15日	第2版第2刷発行

著者	Educational Testing Service
発行者・編者	財団法人 国際ビジネスコミュニケーション協会 TOEIC運営委員会
発売元	株式会社 国際コミュニケーションズ・スクール
	〒100-0014 東京都千代田区永田町2-14-2 山王グランドビル 　電話 (03)5521-5935 　FAX (03)5521-5879
印刷・製本	大日本印刷株式会社